SUMMARY OF OS/2 COMMANDS*

COMMAND	DESCRIPTION	SYNTAX
DATE	Sets the system date in the specified country format	DATE [*mm-dd-yy* | *dd-mm-yy* | *yy-mm-dd*]
DEL	Removes a file from the disk (same as ERASE)	DEL *filespec* [...]
DETACH (DET)	Creates an independently running background task	DETACH *commprog* [*param*]
DIR	Lists files on a disk or in a directory	DIR [*filespec*][/p][/w]
DISKCOMP	Compares two disks sector by sector	[*D:path*]DISKCOMP [*D1*:[*D2*:]]
DISKCOPY	Completely duplicates a disk	[*D:path*]DISKCOPY [*sourceD:destD*:]
DPATH	Adds protected mode path support for data and overlay files	DPATH [*D1:*]*path1*[;*D2*:*path2*...][;]
EDLIN	Real mode line editor supplied with DOS	[*D:path*]EDLIN *filespec* [/b]
ERASE	Removes a file from a disk (same as DEL)	ERASE *filespec*
EXIT	Terminates an additional command processor task	EXIT
FDISK	Partitions a hard disk	[*D:path*]FDISK
FIND	Finds strings in files	[*D:path*]FIND [/v][/c][/n]"*string*" [*filespec*...]
FORMAT	Prepares a disk to accept data	[*D:path*]FORMAT *D1*:[/s][/v][/4][/n:*xx*][/t:*yy*]
GRAFTABL	Makes ASCII codes 128 to 255 viewable on CGA	[*D:path*]GRAFTABL [437 | 850 | 860 | 863 | 865 | /STA][?]
HELPMSG	Display system message help screens	HELPMSG DOS*nnnn*
JOIN	Merges two disks into one at the specified directory	[*D:path*] JOIN [*D:path*] JOIN *D2 D1:path* [*D:path*] JOIN *D2* /d

*See Chapter 5, "OS/2 Command Reference," for a complete description of commands and their parameters.

ESSENTIAL OS/2

ESSENTIAL OS/2™

JUDD ROBBINS

San Francisco • Paris • Düsseldorf • London

Cover design by Thomas Ingalls + Associates
Cover photograph by David Bishop
Series design by Julie Bilski
Illustrations by Karin Lundstrom

To my family: Laura, Joshua, and Eli

ACKNOWLEDGMENTS

I would like to thank Anne Poirier and Phyllis Davies on my staff for their loyalty, devotion, and team spirit (not to mention editing and typing support) during the intense development of this book. I would also like to thank the Sybex staff who turned these words into a published book: Bonnie Gruen, editor; Robert Campbell, technical reviewer; Scott Campbell, word processor; Charles Cowens, typesetter; Winnie Kelly, proofreader; Karin Lundstrom, illustrator and pasteup artist; and Valerie Robbins, indexer. I also wish to thank Kyocera Unison, Inc. of Berkeley, California for letting me use their F-1010 laser printer during the writing of this book.

TABLE OF CONTENTS —

P A R T   3   ADVANCED OS/2 TECHNIQUES

P A R T   4   *APPENDICES* ━━━━━━━━━

INTRODUCTION

Welcome to the world of Operating System/2! Stepping up from DOS to OS/2 is a little like giving up your old sedan for a racy new sports car. However, in order to take full advantage of the power of your new car, you must understand how its engine works. This book is your key to understanding the inner workings of your powerful new OS/2 engine. Your new operating system has the dynamic 12 cylinder engine you see in Figure I.1.

The new OS/2 for 1988 sports an impressive set of features, and represents a dramatic leap forward in the world of operating system engineering. This book is your first owner's manual, and is conveniently organized to enable you to quickly understand and use these new powerful tools. In the chapters following you will explore the components of OS/2 seen in the diagram. There are four major sections in your OS/2

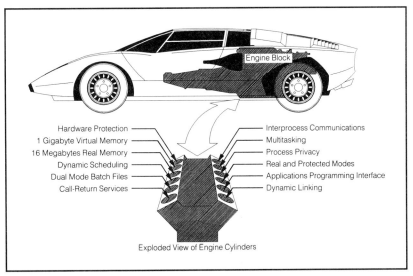

Figure I.1: The new sporty OS/2 for 1988 and beyond

owner's manual: Getting Started, Using OS/2, Advanced OS/2 Techniques, and Appendices. The four appendices provide specific reference information: Glossary, FDISK Command, Exit Codes for OS/2 Commands, and System Service Calls.

WHO SHOULD READ THIS BOOK

This book assumes that you have some background in simpler operating systems. Because many OS/2 commands and features are similar to DOS, a familiarity with DOS terms is particularly helpful. However, the text usually explains DOS references on the spot, and the OS/2 Command Reference (Chapter 5) provides a lot of additional information about DOS commands. The Glossary further augments your understanding of DOS references. Therefore, even if you have never used DOS, *Essential OS/2* can get you started, and explain how to use OS/2 both in an elementary and a more advanced manner.

This book is designed for several types of users:

- First-time purchasers of OS/2 who want to install, start up, and run OS/2 in either single tasking (DOS) or multitasking (OS/2) mode.

- DOS users interested in exploiting the powerful new features of OS/2 and running DOS programs under OS/2.

- Current DOS programmers interested in a first introduction to the protected mode, multitasking environment of OS/2.

- Experienced DOS users curious about the new OS/2 features of multitasking, real and protected mode, memory management, interprocesss communication facilities, and enhanced OS/2 command prompt user interface.

WHY DO YOU NEED OS/2?

You and I most often purchase software based on how well an application package meets our business needs. To run on a microcomputer, any application software must be hosted by an operating system. The earlier and simpler machines used DOS, and DOS successfully hosted thousands of useful and popular software packages. But much of the newest 1988–1989 software is being written under the auspices of Microsoft's OS/2. This operating environment not only provides the key management capabilities for these new pieces of software, but also affords a broader range of support for new types of hardware. OS/2 communicates directly with your hardware, which means that you no longer have to do so.

At the same time, OS/2 affords even more support for software functions. Software designed to run under OS/2 can be much faster, much smaller, and easier to modify and upgrade. These capabilities explain why OS/2 is giving rise to a new generation of more powerful and potentially more popular software products. Those wishing to grow with the newest generation of application software will want to learn how to work with the advanced engineering of Operating System/2.

NECESSARY HARDWARE AND SOFTWARE

This book assumes that you have a microcomputer based on an 80286 or 80386 processing chip. Because not all microcomputers run OS/2, you should check your system's documentation. An IBM/PC AT or compatible, a Personal System/2 or compatible, or the Compaq Deskpro and Portable machines using the appropriate chips will usually run OS/2. This book covers Version 1.0 of MS OS/2 (without the Presentation Manager). You'll need at least the Program and Supplemental disks from the OS/2 package, both of which are high-capacity disks. You'll also need at least one high-capacity floppy disk drive to initially boot the system, or install OS/2 onto a hard disk. But the high capacity drive is not needed once OS/2 is installed on your hard drive.

Microsoft recommends that your hardware contain at least 2MB of real memory, although you can squeak by with a minimum of 1.5MB. In fact, if you are planning to do software development, you'll need a hard disk with at least 10MB free as well. This merely stores the wide range of software tools (compilers, assemblers, editors, etc.) provided with the OS/2 development kit.

A high-capacity floppy disk drive is required for OS/2 installation because all the required files for booting the installation disk cannot fit onto a standard double-density disk.

HOW TO USE THIS BOOK

Read this book in chapter order. The four major sections first present information necessary to get started (Part 1), then move to actually using your system once it and your application programs are installed (Part 2), then look at effective use of advanced OS/2 features and fundamental programming techniques (Part 3), and finally offer handy reference information (Part 4).

As you read through the book, stop as often as possible to experiment with the commands and features on your own computer. The immediate feedback you will get helps you absorb necessary skills quickly and efficiently. You will probably discover some overlap with your own business and operating system experience. Feel free to skim chapters covering topics relatively familiar to you, or even skip the subjects you know from your earlier operating systems experience. Use Appendix A ("Glossary") to verify individual terms, and Chapter 5 ("The OS/2 Command Reference") for detailed descriptions of individual command syntax, restrictions, types, and examples.

HOW THIS BOOK IS ORGANIZED

Part 1, "Getting Started," introduces you to the multitasking world of OS/2. Chapter 1 discusses concepts and techniques of multiple simultaneous programs. You'll learn how OS/2 uses virtual memory, and see how the Memory Manager facilitates programs with very large amounts of virtual memory when it actually has much smaller amounts of real memory available. Chapter 1 also introduces you to the OS/2 Session Manager, which lets you switch between simultaneously running programs. You'll explore both the concept of real mode, which allows you to run DOS programs in OS/2, and protected mode, the heart and soul of OS/2's new multitasking world.

Chapter 2 takes you into the sequence of steps necessary to install and start up your OS/2 system. It tells you about the disks that come with your OS/2 package and details the installation procedure itself. You are taken through the disk partitioning and disk formatting needed to create OS/2 directories for your application or programming environment. Because your environment may be unique and rely on miscellaneous nonstandard hardware, Chapter 2 also focuses on configuration steps required to support both standard and non-standard device drivers.

Chapter 3 explains how you can make a smooth transition from DOS to OS/2. Some distinctions and obstacles are presented, as well as the steps necessary to surmount them. Real mode operations, which allow you to run nearly any DOS applications, are detailed. Chapter 3 is for those of you who wish to minimize any disruption to the business of your office, and prefer to use your existing programs immediately on your new OS/2 machine.

Once you've got your OS/2 system up and running, you'll want to do more than just use your old DOS programs. Part 2, "Using OS/2," goes beyond this introductory level. Chapter 4 compares OS/2 to DOS, contrasting the older configuration features with OS/2's newer and broader features. It compares the single batch file mechanism at DOS startup (Autoexec.bat) with the newer dual batch file mechanism available in both real and protected modes of OS/2. Chapter 4 also presents an overview of the new OS/2 user interface, and classifies the new types of command services OS/2 makes available.

Commands in OS/2 fall into three general categories. The first category includes those commands you know already because they haven't changed from your DOS machine. In the second category are the commands that initially look the same as in DOS, but have enhanced features when run in OS/2 protected mode. The third category includes those new commands that run only in protected mode, and provide the more powerful capabilities such as initiation of background processes from the command prompt. All these old, modified, and new commands are detailed in the command reference in Chapter 5. As you read through *Essential OS/2*, refer to this chapter to get a precise view of syntax, restrictions, type, and examples of use for any particular command.

OS/2 allows commands to be manipulated in new ways called grouping and sequencing. Chapter 6 explores these new command manipulation capabilities that are available at the OS/2 prompt by introducing the techniques of redirection, piping, and filtering in the context of the new, broader arena of OS/2 command operations.

Part 3 of *Essential OS/2* steps up the pace even further. Parts 1 and 2 give you an understanding of how to use OS/2 at a fundamental level. Part 3 takes you into more advanced topics and techniques.

Chapter 7 presents file editing in OS/2. The older EDLIN program has been dusted off and brought out for use in OS/2's real mode. The new protected mode full screen editing program (SSE) is simple to use but limited in capability, representing a cross between restrictive line editing and more expansive word processing. Chapter 7 provides the understanding of file editing essential to the effective use of batch processing.

There are two kinds of batch files in OS/2, one that runs in real mode and another that runs in protected mode. The older style batch programs are supported in real mode with .bat extensions, while the newer batch files running in protected mode must be written with .cmd extensions. Chapter 8 presents the basics of batch processing in both modes and the subcommands available for use in both modes. It demonstrates a number of example applications usable in one or both executing environments.

OS/2 offers an enormously enhanced range of configuration commands. Chapter 9 details each of the possible configuration commands, pointing out those similar to DOS and those that are new to OS/2. The most commonly-used standard commands are presented first, while the more advanced commands affecting operating system internals are presented next. A small, specialized subset of configuration commands controlling national language support or country specific installations are also presented in this chapter.

The last chapter in Part 4 is an introduction to the programming world of OS/2. Chapter 10 looks from a programmer's perspective at descriptor tables, which are used by OS/2 to manage virtual and physical memory. It details the three types of interprocess communication tools available in OS/2: semaphores, pipes, and queues. You will learn about the Applications Programming Interface (API) and the new type of call-return interface for system service calls. The chapter also presents a number of techniques for developing applications that will run on a DOS machine or in the OS/2 protected mode environment. Finally, you will learn a series of programming hints necessary for successful OS/2 coding.

Part 4 contains the appendices. Appendix A is a detailed glossary of operating system terms, both general and specific to OS/2. Use this as a reference whenever you are uncertain about the definition of any term. Appendix B takes you through the somewhat esoteric but occasionally necessary FDISK command for partitioning your OS/2 hard disk. You are shown how to set up a bootable OS/2 partition and how to create an extended partition for additional logical disk drives. Because many commands in OS/2 return exit codes that can be used by programs, commands, and batch files, the actual exit code values for these commands are presented in Appendix C. Finally, Appendix D lists and briefly defines all OS/2 system service calls.

ICONS USED IN THIS BOOK

Three special visual icons are used in this book. ▱ represents a practical hint or special technique. ◪ indicates a special note that augments the material in the text. When you see ◉ , pay particular attention—it represents an alert or warning about a possible problem, or a way to avoid or prevent the problem.

COMPANION DISK TO THIS BOOK

If you wish to use or test any of the large number of batch files presented in this book, you can save yourself the time necessary to type them in by ordering your own copy of the "Essential OS/2 Companion Disk." Complete the order form at the back of this book to get your own copy of this time-saving disk. Wherever appropriate, real mode and protected mode versions of each batch file are included for your convenience.

OS/2 is host to a great wealth of both popular and important business and personal software. In its initial implementation, the great majority of these programs were designed for the DOS world and are supported by OS/2 in real mode. But newer programs, designed by their developers to run within OS/2's protected mode, are appearing weekly. The newest of these are naturally taking advantage of many of OS/2's latest system calls for esoteric, behind-the-scenes manipulation of memory management, multitasking, and interprocess communications capabilities.

As you use your OS/2 system, and as you acquire more and newer software for that system, this book will help you make effective use of your new operating system environment. OS/2 is expected to be a major operating system in the microcomputer world through the 1990s. It's not too early to begin your own immersion into the multitasking world of OS/2.

PART 1

GETTING STARTED

In Part 1, you get a sense of what OS/2 is and what it can do. If you're just beginning to use OS/2 or are thinking about buying it, you should read and become comfortable with the information presented here. Even if you have some experience already, you should read Part 1 to clarify new concepts, as well as refresh your understanding of older concepts that have been upgraded under OS/2.

Chapter 1 explains the fundamental elements of this new operating system: the multitasking, the virtual memory management, the real operating mode (DOS) and the protected operating mode (OS/2). It also introduces the Session Manager and the idea of screen groups. The on-line help facility, a useful OS/2 tool, is also presented in Chapter 1.

In Chapter 2, you will prepare your system for OS/2. You'll partition your hard disk, format it for OS/2, create the necessary directories, then copy the OS/2 system and support files. You'll learn about the automatic Install program, and what goes on behind the scenes during installation. Lastly, you'll learn how to configure your system to understand a range of special purpose devices, some supported directly by drivers supplied with OS/2, and others supported by drivers supplied by the device manufacturer.

The final chapter in this part, Chapter 3, offers a step-by-step approach to running your favorite DOS programs under OS/2. Even though OS/2 has many new features that you will want to take advantage of, you won't want to give up the use of your older DOS software. This chapter shows you how to quickly and easily set up OS/2 to recognize and run your older software.

THE MULTITASKING
WORLD OF OS/2 ─────────

CHAPTER 1

THE OS/2 REVOLUTION HAS ARRIVED. NO MATTER that DOS still reigns supreme in many businesses and on many microcomputers. No matter that it will take time to create and convert programs to run under OS/2. Experienced users need only look back on the 1981 introduction of DOS as heir apparent and supplanter of CP/M. That experience teaches that where innovation leads, users must necessarily follow. And OS/2 is such a quantitative leap forward that it can't be ignored!

But OS/2 represents a much greater advance than the DOS surge in the early eighties. Whereas DOS initially ran on the Intel 8088 and 8086 chips, OS/2 is designed to run on Intel's 80286 chip used primarily by the IBM PC/AT and compatibles, as well as on the even more advanced 80386 chip. For the first time, the full power of these advanced chips is realized with OS/2. The operating system itself takes advantage of the chip power to support improved program operation. In fact, OS/2 offers you power and versatility more like a minicomputer or mainframe than your DOS-run microcomputer.

In this chapter, you'll be hearing about those OS/2 features that account for the wave of anticipation accompanying its release. You will learn how the 80286 chip and OS/2 work together to create the two different modes of operation called *real* (for the sake of compatibility with old DOS programs) and *protected* (the upbeat multitasking mode supported by the sophisticated features of OS/2). The real mode is sometimes referred to as the DOS Compatibility Box, but this book uses the term real mode.

You'll also learn in this chapter how OS/2 extends the former 1MB DOS limit on physical memory to 16MB. You'll see how an OS/2 program can act as if it addresses memory as large as one gigabyte, even if that memory isn't physically there! You will learn about how you can use the OS/2 Session Manager to switch between real and protected modes and between processes while they are running. And you'll explore the benefits of OS/2's on-line help facility, which allows you to get an explanation for every system message as well as a suggested course of action.

RUNNING MULTIPLE PROGRAMS AT THE SAME TIME

DOS and other less-advanced operating systems allow you to run only one program at any given time. This program, which we'll call a task or a process, has to be completed before beginning the next task or process. For example, you usually have to finish working with your word processor before you can begin your spreadsheet, and complete that before you begin your database manager.

DOS does allow you to create the effect of more than one process or program running at a time by using the print spooling capability. While your DOS program is running, the printing mechanism can use some of the idle CPU time to control output to a printer. This *single tasking* might allow you to call one task from another, but you can actually work in only one at a time.

With OS/2, the number of operations that can occur on your system simultaneously is under your control, and depends on the hardware and software configuration that you yourself set up. OS/2 does not force you to complete one task before beginning another, but instead allows for multiple simultaneous tasks. Running more than one program at a time is called *multitasking*.

For example, OS/2 allows you to use a project management software package to create a PERT chart at the same time your general ledger is being prepared and printed. A COBOL program can also be compiling simultaneously, while a financial spreadsheet recalculates, and a consolidated multisite business report is being printed. In

The operating system features of OS/2 are similar to many multitasking operating systems that run on minicomputers and mainframes. It is unfortunate that the terminology for all these machines has not been consistent. What one vendor calls a multiprocessing environment, another calls a multitasking environment. OS/2 documentation uses the terms multitasking and multiprocessing interchangeably, but this book uses only multitasking.

fact, OS/2 allows you to switch between each of these executing programs to check on their status, to interrupt them by pausing or canceling, or to jump into the middle to affect operations. When you are accessing one, none of the others has to end; you have access to all at any time you wish.

Figure 1.1 demonstrates the OS/2 multitasking capability. As you can see, multiple programs—a spreadsheet, a database management system, a Fortran compiler, etc. can all run simultaneously using the available hardware chip (80286 or 80386). You can then use the OS/2 Session Manager to select which output is to be displayed on your video monitor. In other words, although many programs may run simultaneously, only one will be visible to you at a time.

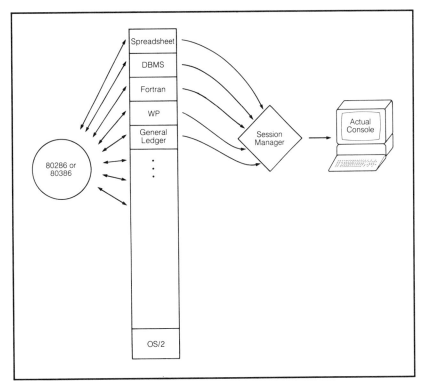

Figure 1.1: Multitasking in OS/2

OS/2 SUPPORTS THE OLD AND THE NEW

The two modes in which the 80286 chip runs are almost like two separate operating systems. In the simpler mode, or *real* mode, OS/2 uses the 80286 chip to emulate DOS 3.x. This real addressing mode is a feature of the microprocessing chip, and offers no hardware protection or multitasking support. When DOS runs on a 80286 machine, it only uses this aspect of the chip. DOS gains speed, but very little else.

The second addressing mode capability of the 80286 microprocessor is called *protected virtual address mode*, or protected mode for short. In this mode, the hardware chip itself offers many improved features, such as memory protection and the ability to run programs that are larger than can fit into memory.

OS/2 is a sophisticated piece of software that manages the advanced hardware features of the 80286 chip, and its successors, in both real and protected modes. For the sake of compatibility, OS/2 can run older DOS programs in the limited real mode of the underlying hardware chip.

Most programs that DOS 3.x runs, with the possible exception of those that make sophisticated use of interrupts, video buffers, and direct BIOS references, run in this OS/2 real mode. Real mode executes DOS programs faster than the 8086 or 8088 chips do. Because DOS on IBM PC/ATs and compatibles uses the 80286 chip in its real mode, programs that used to run on older machines can run on the AT at much greater speed. But using the 80286 chip only in real mode is something akin to tying your hand behind your back; it leaves most of the chip's power unexploited.

The protected mode is the primary operating system in OS/2, and in time it may be the only one that users employ. The protected mode makes multitasking possible. It greatly increases memory addressability and referencing capabilities and makes new user commands and configuration possibilities available, as well as enhanced versions of older, more familiar commands. It also makes significant new hardware instructions and features available to programmers, which enhance both the range and power of the possible new programs.

WORKING WITH REAL AND PROTECTED MODES

When you boot up and switch to either mode, OS/2 indicates whether it is in real or protected mode. Later in this chapter, you'll learn how to switch between modes. The DOS 3.x prompt (C>) appears in OS/2 real mode. The current directory, enclosed in square brackets, appears as the protected mode system prompt: [C:\]. Chapter 4 explains how these startup prompts can be customized and made more distinct by using additional information and even color.

When you run your older DOS program on OS/2, you must use the real mode command processor, called Command.com. Another OS/2 command processor, called Cmd.exe, supports protected mode operations. Each of these programs interprets commands that you enter at the system prompt differently. Chapter 5 presents a complete OS/2 command reference. As you will see, some commands run only in real mode, and look the same as they did in DOS 3.x. Other commands run only in protected mode, and offer unique and powerful new features. Some commands are available in both real and protected mode versions; in some of these cases, the real version runs as it did in DOS 3.x, but the protected mode version offers expanded functionality. This expanded functionality can, for example, give you the ability to reference multiple files with the DIR or DEL commands, without having to use wild cards.

When using the protected mode, the memory required by these different application programs can be separated by OS/2, and the potential of system crashes based on errant programs is significantly reduced. In contrast, DOS allows an application program complete control or access to all memory locations, even if they are not part of the program itself. Between OS/2 and the special features of the 80286 protected mode, large spaces for data that well exceed physical memory can also be created and referenced by application programs. The section on memory management (covered later in this chapter, and in Chapter 10) explores this exciting OS/2 feature in more detail.

Figure 1.2 dramatizes the expanded powers afforded to OS/2 by the 80286 chip. The real mode pie slice was the only one available in

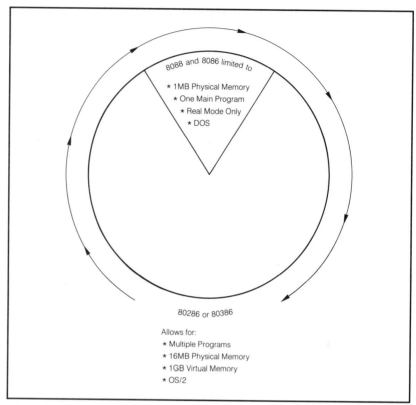

Figure 1.2: Real versus protected mode

the 8086 and 8088 chips; the entire pie is available to OS/2 applications using the 80286 chip.

EXPLAINING OS/2 TASKS OR PROCESSES

In OS/2, a task or process can be defined as simply an instance of a program that uses a set of system resources. This is not unlike DOS-based usage, where programs make use of disk files, system memory, and other system resources, like the system clock or interrupt information from input/output devices.

In Figure 1.3, you can see how an OS/2 process accesses a variety of system resources. Notice that one of those system resources is an output device, enabling you to see the results of the program. The example in Figure 1.3, in this case a monitor, represents one of OS/2's most critical new features: the ability to create *virtual* output devices.

You usually have only one real keyboard and monitor connected to a system. In DOS, this limits you to single tasking. In contrast, OS/2 helps to support multitasking by having each individual program write its output results to special buffers, called *virtual consoles*, that mimic output devices. Figure 1.4 dramatizes the second stage in the user interface: any application process can have a virtual monitor output, without necessarily connecting that process to your system's external, real monitor. Several application processes can share the same virtual output device.

This is how OS/2 manages the execution of multiple processes internally using system resources. At any given moment, OS/2 can map the output from the internal, virtual monitors to the external, real monitor. Each application process that is running has its own output stream, which under DOS would go to an external monitor. But OS/2 allows each of the multiple processes that are running simultaneously to be sent individually to the real screen only when directed.

UNDERSTANDING OS/2'S SCREEN GROUPS

A group of these simultaneously executing processes, all of which are outputting to the same virtual output device, can be called a screen group (see Figure 1.4). There can be only one OS/2 real mode screen group, but multiple screen groups are possible in protected mode. The composition of any screen group depends on whether it is in real or protected mode.

In a real mode screen group, there is normally only one dominant program or application process running and visible on the screen at a time. Just as in DOS, this can be a word processor, database manager, spreadsheet, or any other DOS program now being run in OS/2. If you

Although there cannot be more than one actively running, dominant program in a real mode screen group, a dominant word processor can run at the same time as a spooling program, which is not visible on the screen, but which in fact is running simultaneously. You can initiate the spooling mechanism in this real mode screen group by using the PRINT command at the command prompt.

Similarly, some of you may be familiar with the multitasking programs available under DOS 3.x, such as Windows or DESQview. These allow a limited form of switching between programs, severely restricted by the DOS 640K limits on addressability. Also, there may be memory resident programs that can be loaded and switched to by pressing a *hot key*. A hot key is a special keystroke combination that activates each memory resident program, otherwise idle until commanded to carry out its function.

wish to access a different program, you must go to the real mode command prompt to do so.

When your system starts in protected mode, one screen group is active. This is managed by the program called Cmd.exe, which parallels the command interpretation supported by Command.com in both DOS and OS/2's real mode. A screen group in protected mode usually consists of your choice of one main program. However, it can also run several background tasks simultaneously. It is this OS/2 capability of putting applications in groups that allows for multitasking.

With protected mode you can work with more than one screen group at a time. You will probably want to initiate a word processing program in one screen group, a spreadsheet in another, etc. OS/2 maintains place holders in any programs, so that it can keep track of what you're doing in those programs. Even more importantly,

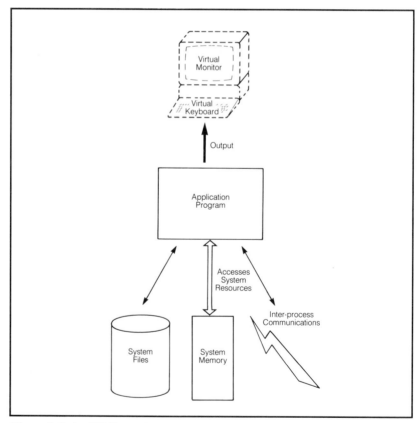

Figure 1.3: An OS/2 process

operations that take a good deal of time can be simultaneously processed by OS/2. For example, your word processor can be doing a time-consuming and automatic spelling check on a large manuscript, while the database manager is simultaneously doing an automatic and time-consuming file sort followed by a resulting report, while a communications program in another screen group is transmitting or receiving a file over telephone lines.

You can separate these screen groups from one another, and request that OS/2 switch the visible screen output from any one screen group to any other at any time. The Session Manager provides this service. By design, separate screen groups represent totally separate address spaces. Each program in any one group is divorced from any other screen group. This form of protection (by hardware and software isolation) explains why you want to put logically separate programs in completely separate screen groups.

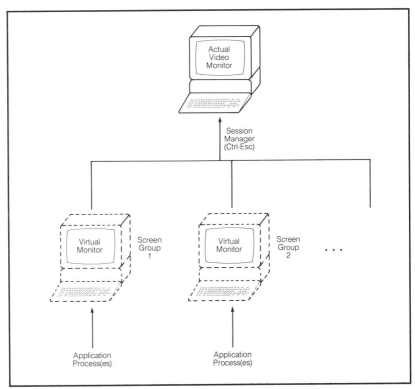

Figure 1.4: OS/2 processes output to virtual monitors

THE OS/2 SESSION MANAGER

The OS/2 Session Manager controls which executing screen group is actually visible on your external monitor and accepting keyboard input at any time. Figure 1.5 shows the Session Manager program selector menu at startup in OS/2.

The left box on the screen in Figure 1.5 allows you start up a new screen group, and the box on the right displays the names of current screen groups to choose from. In this startup screen example, the first of the two screen groups is labeled

MS-DOS Command Prompt

which represents Command.com running old DOS programs in real mode. The second selection is a task that is running the OS/2 Cmd.exe program for protected mode operations. Just as each program can be totally isolated from the impact of other running programs, screen groups can be isolated from one another. Although

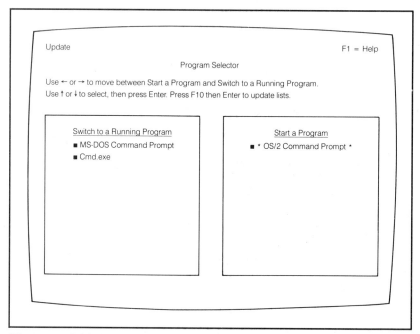

Figure 1.5: OS/2 Session Manager program selector menu at startup

you can exit from the protected mode Cmd.exe task, thereby removing it as a choice from the Session Manager screen, the real mode MS-DOS Command Prompt choice will always remain.

In Figure 1.6, you see the results of extending this concept. By selecting the Start a Program box, you create a new running process, seen on the Session Manager screen as

OS/2 Command Prompt * 1

The next time you select Start a Program, OS/2 will create yet another protected mode process, indicated by the line

OS/2 Command Prompt * 2

Each of these four separate running programs can be selected from the right window of the program selector menu, or Session Manager. Each separate OS/2 command prompt represents a different screen group. You can now switch to each, then initiate separate application

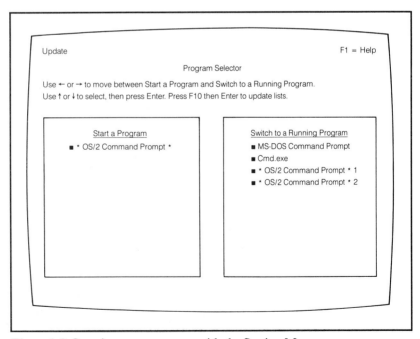

Figure 1.6: Creating new processes with the Session Manager

programs. In other words, when you select Start a Program, you are initiating a new screen group in protected mode. Since real mode does not support multitasking, you must switch to MS-DOS Command Prompt to initiate programs in real mode; but you can only do so for one program at a time, just as in DOS.

Pressing the Ctrl-Esc key interrupts whatever process output is being displayed on your screen, and calls up the Session Manager screen seen in Figures 1.5 and 1.6. The program that had been displayed on the external monitor will keep on running, using its virtual monitor. The right and left arrow keys decide between starting a new program, or switching to a currently executing one. The up and down arrow keys select among the current list of running programs.

In the example in Figure 1.6, you already know the name of the programs that are running in those screen groups. The example shows four separate and isolated screen groups. The MS-DOS command prompt, or a single former DOS program, is in Group 1. The initial protected mode command interpreter (Cmd.exe) is in Group 2. Within this group, any one or more individual OS/2 commands or programs can be run. For instance, you could have initiated a C compilation in that screen group. Then, you could switch to the screen group called OS/2 Command Prompt * 1 to perform some database updating, perhaps in an inventory program. While a possible sort and subsequent inventory report is being prepared in that screen group, you could move over to OS/2 Command Prompt * 2, and be in the middle of performing some spreadsheet calculation. All of these are operating independently, and all can be readily displayed on the external monitor. Simply go to the Session Manager screen by pressing Ctrl-Esc, then select the desired screen group with the cursor keys, and finally switch to it by pressing Return.

An alternate method of initiating programs is the protected-mode-only START command (see Chapter 5). If you enter

START MATRIX

at the OS/2 command prompt, a new screen group Cmd.exe will be started, specifically running the program Matrix.exe (you could replace this with the name of any protected mode program). The more meaningful name of the running program, Matrix.exe, will now appear in the Session Manager list of running programs.

You can also switch screen groups by pressing Alt-Esc. This switches immediately to the next screen group in the list, and bypasses the Session Manager, thus saving some time. However, Alt-Esc runs sequentially through the screen groups, whereas with the Session Manager you can switch directly to a specific screen group.

MEMORY MANAGEMENT UNDER OS/2

OS/2 takes full advantage of the ability of the 80286 chip to reference up to 16MB of physical memory. The *Memory Manager* provides the logic that allows OS/2 to remember where each program is located in memory. This internal manager keeps track of all your requested programs, the memory requirements of each, and the current use of physical memory. The Memory Manager is sophisticated enough to allow individual programs to address more memory than is available, creating what is known as *virtual memory* addressability. It is intelligent enough to run more programs than will fit into the 16MB chip memory. This ability is crucial to multitasking, which may demand more physical resources than the system has available.

The 80286 chip supports the advanced capability called *swapping*, which makes it possible to address virtual memory space much larger than physical memory. When a process addresses a virtual memory location, the Memory Manager will determine whether it corresponds to a valid physical memory location currently belonging to that process. If the location is not in physical memory, the 80286 chip will generate an interrupt signal to convey that fact, and OS/2 can swap a portion of allocated physical memory to a disk file called a *swap file*. Either the now freed-up physical memory can have data written into it, or, if the needed information has been previously swapped out, OS/2 will get that data from another existing swap file. The chip will also generate an interrupt if the process tries to address memory that does not belong to it, allowing the operating system to take appropriate action.

DOS users will recall that the DOS operating system was limited to a maximum physical memory addressibility of 1MB, but that no more than 640K was actually available for DOS itself and your application programs. Swapping allows OS/2 to treat some of that physical memory, whose contents have been swapped out to disk, as if it were extra memory (virtual memory) now available for double duty.

The Memory Manager (see Chapter 10 for more details) keeps track of which programs are in memory and using which physical addresses, as well as which programs have been temporarily swapped out of memory and stored in short-term swap files. The ability to exceed physical memory during the running of programs is known as *storage overcommitment*. OS/2 can even go beyond that, by allowing you to address an apparent memory space of 1 gigabyte, or 2^{30} bytes (see Chapter 10). In fact, OS/2 will run single applications which individually are larger than the available physical memory.

Figure 1.7 shows how OS/2 makes use of memory when running only protected mode applications (i.e., when the system configuration does not allow any older DOS programs to run). Segments of application code and data are placed under OS/2's control throughout the 16MB (or less) of addressable space. The BIOS and the video buffer information are placed just under the 1MB limit, as in DOS. OS/2 itself occupies the lowest memory locations. The space above OS/2 and the 1MB limit can be used for additional OS/2 application code and data information.

If you also wish to run your former DOS programs in real mode, your Config.sys file is responsible for initializing memory as seen in Figure 1.8. See Chapter 9 for more details on the Config.sys file, and Chapter 3 for step-by-step explanations of how to run your former DOS programs in real mode.

As you can see, the OS/2 application code and data information still occupy the upper portion of physical memory, but no more than the physical memory limit of 16MB. In real mode, older DOS .exe or .com files run in the physical memory below 640K. Fundamental OS/2 information still resides in the lowest memory. Above this small OS/2 area, yet still below the 640K limit, is the version of MS-DOS you will be running, along with your application programs. This version of DOS is intended to be compatible with DOS 3.3.

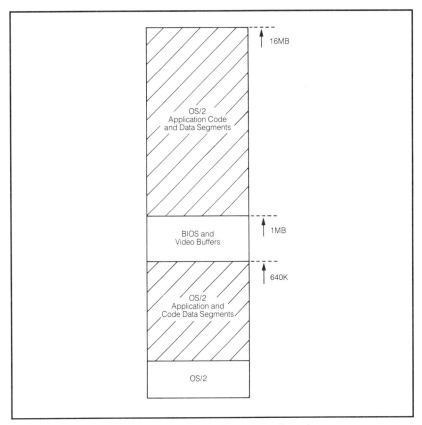

Figure 1.7: Layout of physical memory in protected mode

If you are running suspect programs in real mode, be aware that your entire OS/2 system is more susceptible to crashes when in real mode. Consider upgrading your former DOS programs to protected mode OS/2 versions.

A separate and additional portion of OS/2 resides just above the 1MB limit, but below all of the application code and data segments. Running your former DOS program, then, uses only the bottom 1MB of memory, and running new protected OS/2 programs employs the rest of physical memory. However, when running a former DOS program in real mode, neither the hardware protection of the 80286 chip, nor the software protection of OS/2's protected mode are active. It is possible for any one of your old DOS programs to crash the entire system, including your no-longer-protected OS/2 processes.

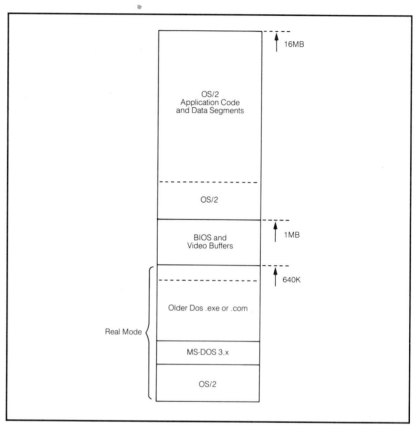

Figure 1.8: Layout of physical memory in real mode

ON-LINE HELP

OS/2 has hundreds of system messages that alert you to various statuses and conditions during system operation. All of these system messages are available to you at the command prompt through a useful on-line program called Helpmsg.exe. This message help facility allows you to request information about any message that OS/2 may display for you. To access it, use the following syntax:

HELPMSG *messageid*

Messageid is the DOS message identifier displayed during system operations when OS/2 wants to alert you to a particular condition. All of the messages are of the form DOS*nnnn*. The *nnnn* represents a four-digit numeric code corresponding to an error message. You can use the HELPMSG command to ask OS/2 for a clarification of the reason for the message, and a suggested course of action. Messages from OS/2 usually occur because of some misunderstanding or misuse of a command. For instance, in the next example, the user attempts to substitute a pseudo disk drive F for the Budget directory, with the following command:

SUBST F: \Budget

If OS/2 is unsuccessful at this substitution, it will display the following message:

DOS 1107: The system cannot complete the process.

If you aren't sure what this message means, you can type the following at the system prompt: HELPMSG DOS1107. You will then see the following result on your screen:

DOS1107: The system cannot complete the process.
EXPLANATION: The command specified can only be run in DOS mode.
ACTION: Retry the command in DOS mode.

Most errors and system messages will be understandable right away. The fact that OS/2 makes *all* system messages accessible to you with both explanation and suggested action makes this system an easier one to use.

SUMMARY

In this chapter, you were introduced to the multitasking world of OS/2. OS/2 brings the power of mainframe and minicomputer operating systems to the microcomputer world.

- OS/2 provides for multiple processes or tasks to run simultaneously. It uses the power of the 80286 or 80386 chip to allow these multiple processes to share system resources and to be protected from each other during program execution.

- Two completely individual operating environments or modes are available through OS/2. Real mode allows all former DOS 3.x programs to run in the lowest 640K of memory, resulting in dramatic underutilization of the power of OS/2.

- The protected mode takes full advantage of all hardware features of the advanced microprocessing chip, and blends those with exciting new software features for supporting multitasking available in OS/2. Each process is protected from violations of its address space from every other executing process.

- A sophisticated memory manager in OS/2 keeps track of all running programs and all memory requirements for each of them. It also manages the swapping of memory to enable more processes to run in your physical memory than would otherwise fit. To accomplish this, it uses disk space in the form of a swap file to temporarily store portions of executing programs, and to facilitate the switching between active and inactive processes.

- OS/2's memory manager even allows processes to run whose memory demands exceed available physical memory through a feature called storage overcommitment. In all cases where memory demand exceeds memory availability, OS/2's swapping feature permits the operation to continue.

- OS/2 provides an on-line help facility, in the form of an external command called HELPMSG, which allows you to call up an explanation for every OS/2 system message, as well as a course of suggested action based on the nature of the message.

In the next chapter you'll take this introductory understanding of the nature of OS/2 and apply it to your system. You will learn how to install and start up OS/2 on your own hardware.

INSTALLING AND STARTING UP OS/2

IN CHAPTER 1, YOU GOT A GLIMPSE OF THE MULTI-tasking world of OS/2. In this chapter, you'll find out how to prepare your hard disk for OS/2, and how you can transfer the appropriate OS/2 files from the disks you received with your system to your hard disk. You'll also learn about the different device drivers accompanying OS/2, some of which are essential for adequately installing and configuring your system. For more extensive details on the advanced customization features of OS/2 that are available during system configuration, see Chapter 9.

AUTOMATIC INSTALLATION OF OS/2

OS/2 comes to you on two high-capacity disks, labeled Program and Supplemental. The Program disk is bootable, and regardless of how your system is currently prepared, you can place it into your high-capacity floppy disk drive, then either turn on the computer or reset it. This will bring up OS/2 on your system. Because OS/2 is much larger than DOS, it takes somewhat longer to load. Don't be concerned with the delay. Once loaded, the commands and programs will actually run faster.

The first thing you will see after the loading process is complete will either be the Session Manager screen (see Chapter 1), or the following protected mode command prompt:

```
[A:\] echo off
[A:\]_
```

OS/2's menu-driven Install program offers you two types of installation. You may choose a simple automatic installation, which directs a set of standard system settings. Alternately, the Install menu provides a customized installation, which asks a number of specific questions about your individual computer and the configuration of its add-on boards, peripheral devices, and memory.

Your dealer or system supplier may have already completed some preparatory steps of the Install program, including partitioning and formatting, so that they are ready to use for your application programs. If this has not been done, however, the Install program can take you through each of the following steps:

1. Partitioning your hard disk

2. Formatting your hard disk

3. Creating the appropriate OS/2 directories

4. Copying the necessary OS/2 files from the program and supplemental disks onto your hard disk

5. Creating the system configuration and startup files

MANUAL INSTALLATION OF OS/2

Occasionally, you may not wish to follow the automatic sequencing of the Install program. You may wish to control each step more closely, for customization purposes, or your disk may already be partitioned (and even formatted), and you may wish to jump right to directory creation. This section presents the individual installation steps; you can select the one(s) most appropriate to your system.

PARTITIONING YOUR HARD DISK

Hard disks are usually so large that they can contain more than one type of operating system. For example, OS/2 can manage one part of your hard disk, while UNIX manages another. Each of these operating system sections is called a partition; a hard disk can have from one to four partitions, depending on the number of different operating systems you intend to place on it.

Partitions make the hard disk, especially a very large one, potentially more economical, because they allow up to four completely different computer systems on one piece of hardware. However, because they do not share a common software environment, they cannot directly share data. And, of course, this isn't even a key issue if OS/2 is the only operating system you intend to place on your hard disk.

You must create partitions before using a hard disk in any manner. Most of the time you will probably want to make the entire disk into one partition and call it drive C, using the FDISK command. However, if you are using one of the increasingly common hard disks with more than 32MB, you must first use the FDISK program to create a primary OS/2 partition of no more than 32MB, then use the remaining space however you like.

Any additional space on your disk, beyond the primary partition's space, can be made into one or more *extended* or additional OS/2 partitions, each of which can also be up to 32MB. Any or all of these extra OS/2 partitions can be divided into additional logical drives, for instance, D or E or F. Only in this way will you be able to store and retrieve information on that larger hard disk. See Appendix B for further information on using the FDISK utility program to prepare your hard disk.

Space on your hard disk that has not been partitioned for an OS/2 primary or extended partition remains available for other operating systems. They are responsible for their own partitioning and formatting of this remaining space.

Do not run the FDISK utility if your hard disk has any information on it that has not been backed up. Partitioning erases all information on a hard disk. If you want to reconfigure your hard disk, back up all desired files first.

FORMATTING YOUR HARD DISK

After partitioning your hard disk, you must prepare the disk itself to receive data. Because you may have partitioned the hard disk into one or more logical disk drives, you will have to use the FORMAT command to prepare each of these logical disks individually. When you prepare the disk yourself, you must use the FORMAT command to specify which hard disk is to receive the system files. The command below does this for drive C:

```
FORMAT C: /S
```

If you have partitioned your disk to include additional logical drives such as D or E, you must repeat the formatting process so that each of those portions of the physical hard disk are also prepared to receive data. A simple line like the following is all that is required:

FORMAT D:

This formats the portion of the hard disk defined as D during the partitioning process. Follow the same procedure for any additional logical drives.

As a result of the formatting process, the system disk (the one you used the /s switch on) is prepared. OS/2 will initialize this disk with copies of Os2bio.com, Os2dos.com, and a host of other necessary system support files. These two files alone occupy more than one quarter of a megabyte, and contain the majority of OS/2's internal instructions. Once this installation process is complete, the information in these files will be sought and read into memory each time you turn on the computer.

The Os2bio.com file contains software that understands how to send data to and receive data from peripheral devices, like printers and disks. The Os2dos.com file contains the logic and routines for managing the data organization itself. The file system is controlled by the logic in this Os2dos.com file, while the more nitty gritty signal and data communications are handled by routines in Os2bio.com. When your system boots up, the [A:\] prompt indicates that these hidden files have been read from disk and loaded into the internal memory of the computer.

Because these two files alone take up several hundred thousand kilobytes and the external disk commands require several hundred thousand additional kilobytes, the use of high capacity disks is mandatory with OS/2. That fact, along with other operating restrictions, makes a diskette-based OS/2 system unrealistic. Although there is a theoretical possibility that such DOS-like diskette-based systems would work, the dependency of many OS/2 operations on the system disk makes it impractical. Disk juggling (switching between the OS/2 Program disk, Supplemental disk, and data disks) is an art greatly scorned by most microcomputer users. In an era of dramatically lowered hard-disk prices, it is not realistic to consider using OS/2 without a hard disk.

CREATING SYSTEM DIRECTORIES
AND COPYING NECESSARY FILES

After your disk has been partitioned and properly formatted, you are ready to selectively create the necessary directories, and to copy the appropriate files into them. The installation program leads you through this stage by creating several directories, resulting in a structure similar to that shown in Figure 2.1. On your own, of course, you would simply use the MD (make directory) and COPY commands to set up your disk structure as desired.

The root directory is created for some critical files, such as the configuration file, the initial batch files, and certain necessary device driver files. Os2, a subdirectory within the root, is created primarily to contain the external .exe and .com command files. These contain familiar OS/2 external commands, such as CHKDSK, XCOPY, and FORMAT, as well as some new ones like ANSI and HELPMSG. If you are using the Install program, you may have another directory called Install, which contains the support files for the installation procedure. If you intend to do considerable programming work with the system, your customized installation procedure may create and populate additional directories, as seen in Figure 2.2.

The minimum system configuration you will need (see Figure 2.1) is a root directory with appropriate configuration and initial batch files, and a subordinate directory called Os2 containing the external commands copied over from the Supplemental disk.

Documentation accompanying any of your additional programming tools offers instruction on initializing the directories seen in Figure 2.2. For example, the Tools directory might include the C compiler routines and the macro assembler files. The Lib directory

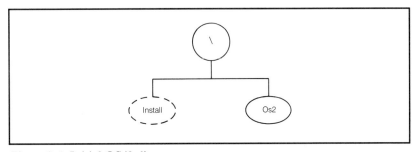

Figure 2.1: Initial OS/2 directory structure

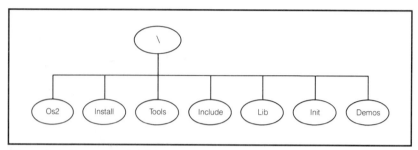

Figure 2.2: Customized OS/2 directory structure for program development

includes the programming library modules and object modules necessary for compilation and assembly. The Include directory is composed of a variety of standard programming modules to be incorporated during program compilation. The Demos directory contains, as you would expect, sample programs using or demonstrating key programming techniques. See Chapter 10 for further information about how these tools and utilities might be used for programming under OS/2.

STARTING UP OS/2 FROM YOUR HARD DISK

You've now completed the entire Install sequence from partitioning your disk to formatting your disk to creating the proper directories and to copying the OS/2 files onto them. At this point, verify that the sequence has worked. Either reboot your system with Ctrl-Alt-Del, turn your system off and on, or press a reset button if your system has one. You should be able to restart your system without a disk in the A drive, and OS/2 should boot properly from your hard disk, resulting in the standard OS/2 prompt, or the Session Manager screen.

If your system has a nonstandard hard disk from which you are intending to boot OS/2, you must configure your system to understand this nonstandard hard disk. Although you will learn about OS/2's configuration in much greater detail in Chapter 9, you need to consider the special conditions of nonstandard hardware now, because so much of the automatic startup operation depends on this nonstandard drive.

The lines below show the default Config.sys file:

```
BUFFERS = 50
PROTSHELL = Shell.exe Cmd.exe
LIBPATH = A:\
```

In Chapter 9 you will learn the meaning of each of the lines in this sample Config.sys file, but for now, you should learn that every nonstandard hard disk has its own device driver. All device drivers are recognizable by a .sys file-name extension. Your hard disk undoubtedly comes with instructions and a disk containing this device driver. For instance, if your device driver is called Hardrive.sys, you must add the following line to the end of the Config.sys file on your OS/2 program disk:

```
DEVICE = Hardrive.sys
```

You must also copy the file Hardrive.sys to the OS/2 program disk.

This adjustment to the Config.sys file assures that when your version of OS/2 boots up from the A drive, OS/2 will recognize and understand the nature and requirements of this nonstandard hard disk drive before you even attempt to work on the C drive. The hardrive.sys device driver file contains all of the necessary information for this purpose. Your own device driver may be named differently from this example. Look in your documentation, or ask your dealer for the information.

INSTALLING ADDITIONAL DEVICE DRIVERS

A wide range of additional devices provide you with broad expanded capabilities for your personal computer. OS/2 is designed to make effective use of these additional devices through special system programs called *device drivers*. As in the example of the preceding section, these programs are written by the manufacturer of the additional hardware, who provides the program on disk. For example, you might buy an add-on board containing a modem, or you might add a 20MB, 40MB, or even 70MB hard disk to your system. Many graphics programs use a mouse, and some printers have nonstandard features like built-in memory. Some specialized application systems even use light pens and bar code readers.

All of these nonstandard devices require that you inform OS/2 of their existence, and that the manufacturer's device driver program is available to OS/2 when it boots (from the hard disk now). You can accomplish this by simply copying the .sys file with the device driver code onto your hard disk, and telling OS/2 where to find it. For example, if you had several device driver files, you could store them all in a directory called \SYS. Then the DEVICE = Hardrive.sys line of the preceding section could be simply revised to tell OS/2 of this different location as follows:

DEVICE = \SYS\Hardrive.sys

OS/2 provides a number of necessary and optional device drivers. The necessary device drivers cover things like the system keyboard, screen, default printer, and clock. The optional device drivers cover things like the ANSI escape sequences, the asynchronous communications ports, the enhanced graphics adaptor, additional floppy disk drives, mouse drivers, and RAM disks. These optional device drivers are available with OS/2, but will only be included in your memory-based system (and therefore take up space) if you include a line of the following form in your Config.sys file:

DEVICE = *drivername*

There are currently six specific optional device driver files provided with OS/2. They are listed in Table 2.1.

The first device driver, Ansi.sys, is a carryover from the DOS days. Installing it allows you to use ANSI escape sequences when in the DOS-compatible (real) mode of OS/2. These escape sequences are normally available in OS/2 mode, but if you want to use them in real mode, you must include the following line in your Config.sys file:

DEVICE = [drive:][path]Ansi.sys

DEVICE DRIVER	FUNCTION
Ansi.sys	Installs escape sequence feature in real mode
Com.sys	Supports asynchronous communications (serial) ports
Ega.sys	Supports EGA-oriented mouse operation
Extdskdd.sys	Supports external floppy disk drive
Mouse*xx*.sys	Supports mouse operations
Vdisk.sys	Supports RAM disk emulation

Table 2.1: Installable Device Drivers in OS/2

Chapter 9 goes into much greater detail about customizing your OS/2 system. The escape sequences available through ansi.sys enable you to control the movement of the cursor and the appearance of a number of graphic designs and colors (for color monitors) on your screen. See the ANSI and PROMPT commands in Chapter 5 for more details about using ANSI escape sequences while in protected (OS/2) mode.

The Com.sys device driver is necessary when using any of the asynchronous communications ports (serial ports) known as COM1 through COM8. This is a new requirement of OS/2. OS/2 allows for up to eight serial ports, whereas DOS 3.3 allows for only four, and DOS 3.2 and earlier allowed for only two.

If you intend to use any serial port during the operation of your system, you must include a line such as this in your Config.sys file:

```
DEVICE = [drive:][path]Com.sys
[/COMn:baud,parity,data,stop,rcv,xmt][,p]
```

Since eight serial ports are permitted, n can range from 1 to 8, and most of the other parameters are similar to but not precisely identical to DOS 3.3 parameters. The variations can be seen in Table 2.2, which specifies each parameter and its possible values.

SUPPORTING
THE ENHANCED GRAPHICS ADAPTER

The Ega.sys device driver should be included in your system if you are using one of the EGA graphics modes and a mouse device that interacts with one of those modes. The required syntax is

DEVICE = [drive:][path]Ega.sys

The three modes supported by this device driver are

mode 14:640 × 200, 16-color display

mode 15:640 × 350, monochrome

mode 16:640 × 350, 64-color display

INSTALLING ADDITIONAL
EXTERNAL FLOPPY DISK DRIVES

As commercial floppy disk research continues, the range of possible disks that can be incorporated into your system broadens. The

PARAMETER	FUNCTION
Baud	Defines the baud rate. Allowable decimal values are 110, 150, 300, 600, 1200, 2400, 4800, 9600, 19200.
Parity	Set the port parity to none (n), odd (o), even (e), mark (m), or space (s).
Data	Number of data bits. Can be 5, 6, 7, or 8.
Stop	The number of stop bits. Allowable values can be one stop bit (1), two stop bits (2), or one and a half stop bits (5).
Rcv	The size in bytes of the receiving buffer.
Xmt	The size in bytes of the transmitting buffer.
P	When used, OS/2 will keep retrying if the printer is busy.

Table 2.2: Com.sys Parameters and Their Possible Values

extdskdd.sys device driver can support any of these external drives. You must include a configuration command of the following sort in your Config.sys file:

DEVICE = [drive:][path]Extdskdd.sys /d:*ddd* [/c] [f:*f*]
[/h:*hh*] [/n:] [/s:*ss*][/t:*ttt*]

Table 2.3 describes the possible values for the switch settings necessary to specify the inclusion of an external disk drive.

For example, if you wish to add an external 1.2MB floppy to your standard AT system, and assuming that you already have one 1.2MB floppy in your system, you would include the following line in

PARAMETER	FUNCTION
/d:*ddd*	Sets the physical drive number. Ranges from 0 to 255. 0 represents drive A, 1 represents drive B, etc.
/c	Indicates that the device driver can ascertain whether the floppy disk drive door is open or closed. Sometimes this is called *change line* support.
/F:*f*	Defines the device type, or form factor. F:0 indicates a disk with a capacity of 160 to 360 kilobytes. F:1 indicates a 1.2MB high capacity drive, and F:2 indicates a 720K to 1.44MB disk drive.
/h:*hh*	Specifies the maximum head number. Ranges from 1 to 99, with a default of 2.
/n	Specifies a nonremovable block device, such as a fixed hard disk.
/s:*ss*	Specifies the number of sectors per track. Ranges from 1 to 99, with a default value of 9.
/t:*ttt*	Specifies the number of tracks per side on the fixed disk. Ranges from 1 to 999, with a default of 80.

Table 2.3: Switch Settings for External Floppy Disk Drives

your Config.sys:

> DEVICE = [drive][path]Extdskdd.sys /d:01 /f:1

This entry specifies an additional floppy disk drive, the second physical drive on your system (d:01), with a form factor or device type of 1.2MB (f:1). Counting of physical drives begins with d:00, the first floppy drive.

INSTALLING MOUSE DEVICES

Different manufacturers' mouse devices understand either real or protected mode application requirements, and some understand both. The code for all three modes is contained in the appropriately-named device driver. You must include the following lines:

> DEVICE = [drive:][path]Pointdd.sys
> DEVICE = [drive:][path]Mousea*xx*.sys
> [,serial = *device*][,mode = *m*][,qsize = *q*]

The italicized variables in this device installation line are explained in Table 2.4.

INSTALLING RAM DISKS

This device driver should be familiar to those of you who have worked in the IBM PC-DOS environment. Vdisk.sys is the device driver that permits use of a portion of physical memory to emulate an additional disk drive. This allows much more rapid application processing for those normally disk-based files that have been placed on this emulated (rapid) disk drive in memory. Those of you who use MS-DOS systems may have known this device driver as Ramdisk.sys. It offers the same kind of support in OS/2, with a few added adjustments.

You must include a line in your Config.sys file of this kind:

> DEVICE = [drive:][path]Vdisk.sys [*bbbb*][*ssss*][*dddd*][/e ¦ /a]

Vdisk.sys normally creates the requested RAM disk in low memory, unless you have specified the /e or /a switches (see Table 2.5). Particularly if you are using real mode, you should use one of these two switches

PARAMETER	FUNCTION
xx	Specifies which of several device drivers to include. If xx is 00, for example, then the Mousea00.sys device driver is loaded. This controls the PC Mouse by Mouse Systems. See your mouse documentation for the driver number (00, 01, 02, 03, etc.) to include here.
Device	Specifies the serial port being used for the serial mouse. Can be COM1, or COM2, with COM1 being the default.
m	Specifies the mode in which the mouse will be used. Can be r for real mode, p for protected mode, or b for both.
q	Specifies the number of bytes to be used for queue buffer space (from 1 to 100) in each protected mode screen group.

Table 2.4: Mouse Device Driver Installation Parameters

to ensure retaining as much available memory for your application program as possible. Don't forget that RAM disks are used most intelligently for increasing speed. You should place files on them that need to be read and accessed rapidly, but that do not need to be updated with any permanent information. This way, if the power is lost during operations, the transient data stored on the RAM disk is not lost forever.

SUMMARY

In this chapter you learned how to install OS/2 on a hard disk, and how to start it up with a configuration that reflects any additional devices that you have in your hard disk.

- OS/2 includes an Install program that leads you through an automatic installation of OS/2 on your hard disk.

- The FDISK utility in OS/2 partitions your disk for use with OS/2 or other operating systems. It also allows you to manage

PARAMETER	FUNCTION
bbbb	Specifies the disk size (in kilobytes) to be emulated. Can range from a minimum of 16 kilobytes to a maximum based on the amount of memory available. The default is 64K.
ssss	Specifies the sector size in bytes. Can be 128, 256, 512, or 1024 bytes. The default is 128.
dddd	Specifies the number of root directory entries. The default value can range from a minimum of 2 to a maximum of 1024, with a default value of 64.
/e | /a	Use the /e if you have installed extended memory beyond 1MB. Use the /a if you have installed an extended memory board that meets the LIM expanded memory specification for a RAM drive.

Table 2.5: Vdisk.sys Setup Parameters

hard disks exceeding 32MB, and to create additional logical drives within that extended memory partition. See Appendix B for further details.

- The FORMAT utility must be run for each logical disk after partitioning. The boot disk must be formatted with the /s switch to reserve sufficient room for the OS/2 system files.

- The Config.sys file is necessary if your hardware includes certain nonstandard devices, such as an extra hard disk, mouse, or modem. (See Chapter 9 for additional configuration information.)

- OS/2 includes a number of optional installable device drivers for managing the ANSI escape sequences in real mode (Ansi-.sys), for managing the configuration of serial ports (Com.sys), for supporting mouse/enhanced graphics adaptor operations (Ega.sys), for installing external floppy disk drives (Extdskdd.sys), for understanding unique mouse hardware (Mouseaxx.sys), and for creating and managing one or more RAM disks (Vdisk.sys).

Naturally, after installing and preparing your OS/2 system, you'll want to use it. The next chapter shows you how to quickly use your OS/2 system for running your favorite older DOS programs.

RUNNING
DOS PROGRAMS IN OS/2

_____

OS/2 PROVIDES MANY DRAMATIC IMPROVEMENTS over DOS. Chapter 1 outlined just how significant those improvements are and discussed an important OS/2 benefit: you are not required to buy or write completely new programs, because almost all of your DOS programs can run under OS/2. It gives you the benefits of a dramatically improved operating system, including the enhanced new features, without losing the functionality of your current programs.

The compatibility between DOS and OS/2 is provided through the OS/2 real mode, which emulates DOS 3.3. Real mode provides an operating environment that allows you to run most of your DOS 3.x programs with no changes. In fact, many programs that predate DOS 3.x will also run in OS/2's real mode.

In this chapter, you will learn the steps necessary to make a smooth transition from DOS to the OS/2 environment including setting up, starting up, and configuring your OS/2 environment to permit DOS programs to run. You will also learn a number of important distinctions between the two operating environments, and potential obstacles to running DOS programs in OS/2. The chapter examines a broad range of issues, from proper configuration to initial batch file contents to some of the more complex programming issues of OS/2 function calls. Special details of interest to programmers are covered in Chapter 10.

WORKING IN REAL MODE

If you follow the instructions in this section and get a message saying **Insufficient Memory**, don't panic and worry that the 2MB of RAM you bought aren't enough to run your old program. They are. The next section on configuration explains how to configure your new OS/2 system to understand the different memory requirements of the DOS programs you'll be running in OS/2's real mode.

You already know that you have to switch from OS/2's protected, multitasking mode to real mode to run DOS programs. When OS/2's protected mode starts up, the first thing you'll see is the protected mode screen prompt [C:\]. Pressing the Ctrl-Esc key combination displays the Session Manager screen, which you saw in Figure 1.5. As you know, you can use your cursor keys and the Return key to start new programs or switch to a running program from the Session Manager.

If you want to run a DOS application, the simplest method is to bring up the Session Manager screen and use the right arrow key to highlight the MS-DOS Command Prompt choice. Then press the Return key. This moves you into real mode and the DOS command line prompt. If you had selected Cmd.exe, you would have been switched to the OS/2 (protected mode) command prompt. Remember that the Cmd.exe command file interpreter handles all protected mode OS/2 command requests, while the Command.com command line interpreter handles all real mode command line requests. Once you have brought up Command.com, you can continue as if your machine were running DOS alone. If you've loaded your disk with your applications, set your PATH and your working directory as required to run the DOS program.

If you try to run one of your DOS programs (.exe or .com) from the protected mode command prompt, you will receive one of the following two error messages:

> DOS0191E: The system has detected an unacceptable signature in the file, *Filename*.

or

> DOS0193E: The system has detected an unacceptable executable format in file, *Filename*.

OS/2 displays one of these two messages when you try to run a file that is either formatted incorrectly for OS/2 or represents an incorrect version of the program. Under most conditions, you would try to find the correct version of the program. In this case, you are trying to run what you know is the real mode or DOS version of the program. Since the .exe and .com files from DOS are unreadable as executable files in OS/2, it is unable to understand the instructions. Any program that was originally compiled, assembled, or prepared to run in DOS mode can be run only in OS/2's real mode. Let's look at some examples.

RUNNING YOUR WORD PROCESSOR

To run a DOS-based word processor on OS/2, you must first switch to real mode and get the familiar C> prompt. In this example, the word processor is located in the WP directory of the C drive. To access it, enter the following commands at the C> prompt:

```
PATH C:\;C:\Os2;C:\Wp
CD \Wp
Wp
```

The first line augments the system search path in order to look for files in the root first, then to search the Os2 directory for any necessary supporting routines (such as the external commands CHKDSK or XCOPY), and lastly to look in the Wp directory (where the word processor in this example can be found). The second line performs the standard change directory (CD) request to make the word processing directory the current default. The final step in real mode is to ask the Command.com interpreter to pass control to your version of Wp.com or Wp.exe, depending on which word processor you are using.

RUNNING YOUR DATABASE MANAGEMENT PROGRAM

Now suppose that you have a database program whose main and support files are located in a directory called Dbms. You want to run your inventory program located in a subdirectory of the Dbms directory called Invntry. You want to switch to the Invntry subdirectory that contains the inventory database information, but you must still ensure that the principal Dbms files are accessible through the

PATH. Use the following sequence of statements in real mode:

```
PATH C:\;C:\Os2;C:\Dbms
APPEND \Dbms
CD \Dbms\Invntry
DBASE
```

In this example, your working directory is now the Invntry directory. This is where the Dbase.com program will look for the appropriate database files or create new ones. The PATH command meanwhile ensures that OS/2 knows how to find its appropriate system files in either the root or the Os2 directory. Because of the PATH command, OS/2 can also find the main DBASE program in the Dbms directory. The APPEND command, on the other hand, enables the system to locate any required overlay files used by the main executable DBASE programs.

RUNNING YOUR SPREADSHEET PROGRAM

Finally, you may wish to run a favorite spreadsheet, like Lotus 1-2-3. All of Lotus's main system files may be located in the Lotus subdirectory, while all of your budget worksheets are located in a subdirectory called Budget, and your accounting worksheets are located in a different subdirectory called Accounts. Like database managers, sophisticated spreadsheets usually work on an overlay basis. You therefore need the following sequence of steps to run this kind of application in OS/2's real mode:

```
PATH C:\;C:\Os2;C:\Lotus
APPEND \Lotus
CD \Lotus\Accounts
123
```

As you can see in Figure 3.1, the CD command makes the Accounts directory the current working directory (pointed to by the arrow in Figure 3.1). To OS/2 this means that your worksheet files will be accessible in that directory. If you want to switch to the Budget

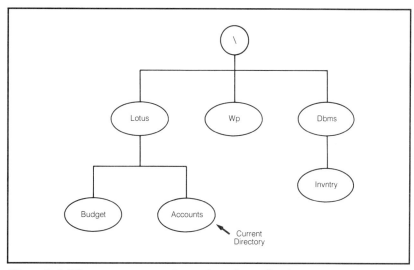

Figure 3.1: Directory structure for real mode applications

directory, do so either from within Lotus, or modify the CD command before running the 123.exe program. The PATH and APPEND lines again direct the OS/2 system to find the main 123.exe program (via PATH), and any subordinate overlay files (via APPEND), in the Lotus directory.

Most DOS programs will run if you follow the instructions above. As mentioned at the beginning of this section, however, some programs may not run directly because they require more memory than the default number of kilobytes allotted by OS/2 to real mode. If this is the only problem, you'll get an **Insufficient Memory** message, and you should follow the guidelines for configuring your system in the next section.

If your program doesn't run in real mode for some other reason, read about potential obstacles in the "Distinctions and Obstacles" section of this chapter. Your program may use certain system interrupts or DOS function calls for manipulating hardware that are not allowed in any program in the OS/2 environment, even in real mode. In these cases, you must either find a replacement program or get the errant program rewritten for the OS/2 environment.

CONFIGURING YOUR OS/2 SYSTEM FOR DOS PROGRAMS

In both DOS and OS/2, the system assumes certain default values if you do not specify new ones with a Config.sys file. In OS/2 as in DOS there is only one Config.sys file. But with OS/2, you can override any and all of a host of initial values for internal systems parameters. The control you have via this initial file is so much enhanced over DOS that Chapter 9 is entirely devoted to initial setup conditions now under your control. This chapter, however, addresses only the minimum required to enable DOS programs to run in real mode. Figure 3.2 shows an example Config.sys file.

When you install OS/2, a slightly different Config.sys file is prepared for you. Though the commands in this example are explained in full in

```
 1    REM
 2    REM      Prototype Config.sys file for OS/2 when booting off a hard disk
 3    REM
 4    REM
 5    REM      If your system has less than 2MB of RAM, shrink the size of the
 6    REM      diskcache and the real mode box.  If you are not going to use the
 7    REM      compatibility mode then remove the REM statement from the line that
 8    REM      reads PROTECTONLY=yes
 9    REM
10
11    BUFFERS=50
12    SHELL=Command.com /p /e:512 c:\
13    RMSIZE=640
14    PROTSHELL=Shell.exe Cmd.exe
15    IOPL=yes
16    LIBPATH=C:\
17    MEMMAN=Noswap,move
18    DEVICE=Ansi.sys
19    DEVICE=Hardrive.sys
20
21    REM      The rest of the file contains commented out lines.  Delete the word
22    REM      REM from the begining of the command lines if that feature is needed
23    REM      or wanted.
24
25    REM PROTECTONLY=yes
26    REM DISKCACHE=512
27    REM SWAPPATH=C:
28    REM DEVICE=C:\Com01.sys
29    REM DEVICE=C:\Vdisk.sys 256 512 16
30    REM DEVICE=C:\Pointdd.sys
31
32    REM    Select one of the following drivers:
33    REM    02 - serial, 03 - Bus, 04 - Import
34    REM DEVICE=C:\Mousea02.sys mode=b
35    REM DEVICE=C:\Mousea03.sys mode=b
36    REM DEVICE=C:\Mousea04.sys mode=b
37
38    REM    The following lines enable the Code Page support drivers.
39
40    REM DEVINFO=scr,ega,C:\Viotbl.dcp
41    REM DEVINFO=kbd,us, C:\Keyboard.dcp
42    REM DEVINFO=lpt1,4201,C:\4201.dcp,rom=(437,0)
43    REM CODEPAGE=437,850
```

Figure 3.2: Sample Config.sys file

Chapter 9, some of the critical commands that have been modified or inserted to allow DOS programs to run are discussed below.

As you can see in line 12, the SHELL command specifies that the DOS Command.com program will be a permanently resident command interpreter for real mode instructions (indicated by the /p switch). All of the lines in this prototype Config.sys file are as they appear during initial installation of OS/2, except lines 13, 18, and 19. Line 13 is essential to DOS programs. During OS/2 initialization, the default is to install a real mode memory size of 256K (RMSIZE = 256).

If the programs that you intend to run require 384K, 512K, or 640K, use your line editor or word processor to change the value in line 13. It is not unusual to use all 640K in real mode for large, demanding programs like computer-aided design programs, or for certain memory resident utility programs that are run in conjunction with standard software. In this case, the DOS real mode will need to occupy 640K and you must make sure that line 13 of your Config.sys file reads

RMSIZE = 640

Depending on need, applications, and installed hardware, you may also have to add extra lines such as lines 18 and 19. Some application programs, like the PreCursor menu management application program, require that the Ansi.sys device driver be added to your Config.sys file (line 18). It is available at all times in protected mode for OS/2 programming and applications. However, you must load the Ansi.sys device driver yourself (by including the line DEVICE = Ansi.sys in your Config.sys file) if you intend to use special ANSI escape sequences in real mode such as cursor movement, graphics characters, and colors on color monitors. (Read the section on the PROMPT command in Chapter 5 for a full explanation of ANSI escape sequences.)

The last example insertion in this Config.sys file is seen on line 19: DEVICE = Hardrive.sys. This line is for a system with a nonstandard hard disk installed, and a hard disk device driver called Hardrive.sys. Your system may have this or other unique installed devices, each of which requires the insertion of a line of this kind:

DEVICE = *drivername*

As you can see in Figure 3.2, there are a number of other sample features that are included as *remarks* (REM statements). These are suggested additions and you can invoke any of the special configuration parameter situations by removing the REM from the beginning of the desired line (as lines 21 through 23 explain). Turn to Chapter 9 if you want further information about any of these additional commands. If you're only interested in the minimum requirements for running DOS programs at this time, continue to the next section on startup programs and procedures.

CONTROLLING AUTOMATIC STARTUP IN OS/2 REAL MODE

When you first boot up your OS/2 system, the internal setup of OS/2 is completely initialized according to the command requests placed in the Config.sys file. These commands influence OS/2 and its internal settings one time only. They are acted upon at system bootup, and are not interpreted or acted upon again until the next time you boot up OS/2.

In contrast to this, Figure 3.3 represents the system flow that can be influenced by you at system start. In DOS, the system would automatically run a special startup batch file called Autoexec.bat immediately after configuration and before giving you control at the command prompt. OS/2 has a similar mechanism.

In real mode, the same Autoexec.bat runs with the same results. If you have a file called Autoexec.bat in the root directory of your boot drive, all of the individual command line entries contained within it will be executed one after the other *the first time OS/2 switches to real mode*. Just as in DOS 3.x systems, all real mode batch files are named with a.bat extension; the Autoexec.bat allows for this automatic execution of a ''batch'' of commands. Paralleling this automatic invocation of the Autoexec.bat file is another batch file called Startup.cmd that is automatically invoked *the first time OS/2 switches to protected mode*.

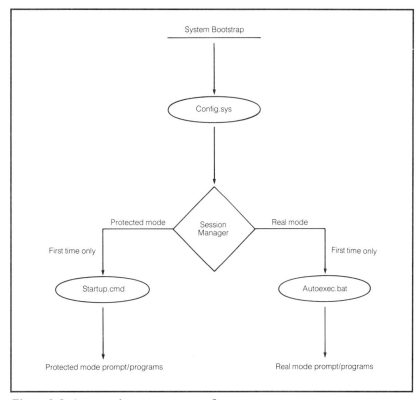

Figure 3.3: Automatic system startup flow

However, unlike the Config.sys file, which can only be invoked at system startup, both these batch files can be run at any time.

The Autoexec.bat file can be a sequence of commands like those you are familiar with from DOS as shown below:

```
SET COMSPEC = C:\Command.com
SET PATH = C:\;C:\Os2
PROMPT $n$g
```

The system PATH is set for system files and external command files. The COMSPEC parameter is also set (for clarification only, because C:\Command.com is the usual default file and directory), which tells OS/2 where it will be able to find the real mode interpreter (Command.com). The PROMPT command in the third line initializes the

Your Autoexec.bat and Startup.cmd batch files must reside in the root directory of your boot disk.

default system prompt to $n (the working drive) followed by $g (a chevron symbol). Chapter 4 explains several additions and modifications you can make to this Autoexec.bat file, allowing a more flexible and utilitarian startup sequence for your system.

You can use this Autoexec.bat file to tell OS/2 how to access your old DOS files automatically. To do so, look at a copy of your own DOS system Autoexec.bat file, and then add your own appropriate adjustments or new lines to OS/2's default Autoexec.bat file. In the simplest case, you can leave the COMSPEC and the PROMPT lines alone. You might adjust the PATH command in your autoexec.bat to include reference to the Dbms and Lotus directories, by changing it as follows:

SET PATH = C:\;C:\Os2;C:\Dbms;C:\Lotus

An APPEND line of the following sort tells the system where the overlay files can be found for your application programs:

APPEND C:\Dbms;C:\Lotus

At the end of your Autoexec.bat file, you can pass control to a hard disk menu management utility you've already set up by adding the following line:

PREMENU

This passes control to the main menu program of a hard disk management package, giving you and other users of your system potential access to all executable DOS programs on your hard disk.

DISTINCTIONS AND OBSTACLES

If you follow the simple guidelines in the previous sections, you should have your old DOS programs up and running in no time. In most cases, it's as simple as adding a couple of lines to the Config.sys file and a couple of lines in an Autoexec.bat file. But life is not always so simple, and certain DOS programs will never run under OS/2. For example, a sophisticated backup system such as Back-It Version

3.0 uses direct memory access (DMA) to achieve very high performance. Data are written to floppy disks at the same time as data are read from the hard disk. This particular program does not work successfully under OS/2, because OS/2 does not allow some of the interrupt-based techniques that are used. However, it can (and probably will) be rewritten using the simultaneous threads technique (presented in Chapter 10) so that it will run in OS/2.

Some programs can be made to run with slight adjustments to the code, but this requires that you are either able to get into the code to adjust it, or that the programmer can provide you with an upgraded version of the code. In this section, you will learn some of the distinctions that should be considered in attempting to make or rewrite these programs.

Let's take a look first at some of the overlapping issues in the DOS and OS/2 operating environments. Figure 3.4 shows a number of the key distinctions between OS/2 and DOS 3.3. It also shows the overlap that allows DOS 3.3 applications to run in OS/2's real mode.

OS/2 uses the hardware features of the 80286 and 80386 chip for protected mode operations, and will not run on machines based on

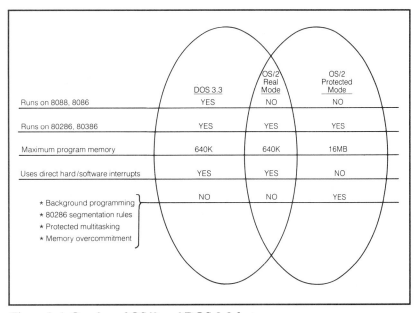

	DOS 3.3	OS/2 Real Mode	OS/2 Protected Mode
Runs on 8088, 8086	YES	NO	NO
Runs on 80286, 80386	YES	YES	YES
Maximum program memory	640K	640K	16MB
Uses direct hard/software interrupts	YES	YES	NO
★ Background programming ★ 80286 segmentation rules ★ Protected multitasking ★ Memory overcommitment	NO	NO	YES

Figure 3.4: Overlap of OS/2 and DOS 3.3 features

8088 or 8086 chips. DOS, although it will run on the more advanced chips, uses only the real mode portion of the chip. Because they do not take advantage of any of the advanced hardware operations of the new chips, DOS programs, whether run under DOS directly or in OS/2's real mode, are limited to 640K of addressable memory.

Although they can make direct use of hardware interrupts, DOS programs running under OS/2 cannot participate in protected multi-tasking. This means that during protected mode operations, your real mode DOS program is frozen. It receives no interrupts and does not continue executing, because it receives no CPU service while you are executing in protected mode. If your program is timer- or clock-dependent, it will not work properly. In addition, the advanced programing features of *segmentation* and *memory overcommitment* can't be used completely by DOS programs.

Segmentation refers to the partitioning of memory by logical addresses rather than physical addresses, enabling you to run programs that can reference more memory than actually exists. Virtual memory, through OS/2's sophisticated memory manager, provides the ability to offer more apparent (virtual) memory to a running process than there is physical (actual) memory available. This is called memory overcommitment. If you are dealing with program writing or rewriting, you will find more information in Chapter 10 on how to solve memory problems with incompatible DOS programs.

Some DOS programs are version specific and will only run on version 2.x or 3.x. These may not work under OS/2, because the version numbering is different.

Those of you accustomed to programming with interrupts may have written your programs to use interrupt 21H services under DOS. Most of the working but undocumented services through this interrupt are no longer supported by OS/2 real mode. Certain service interrupts that access ROM video services by address won't work either, because the management of interrupt 10 has been dramatically changed in OS/2. Since interrupt handling has changed, older special purpose device drivers may not work in the OS/2 environment.

There are many internal distinctions in the methods programmers must use to handle interrupts, manage devices, and code their applications. As a result, Microsoft has defined a special subset of its total system calls that are designed to work in both real mode and protected mode environments. This subset is called the Family Application Program Interface (FAPI) of the complete OS/2 Application Programming Interface (API), and is the suggested subset for programs run in both real mode and protected mode.

If you are writing commercial code that you want to run in either environment, you would certainly do well to write it with the FAPI set of functions. It ensures that users will have much greater ease running your code in either operating system environment, eliminates the drain on physical memory, and enhances the performance and usefulness of the entire OS/2 system. Chapter 10 specifies this subset of FAPI function calls, as well as guidelines for programmers planning to code for both real mode and protected mode execution.

SUMMARY

One of the first ways you will probably use your OS/2 system is to run your DOS programs. Even if you are using OS/2 primarily for new programs, there will probably be times you will want to run DOS programs. This chapter detailed the steps to take to exploit this attractive functionality of OS/2.

- Real mode runs DOS programs in OS/2. OS/2 allows you to reserve (through Config.sys) a portion of physical memory (up to 640K) for emulating a DOS 3.x environment.

- When you switch to real mode, you can run almost any existing application program with standard DOS commands, like CD or PROMPT.

- A Config.sys file initializes both real mode and protected mode operations. Some configuration commands control initial conditions in real mode, and others control these startup system values in protected mode. To run real mode programs, the most important command is the RMSIZE parameter, which must be set equal to the number of kilobytes your DOS program requires.

- The first time real mode is entered from the Session Manager, a batch file called Autoexec.bat executes. All commands within it are assumed to be standard batch file commands, adhering to standard batch file processing rules (see Chapter 8).

- The first time protected mode is entered from the Session Manager, a protected mode batch file (Startup.cmd) executes, enabling you to initialize your working environment for protected mode operations.

- If no Startup.cmd file exists in the root directory of the boot drive, OS/2 starts up with the Session Manager screen.

- The number of overlapping features between OS/2 and DOS 3.3 explains the compatibility that allows many DOS programs to run in OS/2 real mode. But because DOS and OS/2 are not completely compatible, some DOS programs cannot run at all, while others require rewriting.

Now that you understand how to run your favorite DOS programs in your new operating environment, OS/2, you can take a closer look at OS/2 versus DOS in Chapter 4. In this way, you'll gain a better appreciation for the significant improvement in capability and flexibility offered by this new operating system.

PART 2

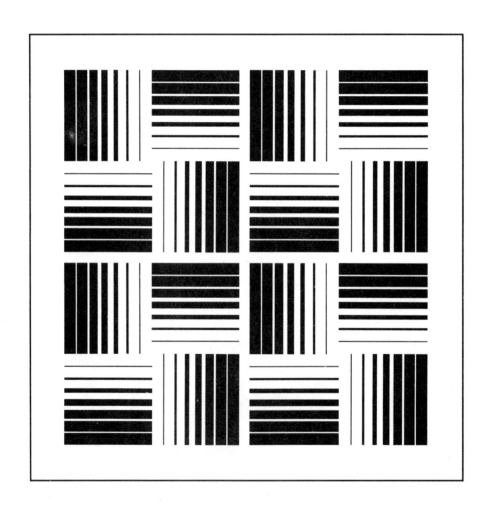

USING OS/2

In Part 2, you will learn how to make OS/2 do much more for you. Chapter 4 starts out with a comparison between DOS and OS/2 that should make you more comfortable with the new operating environment. Chapter 5 then presents all the commands available in OS/2. It distinguishes the ones that can run in conjunction with your old programs in real mode, the ones that have been enhanced or are completely new for the new OS/2 protected mode, and the ones that run smoothly in both modes. Each command is presented with its complete syntax, its type (internal or external), any restrictions, and sufficient examples to ensure easy understanding of proper use.

Chapter 6 takes these commands and explains how they can be used at the command prompt in new ways. Special grouping and sequencing operators are available in OS/2 that allow you to save time and energy by entering multiple commands on the same command line, including commands that are logically dependent on each other. You will also learn how to use pipes, filters, and I/O redirection.

COMPARING OS/2 TO DOS

CHAPTER **4** _____

YOU'VE NOW HAD A CHANCE TO LOOK AT A NUMBER
of differences between OS/2 and DOS, and you've also learned that
the OS/2-DOS overlap permits OS/2 real mode to run DOS programs. In this chapter, you'll get a comparative look at similar commands in DOS and OS/2, and see how the same command can
operate differently in each system. Chapter 1 focused on the key new
features of OS/2, and its advantages over DOS. This chapter
explores differences in major areas: installing DOS and OS/2 and
starting up DOS compared to starting up real or protected mode
applications under OS/2. Also, you'll compare the use of commands
in OS/2 and DOS, as well as the different types of commands.
Lastly, you'll learn about exit codes in OS/2: what they are, which
commands return them, and how they can be used.

COMPARING DOS AND OS/2 INSTALLATION SEQUENCES

DOS has a relatively straightforward installation procedure. You
can format a disk using the /s switch of the FORMAT command.
The FORMAT command itself copies the hidden system files and
the Command.com file to the newly formatted hard or floppy system
disk (see Figure 4.1). This disk is now bootable and can receive any
other application oriented program or data file.

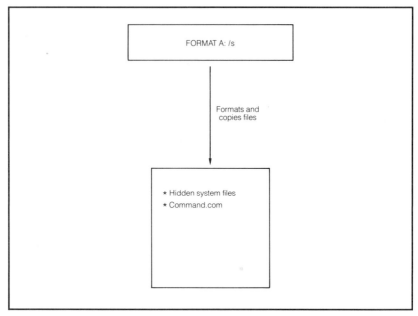

Figure 4.1: Preparing a system disk in DOS

The comparable OS/2 procedure also results in a disk, usually a hard disk, which is formatted to receive the system files. It can boot the system because the special OS/2 system files were transferred to the hard disk during the INSTALL process. These two files, Os2bio.com and Os2dos.com, are no longer hidden. They are visible in the root directory of your boot drive, along with other system support files. However, the OS/2 installation process differs considerably from the DOS system disk preparation process.

As Figure 4.2 illustrates, more steps are needed to install OS/2 than to install DOS. The OS/2 INSTALL process has the potential to go from running the FDISK program (to partition your disk), to formatting your disk, to automatically creating the necessary directories, to copying the appropriate files into those directories, and even to creating certain initialization files. The first result of the OS/2 INSTALL procedure is that the root directory of the boot disk receives the hidden OS/2 system files. Then, the command interpreters for real mode (Command.com) and protected mode (Cmd.exe) and the initialization batch files, are also transferred to

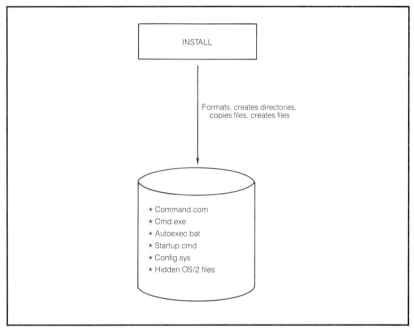

Figure 4.2: Installing OS/2 on your hard disk

the root directory. These beginning control files include the Config.sys file for internal system configuration of both real and protected modes, the Autoexec.bat file for startup operations in real mode, and the Startup.cmd file for beginning operations in protected mode. The OS/2 external command files, such as Xcopy.exe or Helpmsg.exe, are located in large part on the supplemental disk accompanying your OS/2 system. These files are copied into the OS/2 subdirectory. Other files needed for installation are copied into the INSTALL subdirectory.

COMPARING STARTUP OPERATIONS

As you've already seen, only one Config.sys file is necessary in OS/2, and it is created in the root directory of the boot drive during the installation process. Chapter 9 details many new configuration features in OS/2; there are more new commands than there are

Two specific DOS configuration commands, FILES and LASTDRIVE, are no longer useful or necessary. OS/2 will ignore them if it finds them in your configuration file.

unique commands in DOS! Some configuration commands, such as BREAK, FCBS, and SHELL, are appropriate for real mode operations only, and have no meaning for OS/2 protected mode programs. Table 4.1 lists a wide range of additional commands that prepare OS/2 at startup time for operations in both real and protected modes.

Those commands marked with an asterisk are completely new, including commands affecting swapping, scheduling, and memory management. OS/2 operations rely far more on understanding Config.sys possibilities than DOS operations do. Many advanced programming applications available for DOS systems merely suggested that you

REAL MODE ONLY	GENERAL OS/2 SYSTEM
BREAK	BUFFERS
FCBS	CODEPAGE
SHELL	COUNTRY
	DEVICE
	DEVINFO*
	DISKCACHE*
	IOPL*
	LIBPATH*
	MAXWAIT*
	MEMMAN*
	PAUSE*
	PRIORITY*
	PROMPT*
	PROTECTONLY*
	PROTSHELL*
	REM*
	RMSIZE*
	RUN*
	SWAPPATH*
	THREADS*
	TIMESLICE*
* Completely new for OS/2	

Table 4.1: OS/2 Configuration Commands

create a Config.sys file with FILES and BUFFERS parameters appropriately set. In OS/2, your applications will suggest some of these additional parameter settings and you will be able to experiment with the advanced initialization controls inherent in the commands.

As you've learned in Chapter 3, OS/2 has two separate batch file mechanisms where DOS only has one. Both OS/2 batch files are in fact handled similarly, but the naming conventions are different. A batch file written to run in real mode must have a .bat extension; a batch file written to run in protected mode must have a .cmd extension. Following this new convention, the installation process creates two initial batch files, Startup.cmd and Autoexec.bat.

Figure 4.3 shows how these two batch files take control the first time you enter the protected mode (Startup.cmd) or the real mode (Autoexec.bat) from the Session Manager. In both, all the commands listed in these files are performed. As with any batch file, all commands or programs listed in the batch file are run step by step. OS/2 automatically executes each of these two batch files only once at the time of the first switch to real mode or protected mode.

As Figure 4.3 suggests, your OS/2 real mode Autoexec.bat file controls what your real mode prompt looks like, and which programs or .bat files run initially. OS/2 offers a similar startup procedure in its Startup.cmd file, giving you the ability to initialize your protected mode prompt, to begin one or more protected mode processes, or to initiate one or more batch command (.cmd) files.

You can increase your system's overall efficiency by including steps in the beginning batch files that will be executed each time you start up operations in either of the two OS/2 modes. During the installation process, OS/2 transfers initial versions of beginning batch files to do common things like managing the PATH and the PROMPT. You are advised to use your line editor or word processor to customize these startup files.

The Autoexec.bat file will only execute if a real mode compatibility box is configured in your system. As described in Chapter 9, this means that the PROTECTONLY command in the Config.sys file is either set to a value of no (PROTECTONLY = no), or there is no PROTECTONLY command at all in your Config.sys (since the default value is no).

REAL MODE STARTUP

Figure 4.4 demonstrates a customized Autoexec.bat for running DOS applications in real mode on an OS/2 system. Notice that the PATH command is modified to look in the root directory of an additional hard drive (D:\), as well as to search the miscellaneous utility directory (D:\Utility\Misc), the Norton Advanced Edition files (D:\Utility\Nortadv), and the Framework II directory (D:\Programs\Fw). This Autoexec.bat file also sets up three programming-oriented variables (Include, Lib, Init), which direct OS/2 to the subdirectories containing relevant support files.

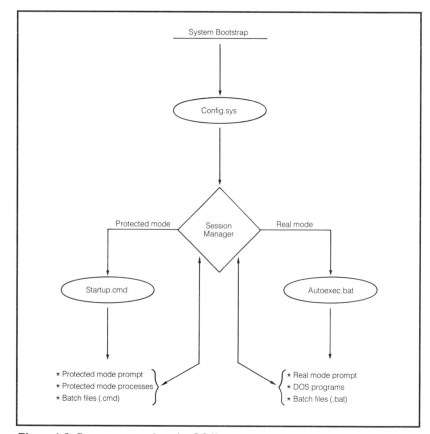

Figure 4.3: Startup operations in OS/2

```
@echo off
REM Autoexec.bat
SET COMSPEC=C:\Command.com
SET PATH=C:\;C:\Os2;c:\Tools;D:\;D:\Utility\Misc;D:\Utility\Nortadv;D:\Programs\Fw
SET INCLUDE=C:\Include
SET LIB=C:\Lib
SET INIT=C:\Init
PROMPT $e[1;37;44m[Real $p]$e[m
PREMENU
```

Figure 4.4: Customized Autoexec.bat for real mode operations

The second to last line in this Autoexec.bat file produces a bold white on blue prompt if you have a color monitor. All text you enter at the keyboard will be echoed as standard white letters on black background, but because of the escape numbers (1;37;44), the message [Real $p] appears in white with a blue background. The $p will be replaced on the screen by the current working directory. This PROMPT command uses the Ansi.sys device driver, which was activated in the Config.sys file in Chapter 3 with the line **DEVICE = Ansi.sys**. (See Chapter 5 for more information on the PROMPT command.)

The last line (PREMENU) in this example Autoexec.bat file runs a hard disk management program that controls the menu display and the subsequent running of any DOS application programs.

PROTECTED MODE STARTUP

Figure 4.5 displays a customized version for protected mode startup operations: a slightly modified variation on the Startup.cmd created by the installation process. The second to last line of the file, the only new line, creates a protected mode prompt that appears as [Prot $p]. This command tells OS/2 to display the prompt as white letters on a red background (due to the escape sequence 1;37;41) while everything else on the screen appears as white letters on a black background.

To use ANSI escape sequences as part of your prompt in protected mode, you can type the command **ANSI ON** at the protected mode prompt, or you can include the line ANSI ON in the startup

```
@ECHO OFF
REM    Startup.cmd
REM    OS/2 will start up a screen group with this file present in the
REM    root directory of the boot drive.  This file is only executed for the
REM    FIRST screen group started at boot time.  After that one must run the
REM    file Initenv.cmd whenever they want to initialize the environment of
REM    another screen group.

REM    Remove the following REM statement to enable the spooler.  The default
REM    action for the spooler is to spool output directed to LPT1:  Also, you
REM    need to make a spool directory "C:\Spool".

REM START C:\Os2\Spool.exe C:\Spool /D:Lpt1 /O:Lpt1

REM    The following command initializes the environment variables

PROMPT $e[1;37;41m[Prot $p]$e[0m
INITENV
```

Figure 4.5: Customized Startup.cmd for protected mode operations

sequence itself, or you can do nothing at all, because OS/2 will then default the value of ANSI to ON (see the ANSI command in Chapter 5). Any one of these methods ensures that escape sequences are always available in protected mode. Be sure to run this command before you try to use the $e escape sequences as part of the prompt.

Finally, note that the last line in the Startup.com file is the name of another protected mode batch file (see Figure 4.6). You use it to initialize new OS/2 working environments. In fact, each time you create a new screen group by initiating a new version of Cmd.exe, or creating a new separate OS/2 process, you should run the batch file, Initenv.cmd. Currently, it only runs during the first protected mode session, because it is invoked from Startup.cmd. This ensures that the new screen group receives a consistent initialization of certain development variables, as seen in Figure 4.6. If you are a programmer developing new applications, you can of course enhance the Initenv.cmd file to perhaps initialize additional useful parameters in your customized environment.

Because the Startup.cmd file is executed for only the first protected mode session, you might naturally wonder if you could automate running the Initenv.cmd batch file for all new protected mode sessions. The answer is yes. In the Config.sys file, there is a command line that loads the protected shell program:

PROTSHELL = Shell.exe Cmd.exe

You can specify a file name to be executed each time a Cmd.exe is started (a new protected mode session). First, add a /k switch to tell OS/2 to keep the command processor in memory, and add a parameter on the line specifying Initenv.cmd as the file to execute when Cmd.exe is run:

PROTSHELL = Shell.exe Cmd.exe /k C:\Initenv

```
REM Initenv.cmd
REM Initialize environment variable for development
PATH=C:\;C:\Os2;C:\Tools
SET INCLUDE=C:\Include
SET LIB=C:\Lib
SET INIT=C:\Init
```

Figure 4.6: Initializing new protected mode environments

This will save you the trouble of running Initenv.cmd each time you select Start a Program from the Session Manager. In fact, this can serve as a model for automatically running any batch file of your choice at the beginning of any new OS/2 protected mode session. Simply replace Initenv.cmd with the desired file name to be executed (batch file or executable program).

COMPARING THE USE OF COMMANDS IN DOS AND OS/2

Now that you've compared configuration requirements, and contrasted the batch file startup procedures, it's time to take a look at the similarities and differences in actual command usage between DOS and OS/2.

The user interface in OS/2 is currently a simple command prompt, somewhat like the command prompt in DOS environments. As you've just seen, you can have different command prompts for real mode and protected mode. In fact, it's advisable that you do just that by using different prompt strings, different colors, or combinations of the two. This way, you'll always know at a glance which mode you are running in. The discussion on the PROMPT command in Chapter 5 gives some additional examples of how to enhance your display by using ANSI escape sequences. Later versions of OS/2 will employ a program called the Presentation Manager, which will offer a full screen windowing environment as an interface to all DOS commands. This Presentation Manager will be similar to the Windows 2.0 overlapping windows environment already seen in DOS.

As you learned in Chapter 1, the Ctrl-Esc keypress can exit any screen group and bring up the Session Manager screen. Alternatively, pressing Alt-Esc allows you to switch from screen group to screen group successively, without going through the Session Manager display.

RESTRICTED COMMANDS

If you select real mode by choosing MS-DOS Command Prompt from the Session Manager menu, the real mode Command.com will be in control, interpreting whatever commands you enter. Table 4.2 displays the groups of commands that are in some way restricted; some work only in real mode, while others work only in protected mode. If your OS/2 is set up to run in a network environment, some of OS/2's commands will not function at all. All remaining commands are unrestricted, working in real mode, protected mode, and network environments. You can find detailed discussions of each command in Chapter 5.

INTERNAL COMMANDS

Many commands in OS/2 execute immediately. They are called *internal commands* and are built into the command interpreter. Those that work in real mode are built into the memory resident portion of Command.com, while those that run in protected mode are built into the memory resident portion of Cmd.exe. The internal commands seen in Table 4.3 are not readily apparent to you, because they are built in and can't be listed as part of any OS/2 directory. All these commands are memory resident and execute very rapidly, because no disk access is necessary to obtain them.

As you can see in Table 4.3, some commands like DETACH, DPATH, and START are completely new to the OS/2 environment. Other commands like COPY, DEL, DIR, and TYPE have

REAL MODE ONLY	PROTECTED MODE ONLY	NONNETWORK ONLY
APPEND ASSIGN BREAK GRAFTABL JOIN	ANSI DETACH DPATH	CHKDSK DISKCOMP DISKCOPY FDISK FORMAT LABEL RECOVER SUBST SYS

Table 4.2: Restricted OS/2 Commands

been enhanced so they can act on multiple files simultaneously (without needing wild cards).

EXTERNAL COMMANDS

In DOS, file names with .com or .exe extensions are considered *external commands* (or *utility commands*). Those provided with your DOS system, like CHKDSK or XCOPY, constitute the formal external commands of DOS. If you write an .exe or .com program yourself or

SAME AS **DOS**	NEW IN **OS/2**	ENHANCED IN **OS/2**
BREAK	DETACH (DET)	COPY
CHCP	DPATH	DEL
CHDIR (CD)	START	DIR
CLS		TYPE
DATE		
ECHO		
ERASE		
EXIT		
FOR		
GOTO		
IF		
MKDIR (MD)		
PATH		
PAUSE		
PROMPT		
REM		
RENAME (REN)		
RMDIR (RD)		
SET		
SHIFT		
TIME		
VER		
VERIFY		
VOL		

Table 4.3: Internal OS/2 Commands

buy one from a utility vendor, these new files are still perceived as external commands because they are disk resident and appear the same to DOS. Also, file names with the extension .bat can also be seen as external commands, because they are accessible through the DOS PATH setting just as .exe or .com files are.

A similar construction occurs in OS/2. File names with extensions of .com or .exe are considered external commands. If you are in real mode, file names with the extension .bat are considered external commands, because they are recognizable as batch files. File names with the extension .cmd are also considered external commands when you are in protected mode, because they can represent batch files written for execution in this protected mode. In both environments, of course, you can create your own new programs (.exe or .com files) or your own customized batch command files (.bat or .cmd).

You don't have to type in the extension when you want to run an external command. For instance, if you type XCOPY, OS/2 knows that it should find and run the Xcopy.exe external command. It is possible to create more than one file with the same *base name* (the name to the left of the period in a complete file name, like Xcopy). OS/2 will decide in these cases that a file name with the extension .com precedes in importance a file name with the extension .exe. Both .com and .exe are given precedence over a batch file with the same name (.bat).

OS/2 protected mode does not recognize a .bat file as a batch file, and in real mode it will not recognize a .cmd file as a batch file. If you have multiple files of the same type with the same base name and same extension, OS/2 runs the one it finds first on your system path. Table 4.4 lists all the external commands available as part of your OS/2 system.

The executable format for programs is, of course, completely different for OS/2. An .exe or .com program has to be written with special care (see Chapter 10) if it is to run in both real and protected modes. Most of the external commands included with OS/2 and listed in Table 4.4 have received that special care; however, some of them are designed to work only in protected mode. Other external commands from outside vendors, or those you write yourself, must

SAME AS **DOS**	NEW IN **OS/2**
ANSI	CMD
APPEND	HELPMSG
ASSIGN	PATCH
ATTRIB	SPOOL
BACKUP	
CHKDSK	
COMMAND	
COMP	
DISKCOMP	
DISKCOPY	
FDISK	
FIND	
FORMAT	
GRAFTABL	
JOIN	
KEYB	
LABEL	
MODE	
MORE	
PRINT	
RECOVER	
REPLACE	
RESTORE	
SORT	
SUBST	
SYS	
TREE	
XCOPY	

Table 4.4: OS/2 External Commands

adhere to the Family Applications Programming Interface (FAPI) presented in more detail in Chapter 10.

As you can see in Table 4.4, most commands are similar to those available in DOS 3.x, although some commands are completely new to OS/2. All of these commands are placed in your OS/2 directory on your boot disk during the INSTALL process.

EXIT CODES FOR OS/2 COMMANDS

When any program runs, it can return an exit code to indicate the final status of the program. This feature is usually important only to programmers who develop modules of code as part of a sophisticated application system. DOS users know how to check for the value of these exit codes in certain DOS external commands, and how to use the results to control subsequent execution in sophisticated batch programs. Although you will explore this in more detail in the discussion of the IF ERRORLEVEL command (see Chapter 8), you should get a sense here that the range of error codes returned in OS/2 is much greater than that in DOS. As you can see in Appendix C, eight commands in OS/2 (as compared to only three in DOS) return a much wider range of exit code values.

An exit code is sometimes called an error code, because it is often used to indicate whether an error occurred during the execution of a program or command. The exit value is usually set to zero if no error occurred, and a value larger than zero if there was an execution problem. You may control processing after an error by using the IF and the GOTO commands explained in more detail in Chapter 8. Table 4.5 lists the external OS/2 commands that provide useful exit codes.

COMMAND	NUMBER OF UNIQUE EXIT CODES
BACKUP	5
DISKCOMP	5
DISKCOPY	5
FORMAT	4
GRAFTABL	3
REPLACE	8
RESTORE	5
XCOPY	5

Table 4.5: OS/2 Commands that Return Exit Codes

Appendix C provides detailed tables that list exit codes, so that you can write effective OS/2 batch files that take advantage of these codes. The examples in Chapter 8 show how these exit codes can be used to control processing when writing your own OS/2 batch files.

SUMMARY

OS/2 offers users a broad extension of DOS capabilities. A great deal of OS/2's enhanced power isn't visible at any command prompt, but is deeply entwined in the multitasking world discussed in Chapter 1. Both OS/2 and DOS use a configuration file called Config.sys that contains commands to initialize the inner workings of each operating system. DOS uses one automatically executing batch file, while OS/2 uses two—one for each operating mode. A number of other OS/2 features are visible and accessible to you and your batch files and programs at the command prompt. All in all, OS/2 offers more commands and more features across the board than DOS does.

- OS/2 installation does more than simply format a disk and copy hidden system files. Both the real mode command interpreter (Command.com) and the protected mode command interpreter (Cmd.exe) are copied to the root directory of the boot drive during installation.

- The installation process copies prototype (simple and representative) versions of the Autoexec.bat file, the Startup.cmd file, and the Config.sys file.

- Config.sys provides an internal system configuration capability similiar to that available in DOS 3.x. However, many more internal system features can be controlled through new configuration commands in OS/2.

- The Autoexec.bat file gives an initial sequence of commands or program executions during the first switchover to real mode operation.

- The Startup.cmd file provides a similar initialization sequence during the first switchover to protected mode operation.

- The current user interface for OS/2 consists of a command prompt interface similar to that seen in DOS. Use the PROMPT command and the ANSI escape sequence to get a dramatically different prompt, either in real or protected mode.

- OS/2 offers a number of new internal commands. These are part of the memory resident code of the active command processor (Command.com) for real operations, or Cmd.exe for protected mode operations.

- OS/2 offers a number of new external commands, presented in detail in Chapter 5. Some of these commands are restricted to real mode operation, protected mode operation, or nonnetwork use only. All others operate in all environments.

- More OS/2 commands return exit codes than was the case in DOS. And these commands return usable exit codes that can be tested and can control error processing, a feature useful for both programmers and those of you who write your own batch programs.

Now that you understand how OS/2 works, how it compares to DOS, and how to get application programs up and running, it's time to take a closer look at the variety of commands available in OS/2. Chapter 5 presents a detailed look at these commands, from the ones that only work in real mode, to the ones that work in both modes (though with enhanced operation in protected mode), to the ones that work only in protected mode.

THE OS/2
COMMAND REFERENCE

CHAPTER 5

THIS CHAPTER PROVIDES DETAILED INFORMATION
on all OS/2 commands, the majority of which can be used in either
real or protected mode. It discusses only commands executable at the
command prompt. Whenever there is a limitation on use, it is noted
in the section on restrictions. Other types of commands are presented
in the appropriate chapter. Chapter 8 presents subcommands used in
batch file processing, and Chapter 9 looks at the configuration commands for your Config.sys file.

Each section covers one command, beginning with a general
description and the command syntax, and followed by the definition
of its switches and parameters. Brackets indicate optional switches
and parameters; solid vertical bars indicate either/or choices. The
command's type and any restrictions on the command's use are then
presented, along with examples and suggestions of typical or suggested uses of each command.

ANSI

ANSI is a protected mode command. It enables the use of ANSI escape sequences when its value is set to ON.

Syntax
ANSI [ON | OFF]

Type
External.

Restrictions
Protected mode only.

Examples and Considerations

ANSI escape sequences are a special series of characters beginning with the escape code (decimal 27). See the PROMPT command for more details about setting up special functions in OS/2 with escape sequences.

If you enter ANSI with no argument, the current status of this parameter will be displayed on your screen. The default value is ON, so that under normal conditions ANSI escape sequences are always supported in protected mode.

Since it is possible that installing the ANSI escape sequence support in protected mode could conflict with one of your OS/2 graphics programs, the instructions for that program may direct you to turn this OS/2 support mechanism off. Do that by entering

ANSI OFF

If you later run a program or enter an OS/2 command sequence that again requires ANSI support in protected mode, you must enter

ANSI ON

before running the program or entering the command.

ANSI escape sequences are supported in real mode through the installation of the Ansi.sys device driver. This is established by including the following lines in your Config.sys file:

DEVICE = [drive:][path]Ansi.sys

Certain ANSI escape sequences supporting some graphics modes are not allowed. These nonsupported video modes are 320 × 200 color, 320 × 200 black and white, and 640 × 200 black and white.

APPEND

The APPEND command directs OS/2 in real mode to search for data files through a predetermined set of directories; it does not include those files ending in .com, .bat, or .exe. It allows a real mode program to open files that will be read from or written to. The PATH command must still be used to find executable files. See the DPATH command for this command's equivalent in protected mode.

Syntax

[*D:path*]APPEND [*D1:*]*path1* [[;[*D2:*]*path2*]...][;]

> *D:path* is the drive and path where the command file itself is located if it is not in the current directory.
>
> *D1* and *path1* are the first drive and directory combinations to be searched after the default drive and directory.
>
> *D2:path2*. . .is the second drive and directory searched after the default drive and directory, and so on.
>
> The semicolon, when used alone after APPEND, erases any current path list on the APPEND command.

Type

External.

Restrictions

Real mode only.

Examples and Considerations

In real mode, the two most common uses of APPEND are to enable OS/2 to locate overlay files for sophisticated application programs, and to locate data files for referencing by those programs. For example, imagine you want to run a simple batch file you wrote for a menu management system. You want it to be able to reference and execute your database program in the Dbms directory, as well as your computer-aided design program in the Cad directory, and also your word processing program in the Wp directory. You must enter the following command that explicitly specifies that the Dbms and the Wp directories are on the C drive, while the Cad directory is on a D drive:

APPEND C:\Dbms;D:\Cad;C:\Wp

This example assumes that any referenced data files also appear in those directories; if in fact they are located in subdirectories, those sub-directory names would have to be added to the APPEND path list.

Clearing the current path list for the APPEND command is one way to force OS/2 to limit its search only to the current working directory.

The APPEND command is also useful in a network environment as a means to locate data files residing on computers other than your own (other nodes on the network).

ASSIGN

The ASSIGN command causes any requests for files on one drive to be carried out on a different drive. The parameter list allows you to assign drive references from one drive to another. With no parameters, ASSIGN cancels all current assignments.

It is used most frequently in real mode to run older applications that reference specific drives, typically A or B drives. Because practical use of OS/2 requires a hard disk, the most convenient use of an older program is to place both program and data files in a directory or directories on the hard disk. The ASSIGN command makes that feasible.

Syntax

[*D:path*]ASSIGN [*sourceD = destD*] [...]

> *D:path* is the drive and path where the command file is located if it is not in the current directory.
>
> *sourceD* is the drive to be rerouted.
>
> *destD* is the drive that will handle *sourceD*'s requests.
>
> ... are additional assignments.

Type
External.

Restrictions

Real mode only. Do not use ASSIGN with any of the following commands: BACKUP, JOIN, LABEL, PRINT, RESTORE, SUBST. Assignments made by the ASSIGN command are ignored completely by the DISKCOMP, DISKCOPY, and FORMAT commands.

Examples and Considerations

As already noted, ASSIGN is most commonly used in older programs that require you to either place your program disk in the A drive, or your data disk in the B drive, or both. For instance, if you have copied all of your program and data files to a directory on the

C drive, and then you made that directory the current directory, you might enter

ASSIGN A = C B = C

This forces all program references to A and B to be dealt with from the current working directory on the C drive.

You can apply the same principle if you have multiple disk drives, and wish to use any other letters to represent floppy disk or hard disk alternatives to the disk drive identifiers originally specified by the application program.

The SUBST command is a more flexible alternative that allows you to work with multiple directories on a hard disk. For instance, if you are running a program called Oldstuff, you can copy all program disk files to a directory called Oldstuff, and all of the former data disk files to a directory called Oldstuff\Data. Then you could issue the following command:

SUBST A: C:\Oldstuff
SUBST B: C:\Oldstuff\Data

See the SUBST command for further details and examples.

ATTRIB

The ATTRIB command is used to change the read/write and archive file attributes. When used with parameters, ATTRIB changes the attributes of a file. When used without the parameters, ATTRIB displays the attributes.

Syntax

[*D:path*]ATTRIB [+ R | – R][+ A | – A][*filespec*][/s]

D:path is the drive and path where the command file is located if it is not in the current directory.

+ R makes *filespec* read-only.

– R makes *filespec* read/write operations possible.

+ A sets the archive bit of *filespec*.

– A resets the archive bit of *filespec*.

filespec is an optional drive and path, plus the file name and extension, of the file that is the object of the command. Wild cards are allowed.

/s causes all matching files in the directory and its subdirectories to be modified.

Type
External.

Examples and Considerations

The ATTRIB command is most commonly used to set one or more files to read-only status. This prevents a file from being accidentally or purposely deleted, and also inhibits any editing or modification of the file. To set read-only status for a file named Budget.wk1, you would enter

ATTRIB + R Budget.wk1

Since wild cards are allowed, you can just as easily turn on read-only status for all personnel data files in the Personel directory, including .txt, .wk1, and .dbf files:

ATTRIB + R Personel.*

The /s switch adjusts the attributes of all files in the entire directory tree starting with the specified directory. For example, you can remove all read-only statuses from an entire disk with the following command:

ATTRIB – R C:\ /s

The other attribute (A) controls the archival status of a file. Since the BACKUP, RESTORE, and XCOPY commands use this archive attribute, you can influence how they work by presetting the +A or – A status of a file prior to executing any of these three commands. See the individual commands for examples of how they treat archive attributes with the /m and /a switches.

ATTRIB is also used in network applications. It enforces read only status of files intended to be shared by multiple users across the network.

BACKUP

This command performs a backup of multiple files from any one disk drive to any other one. BACKUP can save all of your current data, file by file, directory by directory.

Syntax

[*D:path*]BACKUP *sourceD*:[*filespec*] *destD*:
[/s][/m][/a][/d:*mm-dd-yy*]
[/t:*hh:mm:ss*][/f][/l[:*logfilespec*]]

D:path is the drive and path where the command file is located if it is not in the current directory.

sourceD is the drive specification of the source drive to be backed up; this can be a floppy disk or a hard disk.

filespec is an optional drive and path, plus the file name and extension, of the file that is the object of the command. Wild cards are allowed.

destD is where the backups will be stored (a floppy disk or a hard disk).

/s backs up subdirectories of the current specified directory.

/m backs up modified files.

/a appends the backup files to the files already on *destD* instead of writing over them.

/d:*mm-dd-yy* works like /m, but the "modified since" date is specified by *mm-dd-yy,* not the last backup date.

/t:*hh:mm:ss* backs up files on or after the indicated time when /d is used.

/f causes BACKUP to format the destination disk if it has not already been formatted. This switch is not allowed for nonremovable hard disks.

/l creates a log file.

logfilespec is an optional name for the log file (the default name is Backup.log).

Unless the /a
parameter is used,
BACKUP will erase all
the files on *destD*. The
target disk will be formatted according to the
capacity of the drive.

Type

External.

Restrictions

You cannot back up files that you are sharing but do not currently have access to. Do not use BACKUP with JOIN, SUBST, or ASSIGN. FORMAT must be available on the specified path, or in the same directory as BACKUP, because it may be needed to format the target disk.

Examples and Considerations

The OS/2 BACKUP command can process files from different media. Different density 5 ¼-inch disks, different density 3 ½-inch disks, and a wide range of hard disks are all supported. BACKUP manages all of these, despite their varying numbers of different sides, sectors, tracks, or cylinders.

If the /l switch is used to create a log file, the resulting file has a single line indicating the date and time of the backup, followed by separate lines for each file included on the backup. The file name as well as the number of the backup disk containing it are both listed in these individual entries.

Suppose you want to send backup copies of all files in your Dbms/ Data directory with extensions of .dbf to a disk in the A drive. Enter

BACKUP C:\Dbms\Data\ * .dbf A:

OS/2 will instruct you to place your backup disk in drive A:, then issue the following warning messages:

Insert the backup disk 01 in drive A:
DOS1681: Warning! The files in target
drive A:\root will be erased.

Press Enter to continue or Ctrl-Break to cancel.

BREAK

This command makes programs easier to interrupt. Turning BREAK on makes OS/2 check more often for the Ctrl-C key combination. For example, if you are compiling a long program and the compiler encounters an error and gets stuck in a loop, you will want to halt execution. Having BREAK set to ON will make it more likely that you can sucessfully break out of the loop.

Syntax

BREAK [ON | OFF]

> ON enables Ctrl-Break.

> OFF disables the Ctrl-Break function (this is the default).

Type
Internal.

Restrictions
Real mode only.

Examples and Considerations
OS/2 usually checks for Ctrl-C during keyboard, screen, and printer operations. You can turn BREAK on with the following line:

BREAK ON

This line directs OS/2 to check for Ctrl-C combinations when an application program makes other system calls. This is particularly useful for programs that do not themselves check for Ctrl-C, because it increases the likelihood that you can interrupt and break out of those programs quickly. The only disadvantage is a slight additional overhead in OS/2 operations during real mode, which must do the additional checking for Ctrl-C at more frequent intervals.

Entering the command BREAK with no parameter at all causes OS/2 to return the current break status.

CHCP

The CHCP command allows you to change the currently loaded code page (ASCII character set table). It must be run separately for both the real mode command processor (Command.com) and the protected mode command processor (Cmd.exe).

Syntax

CHCP *xxx*

xxx is the code page identifier value.

Type
Internal.

Restrictions

The selected code page, *xxx*, can be only one of two prepared system code pages initialized with the CODEPAGE command in your Config.sys file (see Chapter 9). Table 5.1 displays the five valid code pages, only two of which may be prepared in a system at any one time.

Examples and Considerations

Entering CHCP with no parameters results in the current active code page being displayed, as well as whatever system code pages

CODE PAGE	VALUE
United States	437
Multilingual	850
Portuguese	860
French-Canadian	863
Nordic	865

Table 5.1: Code Page Identification Numbers

may have been prepared. For example, OS/2 might respond in the following way:

Active code page: 437
Prepared system codes pages: 437 863

Each program initiated after a CHCP command uses the specified new code page. Running processes that began before the issuance of this command continue to use the former code page.

The command is intended to initialize the code page for a new screen group. However, you should be aware that issuing a CHCP command will change the active code page, even if the specified code page is not prepared and therefore available for a device. If you choose to reset the active code page to its original value, you must reissue the CHCP command with that original identifier value. For example, you can set or reset the active code page to the multilingual 850 choice by entering

CHCP 850

CHDIR (CD)

When moving through the directory structure, you must change the directory you are in. CHDIR (or simply CD) is an easy way to do that. Executing CHDIR .. will put you in the immediate parent directory of the directory you are in (the two-dot symbol denotes this particular parent directory).

Syntax

C[H]D[IR] [D:path]

D:path is the optional drive and path specifying which directory you wish to make the default directory.

Type

Internal.

Examples and Considerations

The CHDIR (or CD for short) command allows you to change the current working directory. OS/2 looks for *executable files* in the current working directory before searching the path. It looks for *data files* in the current working directory before searching the APPEND list (in real mode) or the DPATH list (in protected mode). It is therefore often desirable to work in the current directory. The CD command is most often used to do this.

For example, if you wish to make the Data subdirectory within the Cad directory your current working directory, enter

CD \Cad\Data

If you want to reset the current working directory to the root of your current drive, enter

CD \

If you wish to make Lotus\Accounts\Judd the working directory, then enter

CD \Lotus\Accounts\Judd

Entering CD with no parameters displays the current working directory on the default drive. If you want to display the current working directory on any other drive, enter the drive name as a first parameter:

CD D:

This will display the current working directory on the D drive.

CHKDSK

A problem in the system area can prevent you from using your disk. The correctional facilities of CHKDSK will help you solve such a problem by resolving errors in the disk's file allocation table.

Syntax

[*D:path*]CHKDSK [*filespec*][/f][/v]

D:path is the drive and path where the command file is located if it is not in the current directory.

filespec is an optional drive and path, plus the file name and extension, of the file that is the object of the command. Wild cards are allowed.

/f allows corrections on the disk.

/v lists all files and their paths.

Type

External.

Restrictions

CHKDSK will not work on drives created by JOIN or SUBST, or on networked drives.

Examples and Considerations

CHKDSK shows the status of your disk and its use of file space. It runs differently in real and protected modes. In protected mode, a standard report will look something like the following:

```
Volume DRIVE-D created Sep26, 1987  6:02pm
22255616 bytes total disk space.
        0 bytes in 1 hidden files.
   11264C bytes in 45 directories.
17446912 bytes in 1552 user
        files.
  4696064 bytes available on
        disk.
```

But in real mode, CHKDSK displays two additional lines for compatibility with DOS 3.x:

```
[DOS mode storage report]
    655328 bytes total storage
    540208 bytes free
```

These additional lines indicate total memory and free memory. They're inappropriate in the OS/2 environment; they are displayed only for compatibility with the DOS 3.x environment, with its limit of 640K of total physical memory.

Because OS/2 multitasking processes can be accessing various files on the disk, don't use the /f switch to try to fix disk errors when any multitasking program is operative. It is normal to have open files during multitasking operations.

Checking the status of your default disk drive is as simple as entering

CHKDSK

Checking the status of another disk drive requires only the addition of the disk drive identifier:

CHKDSK D:

Errors may be reported on a disk, but nothing can be done about them unless you run the CHKDSK command using the /f switch. Using the /f switch is the only way CHKDSK is permitted to make adjustments to the file allocation table. And this occurs only if you answer Y to the question posed by the CHKDSK command about fixing the error, and only if there are in fact any errors discovered on the disk.

You cannot do a CHKDSK/f on the boot drive.

A unique situation occurs if you try to use CHKDSK/f to repair problems on the boot drive. You'll always receive the following system message:

DOS0108: The drive containing the file
is being used by another process.

This is because OS/2 cannot fix FAT errors if there are any files still open on the target drive. Because the system's hard error handler is on the boot disk and is always active, there will always be open files on the boot disk.

CLS

Sometimes the screen becomes cluttered or you have a batch file that does many different things, and you no longer need to see everything put on the screen. To clear the screen, you can use the CLS command. After the screen is erased, the cursor is placed at the top left of the screen.

Syntax

CLS

Type

Internal.

Examples and Considerations

The CLS command is normally used when you want succeeding output from any program or batch file to begin at the top line of a screen. Entering

CLS

erases the screen and leaves the cursor at the top left position. You can also use CLS during batch file operation, when successive screenfuls of messages are displayed. It erases the screen between each set of messages or each block of text being displayed.

CMD

The CMD command initiates a protected mode command processor. Like running Command.com in real mode, this mechanism can be used in protected mode to create new processes.

Syntax

CMD [*drive:*][*path*] [[/c | /k] *string*]

> *drive:path* is the drive and path where the protected mode command processor file is located if it is not in the current directory.
>
> /c directs the command processor to execute the command(s) specified by *string* and then to return automatically to the primary Cmd.exe file active when CMD was entered.
>
> /k directs the command processor to perform the command(s) in *string* and to keep the new command processor in memory after the command is completed.

Type
External.

Examples and Considerations
Each time a protected mode command processor is initiated, a new environment is created. Because it is only a copy of the former parent environment, it may be changed without affecting the parent task's environmental values.

An application process may, for example, want to invoke a special purpose command processor with the sole function of performing a DIR or a CHKDSK command. While that invoked command processor is active, it will be part of the same screen group as the parent command processor, and will naturally have access to all hard disk files for editing, investigating, or modifying. This is the most common application of CMD, and requires you to keep the invoked processor in memory until you no longer need it. The following command invokes the command processor:

CMD /k

The now-active command processor can be used to access files and make adjustments. When you no longer need this extra copy of Cmd.exe, type the command EXIT at the command prompt, terminating that particular session. While the session is active, it represents a separate screen group. It can therefore be switched to by either the Session Manager (Ctrl-Esc), or with the Alt-Esc keypress combination directly.

COMMAND

The Command.com command processor, invoked when you switch to real mode, is the part of OS/2 that takes in, translates, and executes real mode commands. Invoking a second command processor can give you the ability to execute OS/2 commands from inside a program and then return to that program. The COMMAND command also allows you to load a custom command processor that has special functions and abilities or altered command definitions.

Syntax

COMMAND [*D:path*][/p][/c *string*][/e:*xxxxx*]

D:path is the drive and path where the command file is located if it is not in the current directory.

/p makes the new processor the primary processor.

/c *string* executes the command represented by *string*.

/e:*xxxxx* sets the OS/2 environment size to *xxxxx* bytes.

Type

Internal.

Restrictions

COMMAND is used in real mode only. If you use the /e switch, the value of *xxxxx* is limited to a range of from 160 bytes (the default) to 32,768 bytes. OS/2 will default the environment size to one of those two numbers if you specify an environment size outside that range.

Examples and Considerations

As with CMD, starting a new command processor in real mode copies the environment from the parent process. You can make any changes you like to environmental parameters without affecting the old environment.

Note that the /e switch should be invoked to set the environment size *prior to* invoking any other OS/2 command that may increase the resident size of OS/2. The space reserved for environmental parameters cannot be expanded once that resident area has been taken over for other OS/2 purposes.

The required syntax for invoking a permanent secondary real mode command processor is

COMMAND /p

This will invoke another command processor and keep it in memory, returning to the parent Command.com only after you enter the EXIT command at the prompt.

COMP

This command compares two or more files to see if they are the same.

Syntax

[*D:path*]COMP [*filespec1*] [*filespec2*]

> *D:path* is the drive and path where the command file is located if it is not in the current directory.
>
> *filespec1* is the optional drive and path, plus the file names and extensions, of the first set of files to be compared. Wild cards are allowed.
>
> *filespec2* is the optional drive and path, plus the file names and extensions, of the second set of files to be compared. Wild cards are allowed.

Type

External.

Examples and Considerations

The COMP command is used to compare the contents of two or more files. It is commonly used to determine whether two files located in two separate directories are identical copies. For instance, the following command line can verify if the version of Budget.txt in the Accounts directory is a duplicate of the file of the same name located in the Budget directory:

COMP C:\Lotus\Budget\Budget.txt Budget.txt

This example assumes that the second parameter, Budget.txt, is located in the current working directory (presumably the Accounts directory).

It is also possible to use wild cards to compare multiple files with different extensions. In the following example, all word processing files with a .wp extension are compared to all word processing files with a .wpb extension to determine which files are identical to their backup versions (no changes were made in the most recent edit):

COMP \Wp*.wp \Wp*.wpb

This command is most useful for verifying that the contents of two files are the same, but less than useful to most users for determining exactly what the differences are. This is because the results of COMP are presented using hexadecimal notation, and not the original text. If the files are identical, you'll receive the message "The files compare OK." If they are different in any way, COMP returns values for the bytes that are different and for the offset into the files. For non-programmers, this is hardly any use at all.

COPY

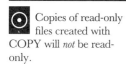 Copies of read-only files created with COPY will *not* be read-only.

The COPY command has three distinct uses. You can use it to duplicate files, to access devices, or to concatenate files.

Duplicating files with COPY, using the first format of this command, allows you versatility in moving files around the disk system. Whole directories can be copied and thus moved to another location or to another disk. Without COPY, you would never be able to transfer newly purchased programs from floppy disks to your hard disk, or copy files to a floppy disk for another system.

The second format of COPY is especially useful for printing multiple files at once, which cannot be done with the TYPE command. It is also the only way for you to directly send information to a device from OS/2.

The third format of the COPY command allows files to be concatenated; that is, ASCII-type files can be added to the end of one another to form one big file.

Syntax

COPY [/a][/b]*sourcefile* [[/a][/b][*destfile*][/a][/b][/v]]
COPY [/a][/b]*source* [/a][/b][*dest*][/a][/b][/v]
COPY[/a][/b]*sourcefile1* + *sourcefile2*[/a][/b] + ... [*concatfile*][/a][/b][/v]

These switches will affect the file immediately preceding the place where the switch is used, as well as all files following it, until the next time the switch is used.

The /a switch is used with *sourcefile, source,* or *sourcefile1, sourcefile2* to read data up to but not including the first Ctrl-Z (end-of-file) character; the file is treated as an ASCII file. This is the default when concatenating (format 3).

The /a switch is used with with *destfile, dest,* or *concatfile* to write a Ctrl-Z at the end of the file.

The /b switch (the default for duplicating files in format 1) is used with *sourcefile, source,* or *sourcefile1, sourcefile2* to copy the entire file, including any Ctrl-Z characters.

The /b switch is used with *destfile, dest,* or *concatfile* to make sure that no Ctrl-Z characters will be written at the end of the file.

/v causes OS/2 to check that all the files were copied successfully.

sourcefile is the drive, path, file name, and extension of the file to be copied.

destfile is the drive, path, file name, and extension of the file to which *sourcefile* will be copied.

source and *dest* can be either device or file specifications, although OS/2 only allows ASCII files to be read from a device.

sourcefile1 and *sourcefile2* are a list of files to be added together (*sourcefile2* to the end of *sourcefile1,* etc.).

concatfile is the file composed of the concatenation of the source files.

Type
Internal.

Not specifying a destination file in the third format of the COPY command will result in all source files being appended to the end of the first source file.

Examples and Considerations
The COPY command is one of the most common and useful in OS/2. It can be used in either real mode or protected mode, and is often employed to copy versions of software between disks, or directories on a hard disk. The simplest example of COPY is to copy a specific file from drive A to drive B. For instance, copying the file Sk.com is done with the following command:

COPY A:Sk.com B:

You can just as easily copy this file from the A drive to a directory of your C drive, such as a directory containing utility software:

COPY A:Sk.com C:\Utility

All copies placed in the utility directory have the same name as the original on the disk in drive A.

You can also make an entire backup directory for housing backup copies of all spreadsheet files. The following command sequence creates a backup directory, and then transfers all .wk1 files into that directory, giving them new extensions (.wkb) in the process. The base name of the entire file name remains the same:

MD \Lotus\Backups
CD \Lotus\Data
COPY *.wk1 \Lotus\Backups*.wkb

COPY is also used to consolidate a group of text files, so that small files can be edited more easily by a word processor, possibly to produce a consolidated report. The following example combines three separate text files into one:

COPY Study.txt + Results.txt + Analysis.txt Summary.rpt

The separate text files—Study, Results, and Analysis—are merged into a new file called Summary.rpt. The new report file is created on the default drive with the current date and time. Be careful to have a destination file. If you do not, OS/2 combines the files and places them all in the first specified file of the collection. This is sometimes a trick used to avoid specifying a separate destination file.

Wild cards can also be used to combine several files. For example, all files with a .txt extension can be combined into one complete report with the following command:

COPY *.txt Total.rpt

DATE

This command changes the date. Use it either to update or to simply find out what day of the week a certain date is. DATE also resets a permanent clock's date, should one be installed.

Syntax

DATE [*mm-dd-yy* | *dd-mm-yy* | *yy-mm-dd*]

mm is the month (01 to 12).

dd is the day (01 to 31).

yy is the year, either 80 to 99, or 1980 to 1999.

If the *mm-dd-yy* specification is left off, you will be prompted for it. The order of *mm-dd-yy* is dependent on the country you have selected.

Type
Internal.

Examples and Considerations
When you enter the month, day, and year, each entry may be separated by either dashes, slashes, or periods. The order of these entries depends on the setting of the COUNTRY command in your Config.sys file. In fact if you are using a code page other than 437 (United States), the separator symbols between your numeric entries may also vary.

You may set the date on your computer system by using the DATE command with one parameter equal to the desired date. For example

DATE 2-3-89

calls up the date routine, which permanently resets your internal computer clock to the date: February 3, 1989. The OS/2 command prompt immediately returns.

If you wish to set the date from a batch file, as you might in Autoexec.bat or Startup.cmd, simply enter the DATE command. OS/2 displays the current date, and prompts you to enter a new date. For example:

Current Date is FRIDAY 2-3-89
Enter New Date (mm-dd-yy);_

DEL

This command removes a file from the directory. The file is still physically present on the disk and can be retrieved by using certain disk utilities (such as Norton Utilities), but it is no longer directly accessible using the directory structure.

Syntax

DEL *filespec* [...]

> *filespec* is an optional drive and path, plus the file name and extension, of each file to be deleted. Wild cards are allowed.

> [...] are additional parameters when DEL is issued from protected mode.

Type
Internal.

Restrictions
You cannot use DEL to delete read-only files.

Examples and Considerations
An alternate command, ERASE, has exactly the same role as the DEL command. Many users prefer to use the ERASE command because it is more distinct from the other three letter command, DIR.

When issuing the command DEL *.*, which deletes all files in the current directory, OS/2 will issue the warning "Are you sure (Y/N)?" to verify that you really wish to take such drastic action. Issuing the DEL command with a subdirectory as the *filespec* parameter deletes all of the files in that subdirectory, but does not remove the subdirectory itself.

You can delete an individual file or use wild cards to delete multiple files at a single time. The following example deletes the specific file, 1985.wk1:

DEL 1985.wk1

A wild card can be used to delete all backup files in any directory:

DEL \Dbms*.bak

This deletes all backup files from the Dbms directory.

The contents of any particular directory can be completely erased by specifying the directory name itself as a parameter to this command. For example, to remove all files from the Cad\Data directory, enter:

DEL \Cad\Data

In protected mode, you can specify multiple file names on the same line without having to use wild cards. For example, three individual files could be deleted in protected mode with the following line:

DEL 1985.wk1 1986.wk1 1987.wk1

Wild cards can still be used in protected mode as in the earlier example, but they can now be combined as only one of the parameters on a line. To simultaneously erase all the backup files in the Cad\Data directory, while also erasing the 1985.wk1 file, enter

DEL \Cad\Data*.bak 1985.wk1

DETACH (DET)

DETACH creates a new process that runs independently in the background. This protected mode command generates an independently running process for any individual command or executable program not requiring user interaction at the keyboard.

Syntax

DETACH *COMMPROG* [*parameters*]

> *COMMPROG* is any valid OS/2 executable program or command that requires no user interaction from the keyboard to the program.
>
> *parameters* are valid additional values or switches for *COMMPROG*.

Type
Internal.

Restrictions
Protected mode only.

Examples and Considerations
DETACH is broadly analogous to the simpler and more focused PRINT command that you may know from DOS. Whereas PRINT creates a simultaneous print queue task in the background, DETACH creates a simultaneous program of your own choosing in the background. In each case, the OS/2 prompt is immediately returned to you so that you can run other commands or programs while the newly detached process runs independently. When OS/2 initiates this detached process, a process identification number (PID) is assigned and displayed. The only way you know this process is operating is through the PID. When your process completes, OS/2 displays another message.

Because it is independent, a detached process will continue to run even if the parent process that created it terminates, is exited, or is deleted in any other fashion. A detached process must terminate on its own. You no longer have any direct control over that process from the command prompt. For that reason, you should only detach processes that can run independent of keyboard input. For example, you may have written a missile simulation program that simulates a complex analysis of probabilistic calculations to intercept incoming missiles. The program, Missile, uses one parameter to indicate how many missiles are coming in at random times. This results in a disk file containing an analysis of intercepted missiles and potential damage. Because the program needs no input from the keyboard once it has been initiated, the DETACH command can be used as follows:

DETACH Missile 2000

You immediately receive a message from OS/2 indicating what process identification number has been assigned. The OS/2 prompt will then return so that you can continue other activities. When OS/2 announces that the DETACH process is complete, you can review the newly created Missile.rpt.

A more common commercial application might be a sort program. For example, you might have a program called FASTSORT, which sorts a dBASE III PLUS file by any field(s) in the database structure. Because this can run independently of the keyboard, you can detach it by specifying only the name of the database, followed by the field name(s) to sort on:

DETACH FASTSORT Personel LastName FirstName

This produces an independently-running process that sorts the Personel database file, using LastName as a primary key and FirstName as a secondary key.

DIR

The DIR command offers several ways to see what files you have. Without this command, it would be extremely difficult, if not impossible, to operate a computer system of any size.

Syntax

DIR [*filespec*] [...] [/p][/w]

filespec is an optional drive and path, plus the file name and extension, of the file that is the object of the command.

[...] represents additional *filespec*s that can be handled by the protected mode command interpreter, Cmd.exe.

/p causes the computer to prompt you to continue listing the directory entries if the listing is longer than one screen.

/w causes the listing to be displayed in wide format (without the size, date, and time, and in a horizontal listing).

Type
Internal.

Restrictions
Hidden files will not be shown when you use the DIR command. Multiple file specifications can only be entered from protected mode.

Examples and Considerations
The DIR command is one of the OS/2 commands most commonly used to discover status information about files on the disk. Its various forms allow you to discover the names of files on different disks, or information about the size and date/time of last modification of the file. You can learn how many bytes remain free on the drive you are referencing, and the total number of files on that drive that match the specified parameter. For example,

DIR C:\Os2

displays the label of the disk (volume) in drive C, and the names, sizes, and date/time of the last modification of each file in the Os2 directory on drive C.

All DIR parameters represented by *filespec* are completely independent from one another. They can be used in any combination, either alone or together, to narrow down the directory listing.

In protected mode, DIR is even more flexible, because it accepts multiple parameters on the same line:

DIR C: D:

This successively displays the same information in the same format for both drives C and D.

In each case, the display can be compacted by eliminating the size, date, and time columns, and displaying only file names in five parallel columns. The /w switch manages the creation of this wide display:

DIR C: D: /w

This will display the same file names as before in the current working directories of drive C and drive D. This time, however, only the file names themselves are displayed, in five columns.

You can of course use wild cards and path names as well as multiple drives (multiple parameters are limited to protected mode only). For example, all .exe files in your Os2 directory on drive C and your utility directory on drive D can be displayed with the following line:

DIR C:\Os2*.exe D:\Utility*.exe

DISKCOMP

Unlike the COMP command, which compares two sets of files, the DISKCOMP command compares two floppy disks. Usually it is used to verify a DISKCOPY operation.

Syntax

[*D:path*]DISKCOMP [*D1*:[*D2*:]]

D:path is the drive and path where the command file is located if it is not in the current directory.

D1 and *D2* are the two drives to be compared.

Type

External.

Restrictions

DISKCOMP can not compare hard disks, network disks, or disks set up with JOIN, ASSIGN, or SUBST commands.

Examples and Considerations

OS/2 automatically determines the number of sides, tracks, and sectors to compare on the two disks, based on the format of the source disk. Both disks must be of the same type to make a valid comparison (single-sided, double-sided, 3 1/2'', 5 1/4''), or OS/2 displays a message that the drive or disk types are not compatible. If the two disks match completely, you will receive the message, ''Compare OK.'' If some portions of the disks do not match, you will receive the message, ''Compare ERROR,'' with details of unmatched tracks and sides. Only true disk replicas can compare exactly; disks that contain the same files resulting from the XCOPY or COPY commands may not match, because placement of those files on the tracks may be different on each of the two disks. If you do have two disks with the same files but with different placement, use the COMP command to compare individual files.

If your system has only one disk drive, you can still compare two disks by issuing the command

DISKCOMP A:

OS/2 will then prompt you to switch disks. If you have two disk drives, just place your disks in the two drives and enter

DISKCOMP A: B:

DISKCOPY

This command gives you a quick way to copy a disk with a lot of data on it that would otherwise take considerably longer to copy with the COPY command. DISKCOPY copies the raw data of the disk, so if the source disk is a system disk, the new copy will also be a system disk. If the source disk is not a system disk, the copy will not be a system disk either, even if the destination disk originally was a system disk. The second disk will be an *exact* copy of the first. This command also formats a nonformatted destination disk during the copying process.

Syntax

[*D:path*]DISKCOPY [*sourceD*: *destD*:]

> *D:path* is the drive and path where the command file is located if it is not in the current directory.

> *sourceD* is the source drive to be copied.

> *destD* is the destination drive to be copied onto.

Type
External.

Restrictions

You cannot use this command with a hard disk; also, it does not recognize an assigned or substituted drive, and should not be used with JOIN. DISKCOPY cannot reliably read a double-sided disk formatted in a high-capacity drive, and it will not work with network drives.

Examples and Considerations

The DISKCOPY command enables you to make a precise replica of a floppy disk. The destination drive should contain either a new and unformatted floppy disk, or an older formatted disk that contains data you no longer need. During the DISKCOPY operation, any existing data on the destination disk will be completely overwritten. As with DISKCOMP, a one-disk system supports DISKCOPY operations. OS/2 will prompt you when it is necessary to switch disks.

If errors are discovered on either disk, DISKCOPY indicates the drive, track, and side containing the problem, but will proceed with the copying operation. You can make your own assessment of the severity of the problem noted. In general, it's better to get a new destination disk if hardware errors are discovered on it, because this would call into question the validity of the copy. If hardware errors are discovered on the source disk, you should examine your original data on that disk before assuming that you are now protected with a backup disk. Both the original and the backup may contain questionable data.

Again, the syntax is straighforward. To copy a disk from the A drive to the B drive, you must enter

DISKCOPY A: B:

If you have only one drive, enter

DISKCOPY A:

In this case OS/2 prompts you to

Enter drive letter for target.

Enter A: at this point, being sure to use the colon.

DPATH

The DPATH command provides the same function in protected mode as the APPEND command in real mode. It specifies the sequence of directories to search for program overlay and application data files (those extensions other than .exe, .com, .cmd, or .bat). The directories listed as parameters to this command are searched if the data file in question cannot be found in the current directory.

Syntax

DPATH [*D1:path1*] [*;D2:path2* ...] [;]

> *D1* and *path1* are the first drive and directory combinations to be searched after the default drive and directory.
>
> *D2:path2.* . .is the second drive and directory searched after the default drive and directory, and so on.
>
> The semicolon symbol when used alone after DPATH erases any current path list on the DPATH command.

Type
Internal.

Restrictions
Protected mode only.

Examples and Considerations
DPATH is an environmental parameter like PATH. Whereas the PATH command specifies the location of .exe, .com, .bat, or .cmd files, DPATH specifies the location of files with all other extensions. DPATH is an environmental variable inherited from a parent process, but it can be reset at any time. For instance, entering the following command line specifies that a search is to be made for data files in two directories, Cad\Data and Dbms\Data:

DPATH \Cad\Data;\Dbms\Data

These settings can be completely cleared by entering the DPATH command with a semicolon as the only parameter:

DPATH ;

In this case, only the current working directory will be searched for data files.

The current list of DPATH directory names to be searched can be displayed by OS/2 if you enter DPATH with no parameters:

DPATH

ERASE

The ERASE command is a synonym for the DEL command. See DEL in this chapter for syntax and examples.

EXIT

The EXIT command has an effect only if you have initiated an additional command processor in real mode (Command.com) or in protected mode (Cmd.exe). It exits that command processor and returns to the previous level. In protected mode, exiting from a new command processor removes an entry from the Session Manager screen (the list of running programs).

Syntax

EXIT

Type

Internal.

Examples and Considerations

A new real mode command processor is initiated by typing the following command:

COMMAND /p

A new protected mode command processor is initiated by typing the command

CMD /k

In either case you can return to the formerly executing command processor (at whose command prompt you typed Command or Cmd) by typing EXIT. In protected mode, you can also initiate a new command processor by selecting the choice Start a Program from the Session Manager screen.

FDISK

FDISK allows you to create a new partition, delete an old one, specify the active one, display current partition information, partition multiple hard drives, and define new logical drives within extended partitions. Appendix B describes the FDISK procedure in depth.

Syntax

[*D:path*]FDISK

> *D:path* is the drive and path where the command file is located if it is not in the current directory.

Type
External.

Restrictions

All data on your hard disk will be destroyed when you create partitions with FDISK.

FDISK can only be used on hard-disk systems. A disk must be reformatted logically after being partitioned. FDISK will not work if another process is accessing the disk.

Examples and Considerations
Refer to Appendix B for a thorough discussion of FDISK.

FIND

FIND allows you to search through a file to locate any particular string of text characters.

Syntax

[*D:path*]FIND [/v][/c][/n]''*string*'' [*filespec*...]

D:path is the drive and path where the command file is located if it is not in the current directory.

/v causes FIND to display each line not containing *string*.

/c counts the number of lines containing *string* and shows the total.

/n shows the relative line number of each line containing *string*.

string is the string of characters to be searched for.

filespec is the drive, path, file name, and extension of each file to be searched. Multiple files should be separated by a space.

Type

External.

Restrictions

Wild cards are not allowed with this command. FIND will end its search at the first Ctrl-Z encountered in a file.

Examples and Considerations

The FIND command searches for your specified *string* in one or more files. It displays any line found to contain this string. Quotation marks around the string are required.

For example, the following command line will display all lines found to contain ''Ace Mfg'' in the file Clients.lst:

FIND ''Ace Mfg'' Clients.lst

If no file specification is made on the line, FIND can act as a filter (see Chapter 6). In this case, FIND takes input from the OS/2 standard input device (usually the keyboard), from a redirected input file, or from a temporary pipe.

FORMAT

The FORMAT command destroys the contents of a disk, so be careful. Write-protecting any disks in other drives during a format may help prevent errors.

When you want to use a new disk with your system, it must be formatted. Certain markings must be placed on the disk to help the computer know where it is when it accesses the disk. The disk is not actually erased but is reset to a state in which nothing appears to be on it.

The FORMAT command can create both a data disk, in which all storage space is available for use, and a system disk, which is bootable and contains OS/2's necessary system files. FORMAT will also check the disk for any areas that have gone bad and mark them accordingly, so that no data will be saved in those areas.

Syntax

[*D:path*]FORMAT *D1*:[/s][/v][/4][/n:*xx*][/t:*yy*]

> *D:path* is the drive and path where the command file is located if it is not in the current directory.
>
> *D1*: is the drive to be formatted.
>
> /s causes a system disk to be made.
>
> /v prompts you for a volume label after the formatting is complete.
>
> /4 causes a high-capacity drive to create a 360K, double-sided disk. Unfortunately, a 360K disk formatted in a high capacity drive cannot be reliably read in a 360K drive.
>
> /n:*xx* specifies that the disk be formatted with *xx* sectors per track.
>
> /t:*yy* specifies that the disk be formatted with *yy* tracks.

Type
External.

Restrictions
FORMAT ignores assignments made with ASSIGN.

When you format a 360K disk in a high capacity drive, it cannot be read reliably in single or double-density drives. If you need a formatted 360K disk in another machine, format it in that other machine; it can then be reliably written on by a high capacity drive.

Examples and Considerations

If you do not specify parameters, OS/2 formats the disk as a standard data disk according to the type of drive that contains it. A high capacity drive will produce an automatic 1.2MB formatted disk, for instance, while a 5 1/4-inch double-density drive will produce a 360K disk.

As an extra protection, if you try to format a hard disk, FORMAT requires you to enter the current volume label. If in fact your hard disk does not have a volume label, press the Return key to begin the formatting. OS/2 will not format a disk if the volume label you enter does not match the label it finds on the disk. For instance, if you enter the command FORMAT D: for a hard disk, and then enter a volume identifier different from the one OS/2 actually finds on the disk, OS/2 informs you

**Incorrect volume label entered for drive D:. Formatting
cannot be completed.**

If the volume labels match, OS/2 gives you a last chance to back out of this potentially traumatic procedure, in which all data on your disk will be lost:

**WARNING!
ALL DATA ON THE FIXED DISK DRIVE D: WILL BE LOST!
PROCEED WITH FORMAT (Y/N)?**

Assuming you wish to format a disk in the A drive, you can use as much space as the drive allows by entering

FORMAT A:

If you want to create a system disk with a volume label, enter the following command:

FORMAT A: /s /v

In this example, OS/2 formats the disk, copies the operating system files onto it, and prompts you to enter a volume label. This volume label identifies your disk, and should be written each time you format a new disk. You can type up to 11 characters of any sort, including spaces, in the label.

GRAFTABL

It is nice to be able to display the full ASCII range of characters on the screen so that you can see exactly what you are dealing with. If you have a Color Graphics Adapter, this command will enable you to display the otherwise difficult to read ASCII characters that have codes from 128 to 255.

Syntax

[D:path]GRAFTABL [437 | 850 | 860 | 863 | 865] [/STA] [?]

D:path is the drive and path where the command file is located if it is not in the current directory.

437 loads the U.S. code page.

850 loads the Multilingual code page.

860 loads the Portugese code page.

863 loads the Canadian code page.

865 loads the Norwegian and Danish code page.

/STA shows the number of the code page currently in use.

? shows the current status, as well as the available options.

Type

External.

Restrictions

Real mode only.

Examples and Considerations

The GRAFTABL command should only be invoked once, by entering the following:

GRAFTABL

OS/2 acknowledges that this special character set has been loaded with the message

Graphics characters loaded

Using the GRAFTABL command increases the size of the resident portion of OS/2. If you need the GRAFTABL command at all, consider including it in your Autoexec.bat or Startup.cmd batch file.

If you wish to load a graphics table other than the default (United States, 437), specify the desired code page identification number. For example, to display the French-Canadian character set in graphics mode, enter

GRAFTABL 863

HELPMSG

Invoking the HELPMSG command brings up an explanation for each possible OS/2 message, as well as a suggested course of action.

Syntax

HELPMSG DOS*nnnn*

> *nnnn* is the four-digit unique identification number OS/2 displays along with the message.

Type

External.

Examples and Considerations

During normal OS/2 operations, a variety of error conditions may occur. These errors can result from program conditions, or from inappropriate command entries. For example, if you tried to initiate spooling in OS/2 real mode with the SPOOL command, you would receive the following message:

DOS1428E: The system cannot accept the SPOOL command in real mode.

You then enter

HELPMSG DOS1428

This will result in your being told that SPOOL is a protected mode-only program. But this self-explanatory example doesn't really show how useful HELPMSG can be.

There are many situations where an error is hidden behind the scenes. You could initiate spooling in protected mode, and then later receive the following message:

DOS1436E: The system found a spool internal error.

If you then enter

HELPMSG DOS1436

you will receive the following very useful clarification from OS/2:

The operating system was configured without enough memory.
End the execution of another program to free up memory for spool to execute.

JOIN

JOIN makes OS/2 treat a whole disk drive as if it were a subdirectory of another drive. The JOIN command has three main formats. The first displays all directory and disk names that have been joined; the second actually performs the joining; and the third disjoins a directory and disk.

Syntax

[*D:path*]JOIN
[*D:path*]JOIN *D2 D1:path*
[*D:path*]JOIN *D2* /d

D:path is the drive and path where the command file is located if it is not in the current directory.

D2 is the drive to which a directory will be attached or released.

D1:path is the drive and path of the directory to be joined.

/d causes any previous joining of *D2* to be unjoined.

Type
External.

Restrictions

Real mode only.

When a drive has been joined to another drive's directory, none of the following commands will work: CHKDSK, DISKCOPY, FDISK, FORMAT, LABEL, RECOVER, and SYS.

Examples and Considerations

The JOIN command is used in two principal ways. You may have a program outputting information to a fixed subdirectory on your C drive, such as C:\Cad\Data. If you wish to output this information directly to a disk in the A drive, enter

JOIN A: C:\Cad\Data

On the other hand, you might have a program designed to send output data to the root directory of the B drive, and want this output to be sent to the current working directory of drive C. You presumably have changed the working directory to that desired subdirectory on the C drive before running the program (with CD). To join the C drive to the root directory of the B drive, enter

JOIN C: B:\

To restore normalcy and nullify a previously-defined JOIN, use a /d switch. For example, to disconnect the C drive from the root of the B drive you would enter:

JOIN C: /d

KEYB

This command is used to load a new keyboard translation table for a specific country to replace the default US keyboard layout.

Syntax

[*D:path*]KEYB *xx*

D:path is the drive and path where the command file is located if it is not in the current directory.

xx is a keyboard code representing a country. It can be one of the following:

US	United States
UK	United Kingdom
GR	Germany
FR	France
IT	Italy
SP	Spain

Type

External.

Examples and Considerations

To switch the keyboard layout from standard US to the layout normally used in France you simply enter

KEYB FR

LABEL

LABEL allows you to give your disks volume labels electronically. You will then see your disk's name each time you call up a directory.

Syntax

[*D:path*]LABEL [*D1*:][*string*]

> *D:path* is the drive and path where the command file is located if it is not in the current directory.
>
> *D1*: is the drive containing the disk whose label is to be changed or displayed.
>
> *string,* when specified, will become the label of the disk in *D1*.

Type

External.

Restrictions

LABEL cannot be used with drives that have been substituted or joined.

The following characters may not be used in a volume label:

> * ? / \ | . , ; : + = < > [ ] ( ) & ^

Examples and Considerations

If you know the contents of a particular disk and want to give that disk a new electronic label, you can do so quickly with a single line entry. For instance, if you want to label the disk in drive B with the name "Budgets," enter:

LABEL B: Budgets

If you are not sure of what is currently on the disk, consider using the LABEL command as follows to display the current volume label. For example, typing

LABEL B:

will result in the following display:

**Volume in drive B is Budgets
Type a volume label of up to 11 characters or
Press Enter for no volume label update: _**

MKDIR (MD)

The MKDIR command (or MD for short) creates a new directory, either in the current working directory or at the specified path location in an existing tree. This new directory will be empty of files initially, but it is usable immediately.

Syntax

M[K]D[IR] [*D:path*] [...]

> *D:path* is the optional drive and path specifying which directory you wish to create.
>
> [...] are additional *D:path* entries, understandable to the protected mode command processor.

Type

Internal.

Examples and Considerations

The MKDIR command enables you to make new directories to help you to organize files on any disk. As with all other file references, you can specify a file name without a complete path and OS/2 will assume that the reference is to the current working directory.

No matter what directory you are in, you can also create a new subdirectory within it called Data, by entering:

MD Data

Assuming that your current working directory is Symphony, you have effectively created a data directory with the full path name of Symphony\Data.

It is not necessary to be located in the directory where the new subdirectory is to be placed. Your working directory can be located on drive A, and you can use the MD command to create a new Info subdirectory within the School directory, located on the D drive:

MD D:\School\Info

Protected mode gives you the ability to create multiple directories by specifying multiple entries on the MD command line. For instance, to create the directories Jr, Pd, and Ap in the Progs directory on the default drive, you would enter

MD \Progs\Jr \Progs\Pd \Progs\Ap

MODE

The MODE command controls and redirects output. There are four formats for this useful command. The first selects various print modes on parallel printers, the second redirects output, the third changes the parameters of the serial port, and the fourth changes the display type.

Syntax

[*D:path*]MODE LPT*x*: [*CPL*][,[*LPI*][,p]]
[*D:path*]MODE LPT*x*: = COM*y*
[*D:path*]MODE COM*y*[:]*baud*[,[*parity*][,[*bits*][,p]]
[*D:path*]MODE *type*

> *D:path* is the drive and path where the command file is located if it is not in the current directory.
>
> *x* is a printer number.
>
> *CPL* is the number of characters per line, 80 or 132.
>
> *LPI* is the number of lines per inch, 6 or 8.
>
> p causes the computer to continuously retry accessing the port during time-out errors.
>
> *y* is a serial-port number, from 1 to 8 (default = 1).
>
> *baud* is a baud rate for the COM port (110, 150, 300, 600, 1200, 2400, 4800, 9600, or 19200).
>
> *parity* is a parity value for the COM port; it can be E (even), O (odd), or N (none) (the default is even).
>
> *bits* is combination of two parameters (separated by a comma) specifying the number of stop and data bits used. Data bits can be 7 (the default) or 8, and stop bits can be 1 or 2. The default value is 1 for all rates except 110 baud where it is 2.
>
> *type* is the display type being used. It is specified as 40, 80, BW40, BW80, CO40, CO80, or MONO.

Type
External.

Examples and Considerations

The MODE command is most often used to prepare a serial port for computer output to a serial device. If you wish to connect Com2 (your second communications port) to an HP plotter, for instance, enter:

MODE Com2:9600,n,8,1,p

This ensures that data is transmitted by OS/2 out of that second communications port to the waiting plotter at a rate of 9600 baud. Similarly, if you want to connect a 1200 baud printer to your first communications port, you can enter

MODE Com1:1200,n,8,1,p

The p parameter assures that OS/2 will continue trying to print a file, even if the printer is not yet ready. To change this setting, you can reenter the MODE command with adjusted parameters.

Suppose that standard parallel printer output must be redirected from Lpt1 to Com1. Assuming that Com1 has just been set up with one of the appropriate preceding MODE commands, you can now control this redirection by entering

MODE Lpt1: = Com1:

All succeeding output to the Lpt1 port (the default PRN port) will now be sent out to the printer connected to the first serial communications port.

After outputting to a serial port, you may wish to use your parallel printer again. Redirection can be disabled by entering

MODE Lpt1:

These kinds of definitions, setups, and redirections are usually done only once in a system. Therefore, it is a good idea to include them in your Autoexec.bat or Startup.cmd files.

MORE

This command is similar to the DIR/p command, which pauses the directory listing after each screenful of data and asks you to press a key to continue. MORE is a filter—that is, data is sent to it, and MORE processes the data and sends it out in a new format. In this case, the filter simply prints the data a screenful at a time and prints "MORE" at the bottom of the screen until you press a key.

Syntax

[*D:path*]MORE

D:path is the drive and path where the command file is located if it is not in the current directory.

Type

External.

Examples and Considerations

The MORE command is typically used as a filter to read information from standard input, from a pipe, or from a redirected file. It always displays a screenful of information at a time, and it is useful when you want to look at long text files one screen of information at a time. For example, you can look at a prepared text report by using the MORE command with redirection techniques:

MORE < Analysis.rpt

With the SORT command, MORE can be used as a filter to provide a sorted display of the contents of any text file, one screenful at a time:

SORT Accounts.txt ¦ MORE

PATCH

The PATCH command enables you to make corrections to any bytes in any position in disk files. The file can even be extended by using PATCH to add bytes to the end of the file.

Syntax

PATCH [*D:path*] [/a]

> *D:path* is the drive and path where the command file is located if it is not in the current directory.

> /a tells PATCH to take its instructions from a specified patching file.

Type

External.

Examples and Considerations

A *patched* program is like a patch on a piece of clothing—it is replacement material for the code originally located at that position in the program file. You normally would enter

PATCH

PATCH will interactively enable you to make corrections and/or additions to a specified file on the disk. In this default interactive mode, you are asked to enter the name of the file to be patched, the offset at which the patch is to be applied, and the new file contents that are to be patched into the existing file. PATCH uses hexadecimal notation, so this command is usually used only by programmers. If you are following step-by-step vendor instructions for program patching (perhaps because of a bug), be extremely careful. An incorrectly patched file may not work at all.

It is best to backup a file before any patches. If you discover that the patch doesn't work or even worsens the situation, you can re-establish the former version of the file by using the COPY command.

Before patching, the current values of bytes located in that area are displayed. A manufacturer supplying a correction will usually indicate what the current values should be; if the displayed values are not what the manufacturer indicates, press the Esc key to cancel patching. If they are as expected, type in the suggested replacement digits (in hexadecimal). You may change 16 bytes at a time. While you are working with these 16 possibilities, pressing a digit replaces the currently highlighted byte, pressing the space bar skips the currently displayed byte, pressing the Backspace key moves backward in the set of 16 bytes, and pressing Return applies the patch to the file. You will then be prompted to reply if you want to make any more patches.

Another mode for experienced users is the /a automatic mode. Using this option tells PATCH to take its patch instructions from a specified patching file containing proper instructions. This is particularly dangerous, because one single error in the automatic sequence of patches can lead to wholesale destruction of your file. A vendor with a complicated patch to the executable file will probably submit a patch file for you to use in automatic mode.

PATH

You often need to access a program in a directory other than the one you are in. The PATH command gives OS/2 a list of drives and directories to search through, in the order given, until it finds the requested program file. Beware of the order given; if there are two different files with the same name in different directories along the path, the first one encountered will be used.

Syntax

PATH [*D1:path1*][;*D2:path2*...]

[*D1:path1*] is the first drive and directory searched.

[*D2:path2*...] is the second drive and directory searched, and so on.

Type

Internal.

Restrictions

PATH will not work for data files, overlay files, or other nonexecutable files (see APPEND and DPATH). You can't specify a drive name before PATH.

Examples and Considerations

PATH is an extremely common command. In fact, it is typically part of the initial environment for every new protected mode process. The Install program automatically places a default startup path in both the Autoexec.bat and Startup.cmd files.

In a simple example, the following entry instructs OS/2 to search the root directory, then the OS2 directory, and lastly the utility directory, to locate any external commands or programs not found in the current working directory:

PATH \;\Os2;\Utility

PRINT

The PRINT command invokes, modifies, and adds files to an internal software-based queue. Queues offer you a way to set up the computer to output multiple files in order automatically.

Syntax

[*D:path*]PRINT [/c][/t][/*d:device*][*filespec*, ...]

> *D:path* is the drive and path where the command file is located if it is not in the current directory.

> /c cancels previous and following entries on the command line.

> /t terminates the queue; everything is canceled and stopped.

> /*d:device* specifies the name of the print device. The default is Lpt1; other possibilities are Lpt2, Lpt3, PRN, or Com*n* (n = 1 to 8).

> *filespec*, ... is an optional list of the paths, names, and extensions of files to be queued for printing.

Type
External.

Restrictions

You cannot use a printer without the PRINT command while a queue is printing. PRINT cannot be used on a network. The disk where the files are located cannot be removed from the drive until the queue has completed printing.

Each queue entry is limited to 64 characters, so overly long path names are not feasible. Also, in protected mode, the required device driver must be installed before printing to a serial port.

Examples and Considerations

The PRINT command is most commonly used to print one or more text files on the connected output printer. In the following example, the printer is connected to your Com1 port, and the file to be printed is called Data.lst. You then enter

PRINT /d:Com1 Data.lst

If you wish to print all the analysis reports on the printer connected to the second parallel port, enter

PRINT /d:Lpt2 Analysis.*

If you want to dequeue or remove the eighth analysis report from the PRINT queue, enter

PRINT Analysis.rpt8 /c

If you want to terminate all printing requests in the Lpt2 print queue, enter

PRINT Lpt2 /t

PROMPT

This command changes the system prompt to whatever you like. It can display the time, the date, a simple message, or a wide range of special symbols and results. This is useful for finding out which directory you are in before you modify or delete any files, or just for constant display of current system information.

Syntax

PROMPT [string]

string is a string of characters that can contain special-purpose entries. (See Table 5.2 below.)

Type
Internal.

Examples and Considerations

The standard adjustments to your prompt can be made with any two character sequence seen in Table 5.2.

Each special result is obtained with a different character preceded by a $. The simplest and most common variation in the default prompt is to make the prompt into the *drive:current directory*. Do this by entering

PROMPT $p

When OS/2 boots up, it provides different default prompts for real and protected mode. Each of these can be changed with the PROMPT command, confirming which mode you are in if you are only looking at a command prompt. For instance, if you have a monochrome monitor you might enter the following command in real mode:

PROMPT Real $p

If your current default directory were \Lotus, your prompt would be

Real C:\Lotus_

In protected mode, your prompt could be slightly different but still informative:

PROMPT [Prot $P]

CHARACTERS	DESCRIPTION
$$	$ sign
$t	Time
$d	Date
$p	Current directory
$v	DOS version number
$n	Default drive identifier
$g	> symbol
$l	< symbol
$b	¦ symbol
$q	= symbol
$a	& symbol
$c	(symbol
$f	) symbol
$h	Erasing backspace
$e	Escape character
$_	Carriage return and line feed

Table 5.2: Special Character Sequences for Creating Special Prompts

If you are working in the Lotus directory while in protected mode, your prompt reads

[Prot C:\Lotus]

If you have a special monitor that supports graphic functions or color and you have installed the ANSI escape sequence support, then you can use the additional escape codes seen in Table 5.3. These are made available by including the symbols, $e[p1;p2;...m] in your prompt sequence. Use the code values from Table 5.3 to substitute for p1, p2, etc.

For example, if the ANSI command in protected mode is set to on, the following prompt will switch your standard prompt to be the current drive and directory, preceded by the word Prot, and nestled

CODE	FUNCTION
0	All attributes off
1	Bold on
2	Faint on
3	Italic on
5	Blink on
6	Rapid blink on
7	Reverse video on
8	Concealed on
30	Black foreground
31	Red foreground
32	Green foreground
33	Yellow foreground
34	Blue foreground
35	Magenta foreground
36	Cyan foreground
37	White foreground
40	Black background
41	Red background
42	Green background
43	Yellow background
44	Blue background
45	Magenta background
46	Cyan background
47	White background
48	Subscript
49	Superscript

Table 5.3: Ansi.sys Escape Code Sequences

inside square brackets. The prompt will also be displayed as bold white letters on a red background:

PROMPT $e[1;37;41m[Prot $P]$e[0m

You can make a similar prompt adjustment in real mode if you include the line DEVICE = Ansi.sys in your Config.sys file during configuration. The command to set the real mode prompt to bold white letters on a blue background, containing the information [Real drive:directory] is

PROMPT $e[1;37;44m[Real $P]$e[0m

RECOVER

Sometimes a part of a disk goes bad—that is, the computer cannot read it, and access to the files in that area may be denied. The RECOVER command reads the file part by part, skipping over the bad data, and rewrites the file without the bad data, allowing the user access to whatever is left. RECOVER can be used to recover specific files or an entire disk.

Syntax

[*D:path*]RECOVER [*D1*][*filespec*]

D:path is the drive and path where the command file is located if it is not in the current directory.

D1 is the drive identifier for the disk to be recovered.

filespec is an optional drive and path, plus the file name and extension, of the file that is the object of the command. Wild cards are allowed.

Type

External.

Restrictions

RECOVER will not work on a network when run from any remote work station, nor does it work on substituted drives or joined drives.

Examples and Considerations

You can recover an individual file from a disk by specifying it as the parameter to the RECOVER command. For instance, if your Salary.dta file is corrupted because of bad sectors on a disk, you can ask OS/2 to try to recover as much of it as possible with the following command:

RECOVER Salary.dta

If much of the disk has gone bad, you can still ask OS/2 to recover as much as possible by specifying the drive letter itself:

RECOVER C:

In this example, all former file names on the disk will be replaced by a sequentially numbered series of newly formed names. In addition, the amount that is recovered will be a function of how badly your disk is damaged. Executable files are usually useless after recovery, while text files can be at least partially reconstructed with your word processor.

RENAME (REN)

The RENAME command (or REN) renames a file.

Syntax

REN[AME] *oldfile newfile*

> *oldfile* is the optional drive and path, plus the file name and extension, of the file that will be renamed. Wild cards are allowed.

> *newfile* is a new file name and extension for *oldfile*. Wild cards are allowed. The *newfile* parameter does not require or accept a pre-fixed drive and path.

Type
Internal.

Restrictions

You cannot use the REN command to move a file from one directory or drive to another.

You cannot use RENAME to give a subdirectory a new name. You cannot specify a drive for this command, and you can only rename a file on a particular drive to a new name on that same drive. This means that you cannot type either a drive or a path name in front of *newfile*.

Examples and Considerations

You can rename the Budget.tmp file to Budget.88 with the following command (this example assumes that the original Budget file is located in the Lotus\Data directory in the D drive):

REN D:\Lotus\Data\Budget.tmp Budget.88

Budget.88 still resides in the Lotus\Data directory.

You can use wild cards to change a set of file names at once. For example, all of the accounting files that begin with the letters Acc and have an extension of .new could be changed to have an extension of

REN Acc*.new Acc*.old

REPLACE

The REPLACE command is an advanced, selective version of the COPY command. It is useful for changing versions of OS/2 when files need to be updated. It is also useful for selective backups of files without the BACKUP command. For example, if you work with a single-disk word processor, then a backup disk might only contain copies of the text files you've worked on. REPLACE would only replace the files on the backup disk that were changed on the original, or it would only make copies of newly created files, not the older, unchanged files.

Syntax

[*D:path*]REPLACE *sourcefile* [*dest*][/a][/p][/r][/s][/w]

D:path is the drive and path where the command file is located if it is not in the current directory.

sourcefile is the optional drive and path, plus the file name and an optional extension, of each file that will be a replacing file.

dest is the optional drive and path of the files to be replaced.

/a adds files to those already present.

/p prompts you before replacing a file.

/r replaces both normal and read-only files on *dest*.

/s replaces all files in the directory structure that have matching file names.

/w waits for you to insert a disk.

Type
External.

Examples and Considerations
The REPLACE command is most often used for two reasons:

- To find the locations of all directories containing a particular piece of software, and to replace the old versions of that software with the latest version of that software.

- To find all of the different files in a particular directory, and update each of these individual files to their latest version.

For instance, let's say you have acquired several software packages over the years, each of which may include its own version of Cmd.exe. These Cmd.exe versions may still be buried in the individual software application package directories, while your root directory contains the most current version of OS/2's command interpreter.

You can upgrade all versions of the protected mode command interpreter at one time by asking OS/2 to replace occurrences of each version throughout the directory structure (/s switch) with the latest version from the system disk in drive A. Enter the following:

REPLACE A:\Cmd.exe C:\ /s

Another application of REPLACE is to upgrade your existing set of files with a new set from an application or system disk. For example, you might leave all current .sys files alone in your device driver directory Sys, but add new system device drivers with the following command:

REPLACE A:*.sys C:\Sys /a

This command leaves all existing files in the Sys directory of the C drive untouched, while adding any new .sys files from the A drive to the Sys directory.

RESTORE

This command is the reverse of BACKUP: it restores files to the disk and directory from which they were backed up.

Syntax

[*D:path*]RESTORE *sourceD filespec*[/s][/p][/b:*mm-dd-yy*]
[/a:*mm-dd-yy*][/m][/n][/l:*hh-mm-ss*][/e:*hh-mm-ss*]

D:path is the drive and path where the command file is located if it is not in the current directory.

sourceD is the drive containing the backed-up files to be restored.

filespec is the optional drive and path, plus the file names and extensions, of the files on *sourceD* to be restored. Wild cards are allowed.

/s restores files in subdirectories of the files specified in *filespec*.

/p prompts you before a file is restored if that file was modified since it was last backed up.

/b:*mm-dd-yy* causes all backed-up files that were last modified on or before *mm-dd-yy* to be restored.

/a:*mm-dd-yy* causes all backed-up files that were last modified on or after *mm-dd-yy* to be restored.

mm-dd-yy represents a date in months, days, and years.

/m compares the backed-up files and the files on the destination disk; it then restores the files that have been changed or erased since the last backup.

/n restores files that no longer exist on the destination disk.

/l:*hh-mm-ss* restores all files changed since the time specified by *hh-mm-ss*.

/e:*hh-mm-ss* restores all files changed prior to the time specified by *hh-mm-ss*.

hh-mm-ss represents time in hours, minutes, and seconds.

Type
External.

RESTORE will overwrite files with the same name if they are in the specified directory. Use the /p switch (or the REPLACE command) to avoid rewriting a file.

Restrictions

Only files created with BACKUP will be restored. Do not use RESTORE if SUBST, JOIN, or ASSIGN was invoked in a BACKUP operation.

The RESTORE command restores standard files other than command interpreters and system files. The SYS command restores the files, Os2bio.com and Os2dos.com. The COPY command can be used to restore command interpreter files from your system disk, Cmd.exe and Command.com.

Examples and Considerations

Any individual file created with the BACKUP command can be restored to a specified drive. For example, the file Payroll.wks can be restored to the Lotus directory on drive C from a backup disk in drive A by using the following command:

RESTORE A: C:\Lotus\Payroll.wks

All the files in the backup set in drive A can be restored to drive D underneath the root with the following command:

RESTORE A: D:\ /s

Batch files can also use named parameters during processing. This ability circumvents the limitation of nine numbered parameters, and makes the potential batch program easier to read, debug, and maintain. For example, a password mechanism can be set up in your batch file that tests for the value of a variable called *password*. You can initialize this variable at the command prompt, or in an initialization batch file, with the following command:

SET password = 020346

With the command

IF %1 = = %password%

the batch file tests to see if a password entered by a user matches the string of digits (020346) stored in the OS/2 environment. See Chapter 8 for further details about using batch files for password protection, resource management, and named environmental parameters.

SORT

SORT is another filter command. Data is sent in and, depending on the parameters, sorted and displayed or routed to another file. Directories may be displayed in a sorted format, but the files will not be physically sorted on the disk.

Syntax

[*D:path*]SORT [/r][/ + *col*]

> *D:path* is the drive and path where the command file is located if it is not in the current directory.

> /r sorts in reverse-alphabetical order.

> / + *col* starts the sorting with column *col* (the default is column 1).

Type
External.

Examples and Considerations

As with FIND and MORE, the SORT command can use filter and redirection features of OS/2 to arrange data in a file. If the /r switch is used, the data is arranged line by line, and sorted in either ascending order (0–9, then A–Z), or descending order (9–0, then Z–A). By using standard redirection and filtering symbols, SORT filters data from the standard input device, or from a file or a pipe.

For instance, the following sequence takes the data from the Person.txt file and alphabetically sorts the lines in that file, sending the results to Newpers.txt:

SORT < Person.txt > Newpers.txt

If the important key in your file is located in any column other than the first, the / + *col* switch arranges the data according to that column. Combining this with the pipes concept (see Chapter 6), the following command arranges the default directory listing according to the file extension:

DIR ¦ SORT / + 10

Sorted results are displayed on the screen. Of course, this can be further combined with output redirection to send a sorted directory listing (by extension) to another file.

SPOOL

The SPOOL command initiates a printer spooling program to support background printing. You can then immediately run other OS/2 commands or programs.

Syntax

SPOOL [*D:path*] [*/d:device1*] [*/o:device2*]

[*D:path*] defines the subdirectory in which any temporary spool files will be created. If you do not specify this parameter, OS/2 creates all temporary spool files in a directory called Spool. You must create this directory before invoking the SPOOL command, or OS/2 displays a self-evident error message saying that it cannot find the specified (default) spool subdirectory.

/d:*device1* assigns a virtual port for the spooling device; it can be a parallel port (PRN, Lpt1, Lpt2, Lpt3), or a serial port (Com*n*, where n ranges from 1 to 8).

Lpt1 is the default device name.

/o:*device2* represents the actual output device. If this parameter is omitted, the entry in *d:device1* is used as a default.

Type

External.

Restrictions

Protected mode only. A drive name cannot be entered before this command.

Examples and Considerations

Assuming that you have used the MD command to create a separate spool directory called Spool, the following command line spools all output to the Lpt2 port through temporary files created in the Spool directory:

SPOOL C:\Spool /d:Lpt2

Any application program output being directed to the print device connected to Lpt2 is stored in a temporary file in the Spool subdirectory. Only when each process completes, or indicates that the file to be printed is complete, will the output information stored in the spool file be routed to the queue for printing. Figure 5.1 demonstrates this procedure, with three processes sending output to the print queue. In this example, Process 3 completes first, and its output moves to first place in the queue. Process 1 completes next, and Process 2 finishes last. This order of completion connects to Lpt2, and dictates the actual printing order. By using the spooler, individual printed page output from each process will not be mixed with output from any other process. The term SPOOL is an acronym for Simultaneous Peripheral Operations On-Line.

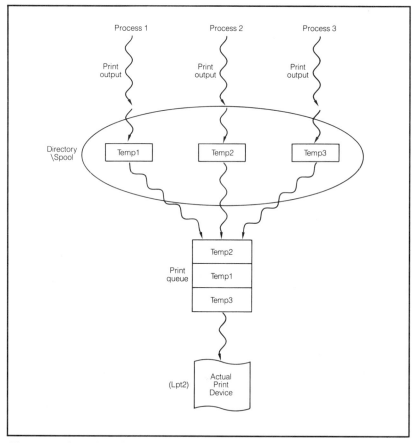

Figure 5.1: Spooling (Simultaneous Peripheral Operations On-Line)

START

The START command enables you to create independent processes in protected mode.

Syntax

START [*drive*:][*path*]filename [*params*]

> [*drive*:][*path*] defines the location of the program to be initiated as a background process.

> filename is the name of the specified program.

> [*params*] are any command line parameters or switches, optional or required.

Type
Internal.

Restrictions
Protected mode only.

Examples and Considerations

In contrast with the DETACH command, which initiates inaccessible and self-running background tasks, START initiates tasks in their own new sessions, or screen groups. For example, you can run the spooler by entering

START C:\Os2\Spool.exe C:\Spool /d:Lpt2

As an alternative to the Session Manager choice, "Start a Program," you can start a new protected mode process session with START by entering the following:

START Cmd.exe

The Session Manager screen displays Cmd.exe as the new running program. In contrast, when you begin a new session with the Session Manager choice, "Start a Program", you will see

* OS/2 command prompt *

displayed as the process title. Any program run with START will have its own name displayed on the Session Manager screen.

SUBST

The SUBST command is the opposite of the JOIN command. It creates a new disk drive corresponding to a directory. Starting with one directory structure, you can take a directory and all of its subdirectories and make that branch of the tree into the root directory of a new, fictitious drive. This new drive accesses all of its data from a physically existing drive, and thus cannot be considered a RAM disk.

Like the JOIN command, SUBST has three distinct formats for its use. The first displays all of the current substitutions, the second actually performs a substitution, and the third cancels out a substitution.

Syntax

[*D:path*]SUBST
[*D:path*]SUBST *newD path2*
[*D:path*]SUBST *newD* /d

> *D:path* is the drive and path where the command file is located if it is not in the current directory.
>
> *newD* is the drive to be created or abolished.
>
> *path2* is the drive and directory specification to be made into drive *newD*.
>
> /d abolishes an existing *newD* substitution.

Type
External.

Restriction
Real mode only.

When a virtual drive is created using the SUBST command, none of the following commands works on that disk: CHKDSK, DISK-COPY, FDISK, FORMAT, LABEL, RECOVER, or SYS.

Examples and Considerations
The SUBST command is often used to cut down on the typing needed to refer to file names located within a complex directory structure. It is easier to type a single letter and a colon than a complete path name. The following example creates a virtual drive, G, as a

substitute for D:\Programs\Wordproc\Wordperf:

SUBST G: D:\Programs\Wordproc\Wordperf

All succeeding references to files in the Wordperf subdirectory can now use either the full path name, or just G.

This technique is also used to fool those older programs understanding only disk drives without a directory structure. For example, you might have a geometric analysis program called Geometry.exe. This program requires that its own system and support files be on drive A, while all its data files must exist or be created on drive B. You can create subdirectories within your disk hierarchy called Geometry and Geometry\Data. Then use SUBST to trick your original programs into accessing program files from the geometry directory, and data files from the data directory:

SUBST A: \Geometry
SUBST B: \Geometry\Data

SYS

If you have made a data disk and want to make it into a system disk, or if you want to transfer a new version of OS/2 to a freshly formatted high capacity disk, this command can be useful. SYS does not transfer Command.com or Cmd.exe, but does transfer the required system files.

You cannot use SYS to install OS/2 by simply replacing the hidden files on a DOS 3.x machine. SYS can not recognize the wide range of different system files loaded onto different machine's boot drives.

Syntax
[*D:path*]SYS *destD*:

> *D:path* is the drive and path where the command file is located if it is not in the current directory.

> *destD* is the drive to which the system files will be transferred.

Type
External.

Restrictions
SYS does not work on substituted or joined commands, nor does it work in a network setting.

Examples and Considerations
This command is typically used to update your version of OS/2 on a hard disk. In OS/2, the /s switch on the FORMAT command does more than just copy the system files, Os2bio.com and Os2dos.com. It also copies a series of additional system files listed in the special system file, called Formats.tbl. For example, if you boot OS/2 from the A drive, and want to transfer the system to your hard disk in drive C, enter

SYS C:

On the other hand, if your system is already on C and you want to transfer it to a 1.44MB, 3½-inch disk in the F drive, enter

SYS F:

TIME

This command is used to set the system time. You can also use it to reset an internal clock. Setting the time comes in handy when errors occur—you can tell exactly when a file was last written to or changed. It also provides a trail by which a programmer can trace the file-saving flow of a program.

Syntax

TIME [*hh:mm*[:*ss*[.*xx*]]]

hh is the current hour, in 24-hour format. (To translate from 12-hour to 24-hour time: if the time is between 1:00 P.M. and midnight, add 12 to the hour. For example, 7:45 P.M. = 19:45.)

mm is the current number of minutes.

ss is the current number of seconds.

xx is the current number of hundredths of seconds.

Type
Internal.

Restrictions

You cannot indicate a drive for this command. In addition, the command format used by TIME is influenced by the COUNTRY command in the Config.sys file.

Examples and Considerations

You can reset TIME on your computer's clock by entering the TIME command along with the new time in the form, hours:minutes:seconds:hundredths, as follows:

TIME 7:58

This entry adjusts your computer's clock to the new time of 7:58 a.m. Remember that OS/2 maintains a 24 hour clock, so that hours from 1 to 11 are always a.m.

If you do not enter a new time as a parameter to the TIME command, OS/2 displays the current time recorded in its clock, and gives you the opportunity to change it:

TIME
Current time is 7:58:27.16
Enter new time:_

TREE

TREE displays a listing of all of your directories and subdirectories and (optionally) the files in them. This is especially useful for identifying long directory specifications that should be cut down.

Syntax

[*D:path*]TREE [*D2:*][/f]

> *D:path* is the drive and path where the command file is located if it is not in the current directory.

> *D2* is the drive identifier of another drive you want TREE to affect.

> /f displays all paths and names of files in the directories.

Type

External.

Examples and Considerations

The primary role of the TREE command is to display the hierarchical tree of directories and subdirectories on a particular disk drive. To display each directory on the drive, and then each subdirectory within each directory, simply enter

TREE

The /f switch enables this command to produce a log of all files, listed by directory on your disk drive. Combining this command with redirection allows you to produce a complete disk file log, store it in a new file, and then print the file when you're ready:

TREE D: /f > Files.log

TYPE

TYPE displays the contents of an ASCII file. ASCII files contain no control codes that would affect the screen display; they appear as straight listings of data.

Syntax

TYPE *filespec* **[...]**

> *filespec* is the optional drive and path, plus the file name and extension, of the file to be displayed.
>
> [...] represents additional *filespecs* that may be typed when this command is issued from protected mode.

Type
Internal.

Using TYPE on a non-ASCII file could have no effect, or it could display meaningless symbols on your screen. And, in real mode, it could even lock up your system entirely. If this happens, you'll need to reboot.

Examples and Considerations

The TYPE command is used principally to display a text file on your screen or on your printer. To type the file Analysis.rpt on your screen, enter

TYPE Analysis.rpt

In protected mode, you can process multiple file specifications on the same line. To type a copy of Analysis.rpt and Budget.rpt on your system printer, enter:

TYPE Analysis.rpt Budget.rpt > PRN

VER

This command displays the current version of OS/2 in which you are working.

Syntax

VER

Type

Internal.

Examples and Considerations

Entering the VER command in either real mode or protected mode displays a similar message, indicating the current version of the operating system. Typing VER in real mode might produce the following result:

MS Personal Computer DOS Version *vv.nn*

The principal version number is denoted as *vv* to the left of the decimal point, and intermediate revisions to that version appear as *nn* to the right of the decimal point. In protected mode the same entry will produce a similar, though not necessarily identical, message:

The MS Operating System/2 Version is *vv.nn*

VERIFY

This command turns the global VERIFY feature of OS/2 on or off. When it is on, everything written to a file will be checked buffer by buffer, to ensure the accuracy of the transmission. This is a useful feature, but your system will run more slowly. Use VERIFY ON when you must be completely sure of the validity of the file data being transferred—for example, during BACKUP operations.

Syntax

VERIFY [ON | OFF]

ON turns VERIFY on.

OFF turns VERIFY off. This is the default.

Type
Internal.

Restrictions
VERIFY will not work with network disks.

Examples and Considerations
The VERIFY command turns the verification mode on when writing to disks. To invoke VERIFY, enter

VERIFY ON

This ensures that any files written to the disk will not be subject to corruption from using bad sectors. VERIFY remains in effect until you turn it off with the reverse entry:

VERIFY OFF

Entering VERIFY with no parameter merely asks OS/2 to display the current value (on or off) of this switch.

VOL

The VOL command shows the volume label of a disk in a specified drive.

Syntax

VOL [*D*:] [...]

> *D* is a specified drive, if different from the default drive.
>
> [...] are other drives that can be specified when the command is issued from protected mode.

Type
Internal.

Examples and Considerations

Entering the VOL command alone causes OS/2 to display the label of the current working disk drive. In protected mode, the command can accept multiple drive parameters, enabling you to obtain the labels of multiple drives with one request. Enter

VOL C: D:

This might produce the following result in protected mode:

Volume in drive C is ROBBINS
Volume in drive D is DRIVE-D

XCOPY

XCOPY is a modified version of the COPY command. It does the same thing, only better. Instead of reading and writing files one at a time, XCOPY reads files into a buffer that is equal in size to available memory, and then writes out the contents of the buffer (this is usually several files). XCOPY can be used for a single file or for several different groups of files. You can combine its switches as well.

Syntax

[*D:path*]XCOPY [*filespec1*][*filespec2*][/a][/d:*mm-dd-yy*] [/e][/m][/p][/s][/v]

> *D:path* is the drive and path where the command file is located if it is not in the current directory.
>
> *filespec1* is the necessary drive, path, and file-name specifications for the files to be copied. Wild cards are allowed.
>
> *filespec2* is the necessary drive, path, and file-name specifications for the files to be written to. Wild cards are allowed.
>
> /a copies only files with a set archive bit.
>
> /d:*mm-dd-yy* copies only files created or modified on or after the specified date; the format depends on the COUNTRY specification.
>
> /e creates corresponding subdirectories on *filespec2* before copying is done (even if *filespec1* contains no files to transfer).
>
> /m copies files with a set archive bit and resets the archive bit on the source file.
>
> /p prompts you before each file is copied.
>
> /s also copies files from all subdirectories within the specified directory. Corresponding subdirectories will be created on *filespec2* for all *filespec1* directories that contain files.
>
> /v turns VERIFY on during execution of this command only.

Type

External.

Restrictions

XCOPY will not copy to or from devices. It also will not copy hidden files from the source and will not overwrite read-only files on the destination.

Examples and Considerations

XCOPY works very quickly because it reads as many source files as it can fit into memory. Only then does it begin to write the files to the destination disk. In contrast, the COPY command reads and then writes files one after the other.

For example, to copy all the files in the Lotus\Data directory of the C drive to a high-capacity disk in the A drive, enter

XCOPY C:\Lotus\Data A:

XCOPY also can copy files from a branch of a directory tree. This means that all batch files in all directories below the root of the D drive can be backed up to a disk in the A drive with the following command:

XCOPY D:*.bat A: /s

The /s switch starts at the directory specified in *filespec1*, and works its way through all lower level subdirectories, searching for files that meet the specification, *.bat.

USING COMMANDS
AT THE OS/2 PROMPT ─────

CHAPTER 6

SEVERAL FEATURES OF OS/2 OFFER YOU SIGNIFICANT
control over command entry, as well as input and output in your system, and the processing of files and information. They are of great
interest to programmers designing automated applications for OS/2
systems; they are also of practical value for anyone using OS/2.

This chapter concentrates on several new features of OS/2 (i.e., multiple command submission and logical operators for command grouping) as well as some sophisticated DOS features (redirection, filters, and
pipes) also available in OS/2. These features enable you to manage your
computer information as it flows from one place to another in your system. In presenting these capabilities of OS/2, you'll also learn about the
ability of OS/2 to accept and process multiple commands on a single
command line in a variety of logical ways.

CONTROLLING THE FLOW OF INFORMATION BY REDIRECTION

Redirection refers to the ability of a program or an OS/2 command
to choose an alternative device for input or output. As you know,
most programs and commands have a default device. For example,
when you enter the DIR command, the computer assumes that you
want a directory to be displayed on the screen. It then displays it on
the virtual screen and you have to use the Session Manager or the
Alt-Esc sequence to map virtual consoles to the one actual console.
The default device for DIR is the console (CON), which consists of
the screen as the output device and the keyboard as the input device.
Your normal interface with the microcomputer system is through the
system console.

SENDING SCREEN OUTPUT TO THE PRINTER

You often need a hard-copy printout of the information that appears on your computer screen. As you know, typing Ctrl-PrtSc prints only one screenful of information at a time. However, it does allow you to see your data on the screen *and* then print it out. OS/2 has a simple way of redirecting the complete output to the printer, no matter how many screenfuls of data are involved.

All you have to do is follow a command with > PRN. Think of the greater than sign (>) as an arrow pointing to the destination. For example, entering the following command will redirect the standard OS/2 directory listing to the printer (PRN) instead of to the video screen:

    DIR > PRN

The same principle of redirection applies to any OS/2 command that sends data to the screen. Entering

    CHKDSK > PRN

will generate a status check of disk (and memory in real mode) and send it to the printer rather than to the video screen.

STORING SCREEN OUTPUT IN A DISK FILE

OS/2 can also direct the output to a text file. This means that the information displayed on the screen can be sent to a file on the disk. Screen displays are temporary; if a directory display is captured and stored in a file, however, its information can be used at a later time.

This redirection technique has many practical uses. If you're in a hurry and don't want to wait for printed output, you can quickly send the information to a disk file and then peruse it at your leisure. You can read it into your word-processing program and make modifications to it or include it in reports. You can read it with a database management program and perform file management functions based on the information sent by OS/2 into the disk file.

Redirection is also useful for creating a file that is a catalog of the contents of several disks. If you are working with a word processor or a database program, you can get a master listing of all the files you have stored on all your working disks. If you are working with a hard disk, you can make a catalog of your backup disks.

The first step in creating your own disk catalog is to decide where you want to place the master list. Let's assume you want to place the data in a file called Catalog. The first cataloged directory will be that of the disk in drive A. Entering

> DIR A: > Catalog

produces no visible result on the screen. You told OS/2 not to display the directory on the screen, but rather to store the information in a file called Catalog.

To check the results of this command, you can ask OS/2 to type the contents of the Catalog file:

> TYPE Catalog

The directory will be displayed just as if you had typed in the DIR command. However, this printout represents the directory when the original Catalog file was created by OS/2; it is like a snapshot of the original directory. It contains only the directory information that existed when the file was created.

Redirecting OS/2 output to a disk file can be misleading. Remember that the information contained in that file will not be current and will not be updated automatically to reflect any future changes to your system.

ADDING OUTPUT TO AN EXISTING FILE

Redirection also allows you to add the directory display of another drive to the Catalog file. This requires a slightly different command. Look at the following two commands:

> DIR A: > Catalog
> DIR A: >> Catalog

They look quite similar. However, the first command has only one > symbol and the second has two. What is the difference?

The first command simply replaces the old Catalog file with a new one. The second command tells OS/2 to add the new directory information to whatever is already in the Catalog file. The directory listing of the new disk placed in drive A will be appended to the directory listing of the disk previously placed in drive A.

You can continue this process by placing other disks in drive A and repeating the > > command. The Catalog file will grow as you store your disk directories on it. If you are a hard-disk user, you can place your floppy disks in drive A, and your Catalog file will be updated on drive C.

To see the contents of this file, you can simply enter

TYPE Catalog

OS/2 will then display a consolidated directory that includes the contents of a number of disks.

If you need a hard copy of the directories, you can redirect the data to your printer and use the TYPE command:

TYPE Catalog > PRN

You can edit this command's output with your word processor, print the results on gummed labels, and attach them to your original disks. Some companies sell programs for $50 that do this simple task.

RECEIVING INPUT FROM TEXT FILES

OS/2 can receive input from a text file. This means that instead of waiting at the console to enter data, make responses, or otherwise generate input for an OS/2 command or a program, you can type your responses in advance and store them in a file. OS/2 will then take each response from the input file as it is needed. Let's look at a simple example.

You may have noticed that some OS/2 commands require the user to enter additional keystrokes after the program has begun. For example, the FORMAT command will always pause and ask you to press any key before actual formatting takes place. This safety precaution protects you from errors, giving you a moment to take a deep breath (and to check the disk in the drive) before actually committing yourself to the formatting process.

You could avoid that extra keystroke by creating an input file to be used with the FORMAT command. The input file would contain any keystrokes that you wanted typed in while the program was running. You can create a file called Keys with your word processor or with the real mode EDLIN program (see Chapter 7) that contains a Return keystroke, and the No response (N) to the FORMAT command's request "Do you want to format an additional disk?"

To indicate that these responses are coming from a file and not from you at the keyboard, use the less than symbol (<):

> FORMAT B:/s < Keys

When you enter this command, the formatting does not pause because the Return keypress has been input from the Keys file. When the single disk is completely formatted, the N tells FORMAT you're done, and the OS/2 prompt reappears. As you can see, this kind of feature can save you time and effort and can be useful in a variety of situations, particularly those situations that are interactive.

PROCESSING YOUR FILE INFORMATION WITH OS/2 FILTERS

Another powerful feature of OS/2 is its use of *filters* to process data directly. Just as a camera filter changes what you see through the lens, an OS/2 filter can process any data that passes through it in unique ways and can change what you see on the screen. OS/2 has three filters: SORT, FIND, and MORE. They are stored on disk as the Sort.exe, Find.exe, and More.com files.

ARRANGING YOUR DATA WITH THE SORT FILTER

Let's look first at one of the most useful filters, the SORT filter. SORT rearranges lines of data. Take a look at the sample data files in Figures 6.1 and 6.2. These lists could have been prepared with a word processor, a database manager, a spreadsheet, or even with OS/2 itself. Lists like these usually grow in size, with the new entries added chronologically as your business acquires new clients or as you make new friends and acquaintances.

Every once in a while, you probably rewrite your own personal phone list. You usually want the list in last-name order, but you

```
C>TYPE  BUSINESS.TXT
Cantonese Imports     134  Roberts   Joseph 212/656-2156
Brandenberg Gates     754  Bennett   Mary   415/612-5656
Sole Survivor,Inc.    237  Evans     Gail   415/222-3514
Presley Plastics      198  Presley   Robert 716/245-6119
Plymouth Granite Co   345  Williams  Peter  617/531-6145
Bucket Dance Wear     276  Lewis     Ann    415/635-2530
Intelli-Strategies    743  Griffiths Robert 415/362-9537
Benicia Balloons      983  Franklin  Marie  212/524-4157
Standard Shelters     690  Rucker    Sally  415/532-1107
Panama Rain Corp.     576  Cook      Freda  408/534-9739

C>_
```

Figure 6.1: A business contact list

```
C>TYPE PERSONAL.TXT
Klaar      Wim      213-968-2345   Ready
Torrance   Stan     415-567-4534   Stan
Quilling   Alan     415-526-4565   Al
Keepsake   Alice    415-249-3498   Jala
Bentley    Robert   415-654-4864   Speed
Hendley    Candice  415-212-3434   Candy

C>_
```

Figure 6.2: A personal phone list

might want a special printout in nickname or first-name order. Even more often, businesses need to reprint their client list in some usable order. Perhaps the telephone receptionist needs an updated list in company-name order. The marketing department may need the same list printed in telephone-number order. Then again, the accounts payable department may want the list in customer ID order. All of these are very easy to obtain with the SORT filter.

Using the redirection concept presented in the previous section, you can take each of these representative lists and rearrange the data to suit your needs. The easiest form of filtering is to enter the following command at the OS/2 prompt:

SORT < Business.txt

The resulting screen will display the file in company-name order (see Figure 6.3), because the company name comes first on the line.

A similar arrangement of your personal phone list could be obtained by entering

SORT < Personal.txt

```
[Prot C:\]SORT < Business.txt
Benicia Balloons      983  Franklin Marie  212/524-4157
Brandenberg Gates     754  Bennett  Mary   415/612-5656
Bucket Dance Wear     276  Lewis    Ann    415/635-2530
Cantonese Imports     134  Roberts  Joseph 212/656-2156
Intelli-Strategies    743  Griffiths Robert 415/362-9537
Panama Rain Corp.     576  Cook     Freda  408/534-9739
Plymouth Granite Co   345  Williams Peter  617/531-6145
Presley Plastics      198  Presley  Robert 716/245-6119
Sole Survivor,Inc.    237  Evans    Gail   415/222-3514
Standard Shelters     690  Rucker   Sally  415/532-1107

[Prot C:\]
```

Figure 6.3: Sorting by company name

The resulting arrangement here is by last name, because last name is already the first data in the file.

In the previous example, the .txt file was directed to be *input* to the SORT command—the < symbol points to SORT. Because there was no redirection specified for output, the sorted results appeared on the video screen. Each of these commands could also specify an output redirection that would place the sorted results in a disk file. You could then work with the sorted file as you liked, perhaps delaying the printing until a convenient time.

The two sorted lists could be saved in the files Clients.txt and Phones.txt with the following commands:

```
SORT < Business.txt > Clients.txt
SORT < Personal.txt > Phones.txt
```

Figure 6.4 shows how this last SORT filter example works.

CUSTOMIZING YOUR OS/2 SORTS

The SORT filter allows you several different ways to sort. For example, the /r switch tells the program to sort in reverse (descending)

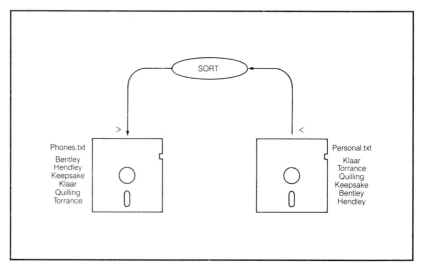

Figure 6.4: The SORT filter at work

order. Entering

SORT < Business.txt /r

produces a listing of the Business.txt file in reverse alphabetical order (see Figure 6.5).

SORT also allows you to specify the column on which you want the sorting to take place. Normally, SORT begins with the first character in the line. However, you can tell SORT to use another position in the data line, which allows you to sort your data files in a variety of ways. The following command will sort by the client contact name rather than by company name (see Figure 6.6):

SORT < Business.txt / + 26

The + 26 in this command tells OS/2 to sort based on the 26th character position. Extending this idea to any other position in the text file, you could just as easily sort the file by client ID number (use a / + 21 switch in the same command line). Character space 21 gets you past the 20-character-long company name, allowing sorting to begin with the ID entries.

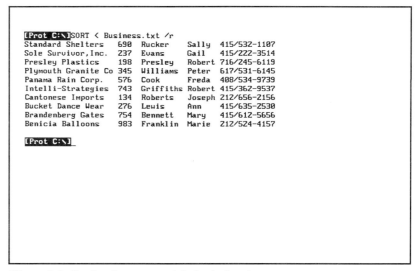

Figure 6.5: Sorting in reverse alphabetical order

The quotation marks around your character strings are delimiters. You must use them. They assist OS/2 in distinguishing a character string from the command line's other characters, which represent commands, file names, or parameters.

PERFORMING TEXT SEARCHES WITH THE FIND FILTER

Let's look at another OS/2 filter, the FIND command. It permits you to scan any text file for a series of text characters and locate any lines in the file that contain the specified characters. For instance, let's take the business contact list from Figure 6.1 and try to find all clients located in the area code 415:

FIND "415" Business.txt

This command will locate all lines in the specified text file (the second argument) that contain the specified character string (the first argument). Figure 6.7 demonstrates the results. Note that the first line of the output identifies the input text file.

This is a typical database extraction request that has been handled by OS/2 *almost* satisfactorily. Notice that the Benicia Balloons company has been included in the results, even though its area code is not 415. You asked OS/2 to find every line in the file that included 415 anywhere in the line, and 415 is in the last four digits of that

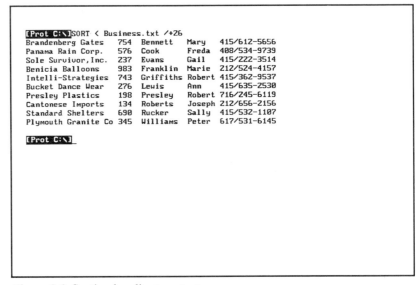

Figure 6.6: Sorting by client contact name

company's telephone number (524-4157). Therefore, the line was filtered into the resulting selection.

To solve this problem, you can specify ''415/'' as the character string. By including the slash you will be sure to extract only the telephone numbers that begin with the desired digits. Enter

> FIND ''415/'' Business.txt

> Make sure your specified character string is unique enough to find only the data you're looking for. The fewer characters in your string, the greater the likelihood that OS/2 will find lines containing those characters.

and you will filter the file correctly, receiving only the five businesses whose area code is 415.

You can also name more than one file as input to the FIND filter. Using the command

> FIND ''617'' Personal.txt Business.txt

you could quickly see if any of your area code 617 business clients appeared on your personal phone list as well. The results are shown in Figure 6.8.

Often, you can creatively combine a number of OS/2 command tools. For example, use the COPY command to join two business

```
[Prot C:\]FIND "415" Business.txt

---------- Business.txt
Brandenberg Gates   754  Bennett    Mary    415/612-5656
Sole Survivor,Inc.  237  Evans      Gail    415/222-3514
Bucket Dance Wear   276  Lewis      Ann     415/635-2530
Intelli-Strategies  743  Griffiths  Robert  415/362-9537
Benicia Balloons    983  Franklin   Marie   212/524-4157
Standard Shelters   690  Rucker     Sally   415/532-1107

[Prot C:\]
```

Figure 6.7: Using the FIND filter to extract data

files (clients and prospective clients) into one temporary file, which you can delete later; then use SORT to filter the resultant file, as shown below:

```
COPY Business.txt + Prospect.txt Temp1.txt
SORT < Temp1.txt > Temp2.txt
```

Even though the business files for clients and prospects may be structurally different, these commands will weed out duplicate entries as long as the telephone numbers were entered in a consistent manner.

You could proceed to find any subset of records of interest (for example, the 617 calling area) with the following FIND command:

```
FIND "617/" Temp2.txt
```

In each case, you would not have to look back and forth between two lists. Duplicates would appear one right after the other, like the two entries for Plymouth Granite Company in Figure 6.9.

Although Figure 6.9 shows the duplicates for the 617 calling area on the screen, remember that the Temp2.txt file still contains the

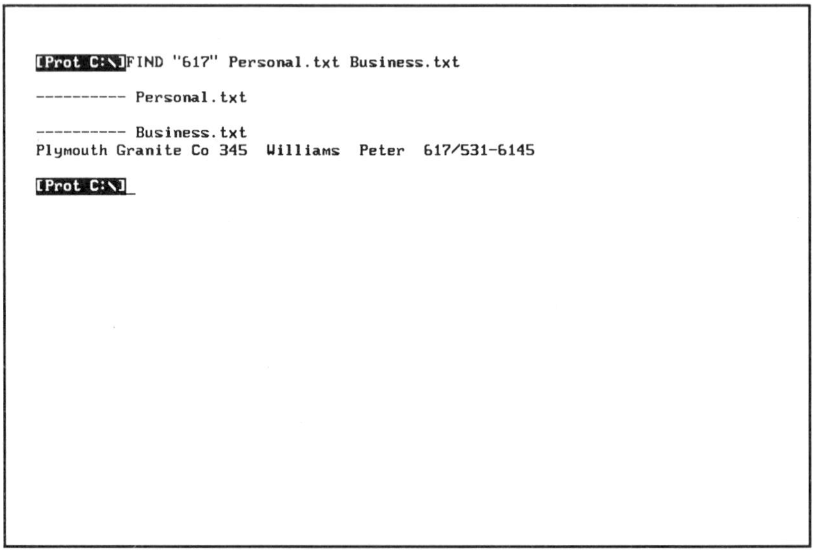

```
[Prot C:\]FIND "617" Personal.txt Business.txt

---------- Personal.txt

---------- Business.txt
Plymouth Granite Co 345  Williams  Peter  617/531-6145

[Prot C:\]
```

Figure 6.8: Filtering multiple files

When you are join-
ing two files to create
a third, or when you are
creating any temporary
file, make sure your disk
has enough space on it for
the operation.

sorted collection of *all* records from both the Business.txt and the Prospect.txt files. This file could be erased now, or you could use it in further processing.

CONTROLLING SCREEN OUTPUT

The last filter available in OS/2 is named MORE. It causes the screen display to pause, just as the /p switch does with the DIR command. However, it is not limited to just one command. It works with all commands that send output line by line to a virtual monitor.

The simplest way to handle very large text files is to display the information within them one screenful at a time. You can use the MORE filter to do this. For example, to direct a text file through the MORE filter, enter

MORE < Prospects.txt

This sequence will display only one screenful at a time from the Prospects.txt file, signaling you at the end of each screen with the

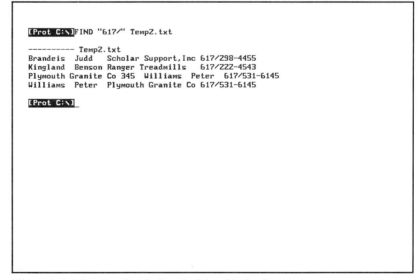

Figure 6.9: Merging files before looking for duplicates

"More" message that more output remains to be viewed. Pressing Return will display the next screenful of information.

CONNECTING OS/2 OPERATIONS WITH PIPES

You've seen how the SORT and FIND filters can work with data files as input. Now you'll explore how filters can work in connection with other programs or OS/2 commands. When these connections are made, they are called *pipes*. Earlier in this chapter, you saw how you could change OS/2's default input and output devices using redirection. Pipes allow you to combine the power of redirection with that of filters. You can simultaneously change (filter) your data while it is being moved (redirected) from one location to another.

Even with the redirection techniques you have learned so far in this chapter, if you want to do several things in a row, you would still have quite a bit of work to do. You might need to run one program, send its results to a disk file, and then run another program to process the resulting data. Then you might have to take the next program's input from that disk file to continue the processing chain, perhaps creating several intermediate files before getting the final result. Piping allows you to take the output of one command or program and make it the input of another command or program. You can do this several times in a row. An entire series of programs that generate intermediate output for one another can be automated by using the sophisticated combination of filters and pipes.

COMBINING PIPING AND SORTING

As you know, the SORT filter can be used to create a sorted directory listing. By adding pipes, you can use any column that appears in a directory listing as the criterion for a sorting order. This is very helpful, because a normal directory display does not arrange the files in any particular order. Using the SORT filter with a pipe, you can produce your directory listings in order of file name, file extension, file size, date of creation, or even time of creation. As you'll see, you can take any text file and arrange it in any way you like as well.

Pipes are created by using the vertical bar symbol (¦). Entering

DIR ¦ SORT

sends the output of a DIR command to the SORT filter before it is sent to the screen. The filtered result is a sorted directory display. Figure 6.10 shows this SORT operation.

This procedure required only a single piping sequence. Without the pipe, you would have to redirect the results of the DIR command into a disk file and then redirect the disk file so that it would be the input of the SORT filter. The pipe handles this job for you.

COMBINING REDIRECTION WITH FILTERS AND PIPES

To make your job easier and quicker, a filter can also be combined with a redirection command. For example, to print a sorted directory listing, you could enter

DIR A: ¦ SORT > PRN

The output of the DIR command is piped forward to become the input to the SORT command; the SORT command's output is then redirected from the screen to the printer.

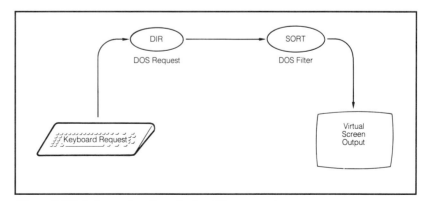

Figure 6.10: Information flow during filter operation

As another example, you can create a text file containing a sorted directory listing by entering

DIR A: ¦ SORT > Sortdir

This is similar to the previous example, except that the final sorted directory listing is not sent to the printer but is instead redirected to the Sortdir disk file. Figure 6.11 demonstrates each of these two examples.

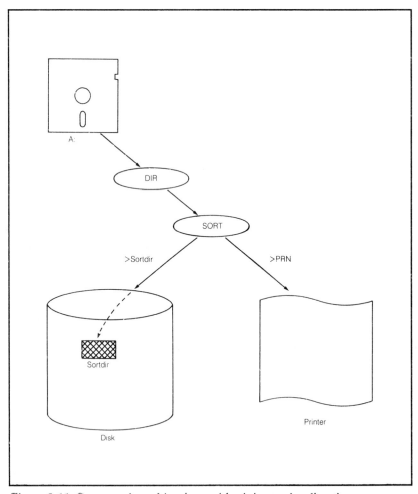

Figure 6.11: Command combinations with piping and redirection

SAVING TIME BY COMBINING FILTERS

When you are doing character searches in OS/2 or any other processing language, the case (upper or lower) of the characters is critical. You must always specify the character string *exactly* as you expect to find it in the file.

Once you are comfortable with OS/2 filters, you can save yourself both typing time and waiting time. You don't need to wait for the SORT filter to finish its work before you ask the FIND filter to begin. Because you can use the SORT and FIND filters together, you can tell OS/2 to execute both filters, one after the other. If you enter

    DIR A: ¦ SORT ¦ FIND ".exe"

you will receive a sorted listing of the .exe files located on the A drive.

You have probably seen advertisements for sorting programs that promise to sort your files by any field within them. You can do all of that kind of sorting with simple OS/2 commands now. You've learned how to use switches on the SORT command to arrange your directory lines by categories other than the first category. You've also learned how to send the sorted results from one filter to another through piping.

For a last example of sophisticated OS/2 manipulation, you could now take the original business contact list shown in Figure 6.1, sort it by telephone number, pipe the results into the FIND filter to extract the 415 entries, and finally pipe the results back into the SORT command to be rearranged alphabetically:

    SORT < Business.txt / + 43 ¦ FIND "415/" ¦ SORT

Figure 6.12 demonstrates the results of this example. Notice that the first sort takes place using character space 43, the first space containing the phone number. If there were several contacts from the same company, their entries would appear in phone number order for each alphabetized company.

This is another example of how a well-written OS/2 command can save you the purchase of a functionally simple piece of additional software. In the next chapter, you'll learn how you can set up a batch file to provide yourself with even more of this kind of customizing capability.

CONTROLLING SCREEN OUTPUT WITH PIPING

The MORE filter works with all commands that send output line by line to a virtual monitor. The proper way to handle pauses with

```
C>SORT /+43  < BUSINESS.TXT | FIND "415/" | SORT
Brandenberg Gates   754  Bennett   Mary    415/612-5656
Bucket Dance Wear   276  Lewis     Ann     415/635-2530
Intelli-Strategies  743  Griffiths Robert  415/362-9537
Sole Survivor,Inc.  237  Evans     Gail    415/222-3514
Standard Shelters   690  Rucker    Sally   415/532-1107

C>_
```

Figure 6.12: Sorting, extracting, and sorting again

piped output is to use the MORE filter as follows:

DIR A: | SORT | MORE

The MORE filter works because it pauses the output of the SORT filter, rather than pausing the input from the DIR command. This sequence will only display one screenful at a time from the sorted directory listing, signaling you with the ''More'' message that more output remains to be viewed. Pressing Return will display the next screenful of information.

GROUPING COMMANDS
IN PROTECTED MODE

As you've seen, redirection and piping enable you to use more than one OS/2 command on a single line. However, these methods require that the commands you use be related to each other; at best, the output of one command must be used as the input to another. Often, what you'd like to have is the ability to enter two or more completely separate commands on the same line.

OS/2 offers several new special symbols for this purpose. (see Table 6.1). The list is in *precedence order*, which means that if more than one of these symbols appear in the same command line, they are treated in the order they appear in this table.

Any of the commands discussed in this section may be grouped with parentheses to alter the order of execution. As you can see in Table 6.1, the use of parentheses for command grouping overrides all other orderings (with the exception of the caret symbol (^)).

SUBMITTING MULTIPLE COMMANDS ON ONE LINE

OS/2 provides a simple new symbol (&) for entering multiple commands on one line in protected mode. In real mode as in DOS before that, you have to wait for one command to finish before you can enter another one. For example, if you enter the CHKDSK command you have to wait until the whole CHKDSK process is complete before you can enter a DIR command. However, using the & symbol, you can enter both together:

    CHKDSK C: & DIR D: /w

This combined command request will result in a normal CHKDSK display for drive C, followed immediately by a directory

PROTECTED MODE SYMBOL	FUNCTION OF SYMBOL
^	Treats following character as text
()	Groups commands
> or < or >>	Redirects input/output
¦	Piping
&&	Logical AND
¦¦	Logical OR
&	Separates commands

Table 6.1: Precedence of OS/2 Protected Mode Grouping Symbols

listing of the working directory in drive D. Notice that the DIR command's switch, /w, will work perfectly in this new combined format. A standard five column wide listing of the file names in the directory will be displayed.

In fact, so will piping and redirection. For example, if you add a redirection request to the sample command line

CHKDSK C: & DIR D: /w >> Status.rpt

the directory listing will be appended to the Status.rpt file. The >> redirection is on the right side of the connecting symbol (&), so it only applies to the command on that side. If you wanted both command outputs to be placed in Status.rpt, you would have to redirect both command outputs as follows:

CHKDSK C: >> Status.rpt & DIR D: /w >> Status.rpt

USING LOGIC IN COMMAND GROUPINGS

Programmers are familiar with logical flow and logical decision making in their code. Those of you who have already used batch files (see Chapter 8) know about similar features with the IF and GOTO commands in OS/2's batch file mechanism.

At the command prompt in protected mode, OS/2 offers similar logical support tools. The simple separator symbol of the previous section (&) executes each command successively, *even if one of those commands fail*. In this section, you'll learn how to submit several commands on one OS/2 command line, and use logic to tell OS/2 which command(s) to actually execute.

CONNECTING COMMANDS WITH THE LOGICAL AND   Any number of multiple commands may be connected with the various grouping symbols presented in this chapter. When any two commands are separated with the logical AND symbol (&&), the command to the right of the connector *only executes if the command to the left executes successfully*. For example, requesting a CHKDSK on a nonexistent disk drive will produce an OS/2 error message:

CHKDSK E:
DOS1333: CHKDSK cannot accept the specified drive.

If you had wanted to save time and had entered the following request for both a CHKDSK E: and a DIR C:\Os2 separated by the AND symbol you would only receive the DOS1333 error message, and no directory listing:

CHKDSK E: && DIR C:\Os2

This is because OS/2 tries to execute each command from left to right on the command line, continuing to the command on the right side, *only if* the command on the left side was able to be successfully executed.

This can be useful with commands that depend on one another in some logical way. For instance, to queue up for printing all .txt files from drive A only if there are text files on the disk in that drive, you would use the following command line:

DIR A:*.txt && PRINT A:*.txt

If the DIR command located no files with .txt extensions, OS/2 would stop immediately, not even bothering to interpret the command request to the right of the && symbol.

CONNECTING COMMANDS WITH THE LOGICAL OR   Another logical command connector, sometimes called an *operator*, is the OR symbol (¦¦). It contrasts sharply with the AND symbol of the last section. An AND connector tries to execute both commands (one *and* the other). If OS/2 can't successfully execute the first of two commands, OS/2 doesn't even try to execute the second.

The OR symbol, however, tells OS/2 to execute only one of the commands on either side of the ¦¦ symbol (one *or* the other). If the command on the left successfully executes, the one on the right is not needed, so it won't be run. If, on the other hand, the command on the left fails, the command on the right is run, in an attempt to get at least one of the two commands to run successfully.

As an example, suppose you wanted to format a series of disks in drive A, but you wanted to check out any remaining files still on those disks before formatting. You might enter

DIR A: ¦¦ FORMAT A:

In this example, you'll receive a directory listing if any files still exist on the disk. Otherwise, OS/2 will immediately execute the command on the right of the ¦¦ symbol, the FORMAT command.

***ENTERING THE SPECIAL CHARACTERS AS REGULAR
TEXT***   Occasionally, you will need to use some of these special OS/
2 symbols as normal text. The caret symbol (^) allows this possibility. Whenever it appears, not in quoted text strings, the character
following it is accepted as standard text, even if it otherwise would be
one of the special characters discussed in this section.

For instance, suppose you have a batch file containing the following ECHO lines, intended for use in an OS/2 tutorial:

>   ECHO OS/2 uses special symbols for command grouping.
>   ECHO The && symbol is used in logical AND operations.

Only the first line of these two will be properly echoed to your
screen. The && symbol in the middle of your second line's text will
be misunderstood by OS/2. OS/2 thinks you want to combine two
separate commands with the AND symbol. The first command
appears to be:

>   ECHO The

which works fine. You'll get the apparently requested phrase ''The''
displayed for you. The next command, as OS/2 sees it, is ''symbol is
used in logical AND operations.'' What you'll receive from OS/2 is
the error message:

>   DOS1041: The system cannot find the filename specified.

This occurs because OS/2 tries unsucessfully to find a file called
Symbol with an extension of .exe, .com, or .cmd (a protected mode
batch file). It thinks the first word after the && symbol is a command
file, and that the rest of the text on the line represents parameters.
Since you actually meant those && characters to be treated as common text, not special symbols, you should use the caret (^) symbol,
as follows:

>   ECHO OS/2 uses special symbols for command grouping.
>   ECHO The ^&^& symbol is used in logical AND operations.

Now, your screen results will be the two echoed lines, minus the caret symbols:

OS/2 uses special symbols for command grouping.
The && symbol is used in logical AND operations.

Each & symbol requires its own preceding caret symbol because a single & symbol could be misinterpreted as a command connecting symbol, as presented earlier in this section.

SUMMARY

In this chapter, you've learned about powerful OS/2 features for specialized utility operations. You've seen that redirection allows you to specify alternative input and output devices for OS/2 commands. Pipes enable you to direct the flow of information with precision from one command to another. Filters permit you to process the data as it flows through your central processing unit under your direction. You've also seen that OS/2 allows the entry of multiple commands on one line, logically combined in a variety of ways. The chapter presented the following important points:

- Multiple OS/2 commands in protected mode may be entered on the same line, and may be grouped in different ways. The symbol & is a simple command separator when more than one command is to be successively entered and processed by OS/2.

- OS/2 commands in protected mode may also be grouped in several ways. Piping and redirection are only one form of command combination. The && (logical AND) and ¦¦ (logical OR) symbols, in conjunction with grouping parentheses, allow for unlimited multiple command groups.

- The escape symbol (^) allows you to enter unique or reserved symbols (like &, ^ , or ¦¦) as normal characters; any special OS/2 interpretation is suppressed temporarily.

- Special symbols are used by OS/2 during redirection operations. The > sign indicates a new output device, and < indicates a new input source. If you use the >> sign, the output is appended to the specified file.

- Certain OS/2 commands can filter data. This data can be input at the keyboard, from an existing file, or even from another program or command.

- The FIND filter selects lines for output based on some selection characters.

- The MORE filter performs the simple task of making the display pause when output fills the screen. This gives you the opportunity to read the complete display before continuing the processing.

- The SORT filter can easily arrange the lines of output from any command or data file. Optional switches add significant power to this command: /r produces a reverse-order listing, while /+n sorts the file by the nth character space instead of the first. This allows you to sort your data in meaningful orders.

- Pipes are preceded by the | symbol. They transmit the output from one command to another, in effect making one command's output the next command's input.

- Pipes can be combined with both filters and redirection in sophisticated ways to produce powerful results.

The examples in this chapter should serve to spark your imagination—you can now create your own useful utility extensions. In Chapter 8, you'll learn more about creating your own real mode and protected mode batch files for even more extensive customized operations.

PART 3

ADVANCED OS/2 TECHNIQUES

In Part 3, you will learn advanced techniques and topics. Chapter 7 prepares you to create and modify text files using the OS/2 real mode line editor, EDLIN, or the OS/2 protected mode line editor, SSE. You will use one of these two programs throughout the rest of the book to generate and update system files, as well as to write your own batch files.

Chapter 8 teaches you how to use batch files to execute groups of OS/2 commands automatically. There are two separate batch file mechanisms in OS/2, one for real mode and one for protected mode. This chapter describes the basic features and limitations of both types of batch files and gives you practice in writing them. It goes on to teach you the OS/2 batch-file subcommands and parameters, distinguishing the ones that are only accessible in protected mode, and demonstrates how to build more complex batch files.

In Chapter 9, you will learn how to customize OS/2 to suit your needs. You will find out how to specify the number of active threads and buffers, manipulate internal multitasking parameters, create and use a RAM disk, and much more. Configuration in OS/2 spans significantly more individual features than it did in DOS. All of these new controls are explained in this chapter.

The final chapter in this section, Chapter 10, introduces the new programming environment of OS/2. You will learn how OS/2's Memory Manager enables references to one gigabyte of virtual memory in systems that have only several megabytes of physical memory. You will also learn about the new group of available system service calls, as well as the new high-level calling interface. Additionally, you will learn how OS/2 can support the development of programs that can be run on older DOS based machines, as well as in protected mode on OS/2 machines.

FILE EDITING IN OS/2 ——

CHAPTER 7

IN ADDITION TO THEIR ABILITY TO PROCESS NUMBERS and large amounts of data, computers are exceptionally good at manipulating text. It comes as no surprise, then, that there are so many different programs available to do this.

These programs are divided into two primary types: line editors and full screen editors. The OS/2 real mode editor, EDLIN, is a line editor. With EDLIN, you can work with only one line of text at a time. Each line has a line number and must be referenced by its number.

The second kind of program, a full screen editor like OS/2's protected mode editor, SSE, displays and lets you work with a full screen of text. A word processor is an advanced form of this kind of full screen editor. In both, you can move the screen cursor to any character position on any line and make changes anywhere on the screen. However, word processors, unlike SSE, usually support additional features such as multiple fonts, boldfacing, and underlining.

Naturally, it's up to you to choose the kind of program you want. You may want to use both at different times. The OS/2 real mode line editor can be fairly restrictive. Referring to your text by line numbers is often inconvenient and uncomfortable, and you may prefer to use the more visually satisfying and flexible capabilities of a full screen editor. Most word processors provide a more extensive set of commands and allow you to edit any character on any line. However, word processors usually require tens of thousands of bytes of disk space merely to contain them, and they have more extensive RAM requirements than line editors. In addition, you must purchase them, whereas EDLIN and SSE are available with your OS/2 system at no additional charge.

EDLIN and SSE are disk-resident and act like any other external utility command. EDLIN is provided for editing files when in real mode, while SSE is provided for editing files when in protected mode. Neither allows the type of text wraparound seen in word processors, so both are suitable for working with batch files and other text files, which limit themselves to command/instruction entries that fit on single lines.

You can use both of these text editors to create and edit text files, which contain standard letters, numbers, and punctuation symbols. Except for the special codes indicating carriage returns, line feeds, and the end of a file (Ctrl-Z), these files have no control codes. Therefore, they do not include such features as underlining on a printer or high intensity on a display. (A text file can be displayed easily on screen with the TYPE command.)

EDLIN can manipulate text files line by line, and it also contains search and replace functions and standard text-editing features. SSE, on the other hand, offers fewer commands for manipulating the text in your file. It's greatest strength is that it shows the lines of your text in standard full screen, and allows you to position the cursor to any character position on any displayed line. You can then make the desired edits without any concern for the actual line number you're affecting.

Use the SSE protected mode editor for batch file editing if you do not need to configure the DOS compatability mode at all.

USING THE
PROTECTED MODE EDITOR

SSE can be run by using the standard invoking convention:

SSE *filename*

If you don't specify a file name, you'll be asked for one. And if the file name you enter does not exist, SSE will ask if you want it to be created. From then on, all text lines in the file will be displayed a screenful at a time. SSE allows you to scroll up and down through the screenfuls of text. Table 7.1 lists the special control keys understood by the SSE text editor, while Table 7.2 lists the additional keys that control scrolling through your text file.

Function keys 9 and 10 are used for the common functions of saving the file and aborting the editing session, respectively. If you press F10, you'll get a second chance in case the keypress was inadvertent:

WARNING: Any edits will be lost (y/n)? _

The only other three control codes in SSE provide minimum capability for inserting and deleting lines. Pressing Ctrl-N inserts a new

KEYPRESS	**PURPOSE**
Ctrl-N	Inserts a new blank line above the current line
Ctrl-B	Inserts a new blank line below the current line
Ctrl-Y	Deletes the current line
F9	Saves the file
F10	Quits without saving

Table 7.1: Editing Control Keys in SSE

KEYPRESS	**PURPOSE**
↑	Moves cursor one line up
↓	Moves cursor one line down
→	Moves cursor one character to the right
←	Moves cursor one character to the left
PgUp	Moves cursor 24 lines (one screen) up
PgDn	Moves cursor 24 lines (one screen) down
Ctrl-PgUp	Moves cursor to first line in file
Ctrl-PgDn	Moves cursor to last line in file
Ctrl-Home	Moves cursor to top of screen (Column 1)
Ctrl-End	Moves cursor to bottom of screen (Column 1)

Table 7.2: Cursor Control and Scrolling Keys in SSE

blank line above the one containing the cursor (the one you are working on), while pressing Ctrl-B places the new blank line below the current line. You may then type a new text line into the blank spaces. Deleting any line is as simple as moving the cursor to the line to be removed (any position on that line is fine), then pressing Ctrl-Y.

The SSE program is simple but efficient. It provides a comfortable user interface and a minimum of necessary features. The EDLIN program provides a less desirable user interface, but does have many more text editing features. The rest of this chapter will concentrate on EDLIN.

GETTING EDLIN STARTED

EDLIN is started from the real mode OS/2 prompt with the command

> EDLIN *FileSpec*

where *FileSpec* is the drive, path, file name, and extension of the file to be edited. You must use the full file name, including any extension. As always, EDLIN must either be resident on the disk you are using, in the current default directory, or on the path to be searched by OS/2.

STARTING A NEW FILE

The optional /b switch (short for binary) can be used with this EDLIN command when the file you will be working on contains Ctrl-Z markers other than the end-of-file marker. As you'll learn later in this chapter, you can use EDLIN to incorporate and then edit control characters in a text file.

If EDLIN is invoked with a *FileSpec* value for a file that does not currently exist, it will respond with the following message and prompt:

> EDLIN has created a new file
> * _

EDLIN is giving you a clean slate, awaiting your commands. Table 7.3 summarizes the commands you can use with EDLIN, their actions, and their general formats. You will learn about each of these as you work through this chapter.

COMMAND	ACTION	GENERAL FORMAT
A	Appends lines	[*Num*]A
C	Copies lines	[*Line*],[*Line*],*Line*[,*Count*] C
D	Deletes lines	[*Line*][,*Line*] D
	Edits line	[*Line*]
E	Updates and exits	E
I	Inserts lines	[*Line*]I
L	Lists lines	[*Line*][,*Line*] L
M	Moves lines	[*Line*],[*Line*],*Line*M
P	Displays full page	[*Line*][,*Line*] P
Q	Aborts and exits	Q
R	Replaces globally	[*Line*][,*Line*] [?] R[*String*][^ Z*NewString*]
S	Searches globally	[*Line*][,*Line*] [?] S[*String*]
T	Merges files	[*Line*] T [*FileSpec*]
W	Writes lines	[*Num*] W

Table 7.3: Summary of EDLIN Commands

Additionally, the standard editing keys (F1–F6, Del, Esc, Ins, and Bksp) that were active in DOS are also active in OS/2. Table 7.4 summarizes these keys that are active at both the command prompt as well as in the EDLIN real mode editor.

CHANGING AN EXISTING FILE

Invoking EDLIN with the *FileSpec* of an existing file will yield the following:

```
The entire input file has been read.
*_
```

EDLIN tries to load your entire text file into available real mode memory. When it tries to load a file that is longer than 75 percent of the currently available RAM, it will load only the first part of that file and will use only 75 percent of the available memory. You may then edit the lines that were loaded. When you are done editing these lines, you can use EDLIN commands to write the edited lines out to a disk and bring in additional text lines to edit.

BRINGING NEW TEXT INTO MEMORY

The command needed to add new, unedited lines of text from a disk file is the Append command, abbreviated as the single character A. This

The brackets around parameters in this chapter indicate that they are optional EDLIN parameters. The brackets themselves are not entered as part of the command.

KEY NAME	FUNCTION
F1	Retypes one character at a time from the last command
F2	Retypes all characters from the last command up to the one identical to your next keystroke
F3	Retypes all remaining characters from the last command
F4	Retypes all characters beginning at the first match with your next keystroke and ending with the last character from the last command
F5	Permits direct editing of all the characters from the entire last command
F6	Places a special end-of-file code at the end of the currently open file; sometimes referred to as a Ctrl-Z end-of-file code
Ins	Permits insertion of characters at the cursor
Del	Permits deletion of the character to the left of the cursor
Esc	Abandons the currently constructed command without executing it

Table 7.4: The OS/2 Editing Keys

command is only used when you have loaded a file that is larger than 75 percent of current memory. Entered at the EDLIN * prompt, its general format is

[*Num*]A

This command loads *Num* lines from the rest of the file (where *Num* is the number of lines to load), provided there is room. If there is insufficient room to load any more lines from your file, the command will not load anything. You must then use the W command (described shortly) to write some of your edited lines from EDLIN to disk.

If you successfully load the rest of the file into memory, the following message will appear:

The entire input file has been read.

You can then continue editing using any of the EDLIN commands.

COMBINING SEPARATE TEXT FILES

The Transfer command (T) is used to combine two text files: one in memory and another somewhere else. When you specify the file to be transferred into the middle of your current file (*FileSpec*), the whole file is read in and inserted before the line number specified by *Line*:

[*Line*] T *FileSpec*

If *Line* is not specified, the file's contents are inserted before the current line.

This command can be quite useful. For example, suppose you have the following two files:

File1	File2
1: Line 1, File 1	1: Line 1, File 2
2: Line 2, File 1	2: Line 2, File 2
3: Line 3, File 1	3: Line 3, File 2
4: Line 4, File 1	4: Line 4, File 2

If File1 is the current file being edited in memory, and you enter the following command:

    3 T File2

the result is a new combined file, which looks like this:

        1: Line 1, File 1
        2: Line 2, File 1
        3:*Line 1, File 2
        4: Line 2, File 2
        5: Line 3, File 2
        6: Line 4, File 2
        7: Line 3, File 1
        8: Line 4, File 1

Note that the current line is now the first line of the transferred file, as indicated by the EDLIN * prompt.

MAKING SPACE FOR LARGE FILES

The Write command (W), like the Append command, is only needed when your file is too large to fit in 75 percent of available memory. In that situation, only 75 percent of your file will have been loaded. If you want to edit the rest of the file, you need to make some room. You must transfer lines from the file in memory to disk, thus freeing up enough space to let more if not all of the rest of the file be loaded. The general format of this command is

    [Num] W

where *Num* is the number of lines to be written. After you execute this command, you can load the rest of the file with the A command.

If you do not specify the number of lines to be written, the W command will keep writing lines to the disk, starting with line 1, until 75 percent of available memory is free. If there is already 75 percent of available RAM freed for EDLIN text lines, then no lines will be written to disk. If, for example, the first 200 lines were written to disk, then line 201 of the total file would become the first line of the memory portion being worked on by EDLIN.

DISPLAYING EDLIN FILES

Perhaps the most common activity you'll ask your line editor to perform will be to show you the text in your file. EDLIN offers two commands for this purpose: the L command for listing any range of lines, and the P command for rapidly looking at complete screenfuls of your file.

LISTING YOUR TEXT FILE

Since line numbers change each time you add or delete a line, the List command (L) will probably be your most frequently used command. You will always want to see the new numbers assigned to each of your text lines before you execute new line-oriented commands.

You can list a block of lines in a variety of ways. If you don't provide explicit line numbers for starting and stopping, EDLIN will attempt to display 23 text lines—a screenful. The size of the display range can extend from 11 lines before the current line to 11 lines after the current line.

Perhaps the most common format for this command is to specify the precise line numbers at which to begin and end the listing. For example,

    6,19L

displays lines 6 through 19 on your screen and then redisplays EDLIN's prompt.

Simply typing L with no line-number specification will display the 11 lines preceding the current line, then the current line, and then the 11 lines after the current line. If your file has less than 23 lines, the entire file will be listed.

LISTING YOUR TEXT FILE RAPIDLY

The Page command (P) is like the L command, except that it redefines the current line number to whatever line has been displayed last on the screen. This command provides you with a rapid way to list all the lines in your text file, a screenful at a time.

Entering a line number alone, as in

17 P

will display up to 23 lines starting with line 17. The last line listed becomes the current line. You can also display a specified range of lines and make the last line the current line, as in

14,28 P

If you simply enter P, EDLIN will make its standard assumptions, giving you a 23-line display, starting with the line after the current line and making the last line displayed the new current line.

EDITING EDLIN FILES

As you have worked through the previous sections on getting EDLIN started, you have seen that EDLIN is *command-oriented;* that is, it does not display menus, but rather expects you to enter individual commands, just as you must at the command level of OS/2. Because of this, you can move around and do things in EDLIN much more quickly than you could with a menu system, but you must know the commands in order to execute them quickly.

You have also seen the EDLIN prompt, the asterisk symbol (*). Whenever you see this on the screen with a blinking cursor next to it, EDLIN is prompting you for a command. An additional asterisk indicates the current line of the file being edited. Any EDLIN command you enter will deal with the text on this particular line (and possibly others as well). You can move a certain number of lines forward or backward from the current line, and you can insert, edit, or delete in relation to it.

Here are some useful tips to keep in mind as you work with EDLIN:

- Most commands can be entered using just the first letter of the command.

- The EDLIN letter commands can be entered in uppercase, lowercase, or a combination of the two.

- When you are performing an operation on a specific line or group of lines, specify the line numbers first.

- Line numbers can be specified in a number of ways; however, they must be whole numbers between 1 and 65529. When you enter more than one line number, you must separate them with commas. If you enter a line number higher than the highest line number in memory and you are going to add a line, the line will be added after the highest line number.

- You can use the pound symbol (#) to refer to the as-yet-nonexistent line following the highest line number in memory.

- You can use a period to specify the current line.

- The + and − keys can be used to specify lines *relative* to the current line number. For example,

      − 20, + 5D

  will delete the 20 lines preceding the current line number, the current line number, and 5 lines after the current line number. If the current line number was 50, lines 30 through 55 would be deleted.

- You can enter more than one command on a line. If you do this, separate each complete command by a semicolon (;).

- It is possible (although not often necessary) to enter a control character into your file. To do this, you must press Ctrl-V first and then the desired control character (in uppercase).

- If you are displaying a lot of data, you can pause the screen output by pressing the Break key, Ctrl-ScrollLock. Press Ctrl-ScrollLock again to restart the output. Note that the processing of the command will have stopped also.

Now let's take a look at the editing tasks you'll want to do with EDLIN, and the commands that perform these tasks.

INSERTING NEW LINES

The Insert command (I) is used to insert lines. Its general format is

[*Line*]I

Again, *Line* may be specified as either a specific or a relative line number. Not including *Line* will result in lines being added before the current line. If you created a new file called Lincoln.txt by calling up EDLIN, you would use the I command to insert text for the first time at line 1. Entering 1I at the EDLIN * prompt like this:

    *1I

would yield

    1:*_

which places you in insert mode. As you can see in Figure 7.1, EDLIN shows you each line number as you type it.

Notice the ⌃ C on line 4. This is EDLIN's response when you press Ctrl-C during text insertion. Use the Ctrl-C key combination to exit from text insertion and return to the EDLIN prompt.

The I command can also be used to insert new text before any existing text line in the file. Simply specify the line number in the file before which you want the new text to be placed.

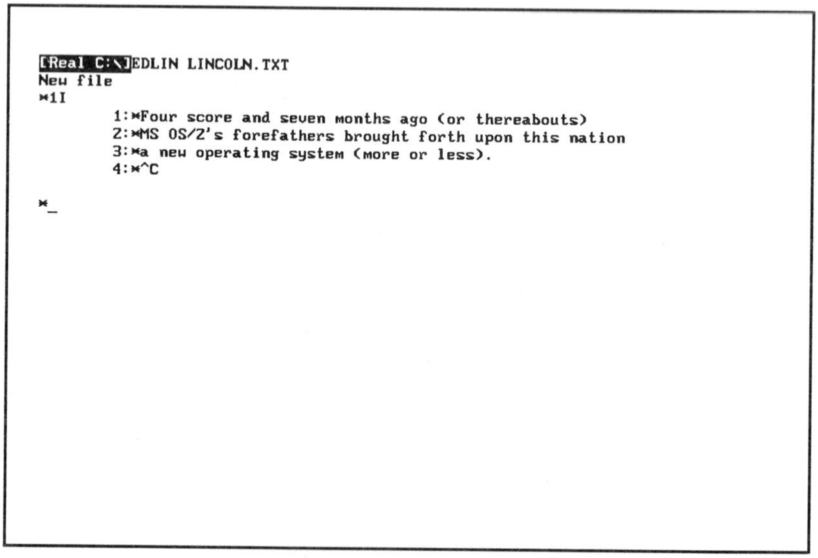

Inserting lines will change all line numbers after the insertion. For example, if you insert new text at line 3, remember that all line numbers after 3 have been changed. It's best to list the file again (L) to discover the new numbering before issuing any new commands.

```
[Real C:\]EDLIN LINCOLN.TXT
New file
*1I
        1:*Four score and seven months ago (or thereabouts)
        2:*MS OS/2's forefathers brought forth upon this nation
        3:*a new operating system (more or less).
        4:*^C
*_
```

Figure 7.1: Inserting text for the first time

CHANGING EXISTING LINES

Editing a line merely means that you are changing the information on the line, *not* adding or deleting a line. Usually, you can enter any line number to put you into edit mode for that line. When you are put into edit mode (for example, by entering 3 and pressing Return), the display looks something like this:

```
3:*a new operating system (more or less).
3:*_
```

The arrow keys or any of the function keys will work as they do at the OS/2 prompt. For example, pressing F3 will do the following:

```
3:*a new operating system (more or less).
3:*a new operating system (more or less)._
```

The original line 3 is completely retyped, with the cursor waiting at the end of the line for additional input.

While editing any line, pressing the Right Arrow key will move the cursor one character to the right and display the character it was on (or under). Pressing Esc-Return, or the Break key combination, anywhere on the line will take you out of edit mode and leave the line unchanged.

If you want to add something to the end of the line, simply press F3 and start typing. You will automatically be put into insert mode. If your cursor is located anywhere else on the line, you must press the Ins key to enter insert mode, and press it again to leave that mode. In Figure 7.2, you can see how line 3 of our example was changed. F3 was pressed, the Backspace key was used to erase the period, and then the new characters '', dedicated'' were typed. Both before and after the change, the L command was used to list the current contents of the file.

The edit to line 3 is only the first step in a common sequence, as shown in Figure 7.3. A change is made, followed by a listing of the file. Then another editing command follows (in this case, a new text insertion at the end of the file), and yet another L command is used to verify the results of the last edit. Continuing this process and adding

```
[Real C:\]EDLIN LINCOLN.TXT
New file
*1I
          1:*Four score and seven months ago (or thereabouts)
          2:*MS OS/2's forefathers brought forth upon this nation
          3:*a new operating system (more or less).
          4:*^C

*3
          3:*a new operating system (more or less).
          3:*a new operating system (more or less), dedicated
*L
          1: Four score and seven months ago (or thereabouts)
          2: MS OS/2's forefathers brought forth upon this nation
          3:*a new operating system (more or less), dedicated
*_
```

Figure 7.2: Making corrections to a line

```
*1I
          1:*Four score and seven months ago (or thereabouts)
          2:*MS OS/2's forefathers brought forth upon this nation
          3:*a new operating system (more or less).
          4:*^C

*3
          3:*a new operating system (more or less).
          3:*a new operating system (more or less), dedicated
*L
          1: Four score and seven months ago (or thereabouts)
          2: MS OS/2's forefathers brought forth upon this nation
          3:*a new operating system (more or less), dedicated
*4I
          4:*to the proposition that all computers (with the same
          5:*microcomputer chip) are created equal.
          6:*^C

*L
          1: Four score and seven months ago (or thereabouts)
          2: MS OS/2's forefathers brought forth upon this nation
          3: a new operating system (more or less), dedicated
          4: to the proposition that all computers (with the same
          5: microcomputer chip) are created equal.
*_
```

Figure 7.3: Adding new lines at the end of a file

still more text (with a correction to line 10 along the way) results in the 12-line text file shown in Figure 7.4.

MOVING LINES (CUTTING AND PASTING)

The Move command (M) allows you to move one line or a body of lines in a file to a new location in the file. (A group of lines to be moved is called a *block*.) For example, entering

```
9,12,6M
L
```

at the EDLIN prompt will move lines 9 through 12 in the file shown in Figure 7.4 to a new position—in front of line 6, as shown in Figure 7.5. This is commonly called *cutting and pasting*. Naturally, when the operation has completed, all affected lines are renumbered. Notice that the current line has moved to the new sixth line, since this was the first line in the block that was moved.

```
        7:*uars.  It is altogether fitting and proper (some may
        8:*disagree) that ue should do this.
        9:*Nou, ue are engaged in a great computer war (more
       10:*have fallen than have risen), testing uhether OS/2
       11:*or any other DOS so conceived and so dedicated can
       12:*long endure.
       13:*^C

  *10
       10:*have fallen than have risen), testing uhether OS/2
       10:*have fallen than have risen), testing uhether MS OS/2
  *1
        1: Four score and seven months ago (or thereabouts)
        2: MS OS/2's forefathers brought forth upon this nation
        3: a neu operating system (more or less), dedicated
        4: to the proposition that all computers (uith the same
        5: microcomputer chip) are created equal.
        6: We are met today to chronicle a part of these DOS
        7: uars.  It is altogether fitting and proper (some may
        8: disagree) that ue should do this.
        9: Nou, ue are engaged in a great computer war (more
       10:*have fallen than have risen), testing uhether MS OS/2
       11: or any other DOS so conceived and so dedicated can
       12: long endure.
  *
```

Figure 7.4: Intermediate version of the text file

```
          3: a new operating system (more or less), dedicated
          4: to the proposition that all computers (with the same
          5: microcomputer chip) are created equal.
          6: We are met today to chronicle a part of these DOS
          7: wars.  It is altogether fitting and proper (some may
          8: disagree) that we should do this.
          9: Now, we are engaged in a great computer war (more
         10:*have fallen than have risen), testing whether MS OS/2
         11: or any other DOS so conceived and so dedicated can
         12: long endure.
     *9,12,6M
     *1
          1: Four score and seven months ago (or thereabouts)
          2: MS OS/2's forefathers brought forth upon this nation
          3: a new operating system (more or less), dedicated
          4: to the proposition that all computers (with the same
          5: microcomputer chip) are created equal.
          6:*Now, we are engaged in a great computer war (more
          7: have fallen than have risen), testing whether MS OS/2
          8: or any other DOS so conceived and so dedicated can
          9: long endure.
         10: We are met today to chronicle a part of these DOS
         11: wars.  It is altogether fitting and proper (some may
         12: disagree) that we should do this.

     *_
```

Figure 7.5: Cutting and pasting text

COPYING LINES

The Copy command (C) is used to copy blocks of lines to other places in a file. It is similar to the M command, although not as frequently used. When you use the C command, the original lines are not bodily moved to a new place in the file; instead, they are replicated in the new place, leaving the original lines intact. After the copy has been made, all line numbers will be recalculated, and the first line that was copied will become the new current line.

There are three versions of the C command. You can make a replica of the current text line anywhere else in the file. The copy of the current line will be inserted in front of the line specified by *Line:*

> ,,*Line*[,*Count*] C

The commas represent placeholders for values that haven't been entered by you; the default (that is, the current line) is used. The optional *Count* parameter can be used to specify the number of times the operations should be repeated.

In any EDLIN
command that
allows the specification of
multiple lines, the beginning line number must be
less than or equal to the
ending line number.
EDLIN cannot work
backwards.

You can also copy multiple lines all at once using the C command. The following format causes all of the lines from *Line1* through the current line to be copied to the position before *Line2:*

> *Line1,,Line2*[*,Count*] C

The third possible format of the C command allows you to explicitly specify the range to be copied:

> *Range,Line3*[*,Count*] C

Range represents a pair of delimited line numbers. This version of the C command is similar to the previous version, except that in *Range* you specify the last line number to be copied, instead of defaulting to the current line number.

Here's an example of using the *Count* parameter with the C command. If you were editing any text file of at least five lines and executed the following,

> *1,4,5,3 C

you would be telling EDLIN to make a copy of lines 1 through 4 in your file, then to place them at a point just before line 5, and then to repeat this operation twice more (a total of 3 for *Count*).

SEARCHING FOR TEXT STRINGS

The Search command (S) locates lines. You can ask EDLIN to carry out the search over a variety of ranges. The general format of this command is

> [*Scope*] [?] S[*String*]

Scope can be defined as any of the following parameters:

- *Line* causes the search to start at *Line* and stop at the end of the file

- *,Line* causes the search to start at the line after the current line and end at *Line*

- *Line1,Line2* causes the search to cover only the lines within the block between *Line1* and *Line2*

- Not using the *Scope* parameter results in the search starting at the line after the current line and ending at the last line in the file

The *String* parameter specifies the text that you are looking for. The first character of this text should immediately follow the S. If *String* is not included on the command line, the search string last used in a Search or Replace command is used. If no Search or Replace command has yet been used in the session, then the message "Not found" will be displayed.

If you specify ? in this command, EDLIN will stop each time it locates the specified string, and it will ask you for confirmation that the string is the correct one.

As an example of using the Search command, let's look for all occurrences of the word *is* in the following file:

```
1: This is the first line
2: of a test file to demonstrate
3: the use of the Search command.
4: It is included for your own
5: information.
```

You would enter the following command:

```
*1,5 ? Sis
```

You would then see

```
        1: This is the first line
O.K.? n
        4: It is included for your own
O.K.? n
        Not found
        *_
```

If you answer "y" to the question "O.K.?", that line becomes the current line, as it was the last line to contain a match with *String*. Otherwise, the current line remains what it was before you initiated the

The Search and Replace commands are case-sensitive—they will look for *exactly* what you type. For example, the S command will consider *Judd* and *judd* to be two different words because of the different capitalization.

search. Notice that Line 1 only came up once in the search. This is because the search finds a whole line with a match on it. If there is more than one match, it's a waste of time to successively redisplay the same line.

SEARCH AND REPLACE CAPABILITIES

R is the Replace command. It gives you the ability to search through any specified range of lines and replace every occurrence of specific text (*String*) with new replacement text (*NewString*).

The general format for the R command is

[*Scope*] [?] R[*String*][Ctrl-Z*NewString*]

The *Scope* and *String* parameters are the same as those for the Search command. If you are going to enter replacement text (*NewString*), end *String* by pressing Ctrl-Z. (This is optional, since you may only want to search for and remove the specified string wherever it is found.)

NewString is the text that will replace the *String*. It does not need to be the same size as *String,* since it will be inserted after *String* has been deleted. If *NewString* is left out, then *String* will be deleted in the specified block. If *String* is left out as well, EDLIN will use the *String* value from the last Search or Replace command, and the *NewString* value from the last Replace command. If Search and Replace have not been used during the current session, you will get the message "Not found."

When ? is specified in this command, EDLIN will display the replaced or modified line and ask whether you wish to confirm the changes that were made ("O.K.?"). You should answer Y or press Return if you want the change to become permanent.

Once an occurrence of *String* has been found and you have accepted or not accepted the change, the search will continue in the specified block. Multiple occurrences on the same line are included in the replacements.

Let's try this command on the example you worked with earlier in this chapter. You can quickly ask EDLIN to search in the file for each occurrence of the text string *DOS*. When found, the command will replace *DOS* with *OS* (see Figure 7.6).

In this example, you specified that all occurrences in lines 1 through 12 are to be acted upon. You can see by the EDLIN prompt that line 10 has become the current line, since it was the last line changed. Notice also that each line that contained the sought-after string of characters was displayed after the change was made (lines 8 and 10). As shown in the figure, you usually execute the L command to verify the results of your command request.

DELETING LINES

The Delete command (D) is used to delete one or more lines from the file. Its general format is

[*Line*],[*Line*]D

The *Line* parameters specify the line or lines that you want to delete.

Suppose you had written some new text and added it to the current file beginning at Line 13 (see Figure 7.7). Then you decided (either immediately or later) that this new text was not appropriate, so you needed to delete it with the D command. Figure 7.8 shows the results of deleting the lines and then listing the remaining file.

Deleting lines causes all line numbers after the deletion to be renumbered. Even if you do not request a listing of the lines (with L), they are still renumbered. For example, if you execute the command 1D twice, you will have deleted lines 1 and 2.

```
         5: microcomputer chip) are created equal.
         6:×Now, we are engaged in a great computer war (more
         7: have fallen than have risen), testing whether MS OS/2
         8: or any other DOS so conceived and so dedicated can
         9: long endure.
        10: We are met today to chronicle a part of these DOS
        11: wars.  It is altogether fitting and proper (some may
        12: disagree) that we should do this.
    ×1,12RDOS^ZOS
         8: or any other OS so conceived and so dedicated can
        10: We are met today to chronicle a part of these OS
    ×1
         1: Four score and seven months ago (or thereabouts)
         2: MS OS/2's forefathers brought forth upon this nation
         3: a new operating system (more or less), dedicated
         4: to the proposition that all computers (with the same
         5: microcomputer chip) are created equal.
         6: Now, we are engaged in a great computer war (more
         7: have fallen than have risen), testing whether MS OS/2
         8: or any other OS so conceived and so dedicated can
         9: long endure.
        10:×We are met today to chronicle a part of these OS
        11: wars.  It is altogether fitting and proper (some may
        12: disagree) that we should do this.
    ×_
```

Figure 7.6: Search and replace operation

```
        11: wars.  It is altogether fitting and proper (some may
        12: disagree) that we should do this.
  ⋈1,12RDOS^ZOS
         8: or any other OS so conceived and so dedicated can
        10: We are met today to chronicle a part of these OS
  ⋈1
         1: Four score and seven months ago (or thereabouts)
         2: MS OS/2's forefathers brought forth upon this nation
         3: a new operating system (more or less), dedicated
         4: to the proposition that all computers (with the same
         5: microcomputer chip) are created equal.
         6: Now, we are engaged in a great computer war (more
         7: have fallen than have risen), testing whether MS OS/2
         8: or any other OS so conceived and so dedicated can
         9: long endure.
        10:⋈We are met today to chronicle a part of these OS
        11: wars.  It is altogether fitting and proper (some may
        12: disagree) that we should do this.
  ⋈13I
        13:⋈The world will little note nor long remember what we
        14:⋈say here (excepting book reviewers, of course), but you
        15:⋈can never forget what you learn here (the author hopes).
        16:⋈^C

  ⋈_
```

Figure 7.7: Additional text entries

```
         5: microcomputer chip) are created equal.
         6: Now, we are engaged in a great computer war (more
         7: have fallen than have risen), testing whether MS OS/2
         8: or any other OS so conceived and so dedicated can
         9: long endure.
        10: We are met today to chronicle a part of these OS
        11: wars.  It is altogether fitting and proper (some may
        12: disagree) that we should do this.
        13: The world will little note nor long remember what we
        14: say here (excepting book reviewers, of course), but you
        15: can never forget what you learn here (the author hopes).
  ⋈13,15D
  ⋈1
         2: MS OS/2's forefathers brought forth upon this nation
         3: a new operating system (more or less), dedicated
         4: to the proposition that all computers (with the same
         5: microcomputer chip) are created equal.
         6: Now, we are engaged in a great computer war (more
         7: have fallen than have risen), testing whether MS OS/2
         8: or any other OS so conceived and so dedicated can
         9: long endure.
        10: We are met today to chronicle a part of these OS
        11: wars.  It is altogether fitting and proper (some may
        12: disagree) that we should do this.

  ⋈_
```

Figure 7.8: Multiple lines deleted

ENDING THE EDITING SESSION

There are two ways to exit EDLIN, depending on whether you want to save the changes you've made to the file or not. You can abort the entire editing operation and restore the file to its original condition, or you can save all your edits to the disk file, permanently engraving those changes in the original file.

QUITTING THE EDITING SESSION WITHOUT SAVING

Entering the Quit command (Q) all by itself is one way of getting out of EDLIN and back to OS/2, without saving any of the work you have just done. EDLIN will ask you if you are sure you wish to leave without saving your file. Anything other than an answer of Y will abort the Q command, and you will be back at the EDLIN prompt.

This exit path usually is used when you have made a serious mistake. Suppose, for example, that you changed your mind about the deletion of lines 13 to 16 done in the last section. You've decided to keep those lines in the text after all. You could type them in all over again; or, if there are no other edits at stake, you could abort the entire editing process, go back to OS/2, and then call up the text file for editing once again. Figure 7.9 demonstrates this process. Using Q to abort the editing process, returning to OS/2, and then immediately recalling the Lincoln.txt file returns the unchanged text file to you.

⊙ Make sure that there is enough room on your disk for the file to be saved. If there is not, the part of the file that *can* fit will be saved with an extension of .$$$. The original file will be retained on the disk, no new .bak file will be created, and the part of the edited file not saved will be lost.

SAVING YOUR WORK AND EXITING TO OS/2

The usual way to exit EDLIN and save your changes is to use the End command (E). With this command, the file you originally named when you started EDLIN will be given a .bak extension; the edited file will retain the original extension. If you created a completely new file, no .bak file would be created.

At the end of the file, EDLIN will insert a carriage return and line feed if they are not already there. It will also insert a Ctrl-Z code to be used for an end-of-file marker.

```
        9: long endure.
       10: We are met today to chronicle a part of these OS
       11: wars.  It is altogether fitting and proper (some may
       12: disagree) that we should do this.
*q
Abort edit (Y/N)? y
[Real C:\]edlin lincoln.txt
End of input file
*l

        1:*Four score and seven months ago (or thereabouts)
        2: MS OS/2's forefathers brought forth upon this nation
        3: a new operating system (more or less), dedicated
        4: to the proposition that all computers (with the same
        5: microcomputer chip) are created equal.
        6: Now, we are engaged in a great computer war (more
        7: have fallen than have risen), testing whether MS OS/2
        8: or any other OS so conceived and so dedicated can
        9: long endure.
       10: We are met today to chronicle a part of these OS
       11: wars.  It is altogether fitting and proper (some may
       12: disagree) that we should do this.
       13: The world will little note nor long remember what we
       14: say here (excepting book reviewers, of course), but you
       15: can never forget what you learn here (the author hopes).

*_
```

Figure 7.9: Aborting the editing process

```
       11: wars.  It is altogether fitting and proper (some may
       12: disagree) that we should do this.
*q
Abort edit (Y/N)? y
[Real C:\]edlin lincoln.txt
The entire input file has been read
*l

        1:*Four score and seven months ago (or thereabouts)
        2: MS OS/2's forefathers brought forth upon this nation
        3: a new operating system (more or less), dedicated
        4: to the proposition that all computers (with the same
        5: microcomputer chip) are created equal.
        6: Now, we are engaged in a great computer war (more
        7: have fallen than have risen), testing whether MS OS/2
        8: or any other OS so conceived and so dedicated can
        9: long endure.
       10: We are met today to chronicle a part of these OS
       11: wars.  It is altogether fitting and proper (some may
       12: disagree) that we should do this.
       13: The world will little note nor long remember what we
       14: say here (excepting book reviewers, of course), but you
       15: can never forget what you learn here (the author hopes).
*e

[Real C:\]_
```

Figure 7.10: Normal EDLIN termination sequence

EDLIN will *not* prompt you to make sure you want to leave. Entering E followed by a press of the Return key is all you need to save all of your editing changes and return to OS/2 (see Figure 7.10).

SUMMARY

In this chapter, you've learned about the text editing capability in OS/2. You've learned that text files can be edited in real mode by the EDLIN program, or in protected mode by the SSE program. You've seen information about the commands available for creating and manipulating text files, as well as for modifying the text within them. Here is a brief review:

- SSE is a full screen editor, although it does not have a word processor's capability for word wraparound.

- EDLIN is a line oriented text editor. All its commands reference line numbers and the text on those line.

- The control codes in SSE provide the ability to insert and delete lines while in full screen mode, and to save or abandon edits.

- All of EDLIN's capabilities are accessible with simple one-letter commands. These commands act on one or more lines within the text file, and act on the text within those lines.

- You can create a new file simply by typing EDLIN *FileName*. The file will be created and you can execute any of EDLIN's editing commands by typing in the appropriate command at the asterisk prompt.

- If the available memory in your system is not sufficient to hold your entire text file, you can use the Write command with the Append command to write edited lines to disk and then add unedited lines to memory.

- You can enter new text with the Insert command. The Break key allows you to terminate the data entry.

- You can list any or all text lines with the Line command. You can also list the entire file a screenful at a time with the Page command.

- Once entered, text can be modified in a variety of ways. The OS/2 function keys can be used to modify any line once you've brought up that line by typing its number.

- You can move one or more lines around in the file with the Move command. You can also leave those lines in place, while making a complete copy of them elsewhere with the Copy command.

- Besides the Move and Copy commands, which manipulate large blocks of text, the Transfer command can insert one complete text file into another.

- What goes in can always come out. The Delete command can remove one or more text lines permanently.

- Any text string can be searched for with the Search command. The even more powerful Replace command can search for any text string and replace it with another string. If you like, the Replace command can be used to replace one string with *nothing,* effectively creating a large-scale (global) deletion capability.

- You can end your EDLIN editing session with the End command, which saves your edited work under the original file name and then returns you to the OS/2 prompt. Or you can abort the entire editing session with the Quit command, which, after confirming that you really mean to do it, restores your file to its previous condition.

Now that you know how to create and modify text files with either EDLIN or SSE, you should turn to Chapter 8 on batch files in OS/2. Having beautifully sculpted text on a disk may be satisfying, but having that text represent commands that control OS/2 operations can be even more exciting.

THE POWER OF
OS/2 BATCH FILES

CHAPTER 8

IN THIS CHAPTER, YOU WILL LEARN ABOUT BOTH kinds of batch files available in OS/2. You've already learned many OS/2 features that give you added power. Batch files can multiply the power of OS/2 dramatically, not just add to it. This chapter will show you what batch files are, how they can be created and used, how they differ in real and protected modes, and how to use some new OS/2 batch commands. You will learn why batch files are so important to you and to your effectiveness as a OS/2 user.

You will see a wide range of batch files throughout this chapter. These examples provide you with usable programs: you can type them in yourself, or you can send for the disk with the files already on it (see the coupon at the end of this book). The disk contains both protected mode and real mode versions of all the batch files in this book, as well as other representative batch files for your study and unrestricted use. These examples will also give you ideas for creating similar programs for your own computer system.

Batch files allow you to enter a group of OS/2 commands automatically. A batch file is a series of ordinary OS/2 commands that the computer can execute automatically as a group (a *batch*) instead of one at a time.

You create batch files to automate OS/2 activities that require more than one OS/2 command. As you will see, this simple idea has some unexpected benefits. OS/2's ability to understand simple batch files allows you to create sophisticated OS/2 programs. These are more complex batch files containing a series of commands and also special elements called variables, conditional statements, and subroutines.

If a batch file you write works, *it's right*. It may not be the fastest, most efficient, or most elegant file, but it's still right.

WORKING WITH BATCH FILES

Batch files can be as simple or complex as you want them to be. In Chapter 3, you saw some simple ones. The Autoexec.bat file represented a sequence of steps that OS/2 performs the first time it switches to real mode. And the Startup.cmd represented a similarly simple batch file, executable at the startup of protected mode operations.

In order for OS/2 to properly recognize and process a file as a batch file, there are several rules you must follow:

- File Type: batch files must be standard ASCII text files. You can create them with the EDLIN or SSE programs described in Chapter 7. They must contain only normal ASCII characters, and each line must end with a carriage return (CR) and a line feed (LF).

- Naming Conventions: You can give a batch file almost any name you like, as long as you use the .bat or .cmd extensions. Of course, the name must adhere to standard OS/2 file-naming rules, with no more than eight letters or numbers in the base name. OS/2 looks for a .bat extension when in real mode, and looks for a .cmd extension when in protected mode. All techniques presented in this chapter apply to both real and protected mode batch files, unless otherwise noted.

- Command Conventions: Any command that works at the OS/2 prompt can be included in a batch file. You'll soon see that there are some additional controlling commands (called subcommands) that can be used in a batch file; you can also use variable input parameters, which will be covered in detail later in this chapter. However, the primary commands are always going to look just as they would if they were typed at the OS/2 prompt.

- Running Batch Files: Executing all the instructions within a batch file is as simple as typing the name of the .bat or .cmd file containing those instructions. As with commands and programs, however, if you don't precede the batch-file name with a drive identifier and a directory name, the assumption will be the current drive and current directory.

- Stopping Batch Files: You can stop batch-file execution at any time by pressing the Break key, or Ctrl-C. In protected mode, the batch processing will be terminated immediately. In real mode, however, OS/2 will ask you if you really want to terminate the batch job. If you have a change of heart and answer N, the current step in the batch file will be ignored and the rest of the commands will be executed.

USING VARIABLES IN BATCH FILES

Until now, you've only seen batch files that have been designed for a specific use: for example, a batch file that quickly and easily initializes a programming environment, or one that sets up a unique screen prompt. In such cases, the batch file works with constant values, like specific directory names or specific ANSI escape codes, each time it runs. If batch files could accept variables, as more sophisticated programming languages do, they could be much more flexible.

You can create OS/2 batch files that will do just that. Variables in any language allow you to construct programs that differ each time the program is run. In other words, the program stays the same, but the value used by the program to complete its tasks varies. You can consider the OS/2 batch-file feature to be a simple programming language.

Let's take a moment to look at the terminology involved. As you saw in Chapter 5, many OS/2 commands accept a variety of parameters. These parameters are just additional pieces of information needed by OS/2 to clarify the task specified in the command. For example, the command

COPY Report.doc February.doc

contains the COPY command, and the Report and February documents are its respective source and destination parameters. Next month, however, you might want to run the COPY command again, with a different report file as the source and the March.doc file as the destination. Thus, these two file names can be considered as variable parameters, because they need to be changed each month.

Batch files can accept variables as easily as they can accept OS/2 commands. Variables always begin with a percentage sign (%) and are followed by a number from 0 to 9. Thus, OS/2 allows variables named %0, %1, %2, and so on.

To see how this system works, create a simple batch file and call it Demo.bat (or Demo.cmd in protected mode), consisting of the following two lines:

```
CLS
DIR *.%1
```

The intention is that this batch file will clear the screen and then display a directory of all file names that have similar extensions (.com, .cmd, .exe, .wp, and so on).

Note that instead of entering .exe or some other extension, you used the variable %1. The batch file is not "locked in" to DIR *.exe, DIR *.cmd, or anything else. Instead, %1 can stand for anything you want.

Here's how the % symbol works. When you type any OS/2 command, OS/2 assigns variable names to each section of that command. Look at the following command:

```
DEMO exe
```

If you enter this command at the prompt, OS/2 would internally assign %0 to the first phrase (DEMO), %1 to the second phrase (exe), and if there were other parameter entries on the line, % values up to %9. This then allows you to reference these phrases within your batch file. Because the DEMO batch file makes reference to %1, DEMO will actually use whatever phrase follows DEMO (in this case exe) to complete the DIR command. Thus, the command

```
DIR *.%1
```

will be treated as if you had originally typed

```
DIR *.exe
```

and the batch file will display all files with an .exe extension.

Running the batch file again with a different value for the first parameter generates a different result. Entering

```
DEMO com
```

causes only the .com files to be listed. You can refer to parameter %1 any number of times inside the batch file, even though the DEMO batch file referred to it only once.

This technique is called *deferred execution,* because the decision as to what parameter will be used is deferred until the time of batch-file execution. In this example, a DIR command will be executed, but the decision as to what specific directory listing will be produced is deferred until the batch file has actually been called and the %1 parameter has been specified as the first parameter after the batch-file name.

Let's take another example of a batch file using variable parameters. This time, you'll use a second variable to create a batch file called MOVE, whose purpose will be to move files from one drive or directory to another. Your task is to create a generalized batch file that will issue all the necessary commands, so that you only need to supply the file names to be moved and the identifier of the new drive. To do this, your batch file should COPY the old files, verify with DIR that the copy was successful, then ERASE the old versions.

The batch file Move.bat (or Move.cmd in protected mode) requires two variables, %1 and %2. The first one will be a file name or a wild card to use for selecting a file or files. The second variable will be the letter specifying the destination drive. For example, you might want to move all the .exe files from the current directory to drive B. To do that, you could enter the following lines:

```
CLS
COPY *.exe  B:
DIR/w B:
PAUSE OK to Continue?
ERASE *.exe
```

Then again, you might want to move all the .prg files from your Dbase\Test subdirectory on drive C to the Active directory on drive C:

```
CLS
COPY C:\Dbase\Test\*.prg C:\Active
DIR/w C:\Active
PAUSE OK to Continue?
ERASE C:\Dbase\Test\*.prg
```

There will probably be many occasions when you need to perform this operation between drives, between directories, or both, so this is

a perfect chance to use variables. You could write a batch file called
Move.bat or Move.cmd that does the same job:

```
CLS
COPY  %1  %2
DIR/w  %2
PAUSE OK to Continue?
ERASE %1
```

This batch file issues the proper commands for you if you merely
indicate the desired file source and destination. For example,

```
MOVE  *.exe  B:
```

will move all the .exe files from the current directory to drive B. And

```
MOVE  C:\Dbase\Test\*.prg  C:\Active
```

will move all the .prg files from the Dbase\Test subdirectory on drive
C to the Active directory on drive C.

The same batch file can be used to move the files the other way.
Simply reverse the parameters. Entering

```
MOVE B:*.exe  C:
```

will move all the .exe files from drive B to drive C.

Variable parameters are a mainstay of batch-file creation. Later in
this chapter, you'll see other more sophisticated examples of batch
files that use this technique. You'll find it to be one of the most powerful and useful aspects of batch files in OS/2.

USING SUBCOMMANDS IN BATCH FILES

Batch files have their own set of specialized support commands,
known as *subcommands*. You don't need them to create simple batch
files, but you greatly expand your possibilities when you learn them.
Depending on what type of batch program you write, you may need
to use one or several subcommands. These subcommands only work
within batch files, and increase your overall control when used in conjunction with the standard OS/2 commands seen in Chapter 5.

Some subcommands will be commonplace in your batch files; for example, you will frequently use ECHO or REM to insert messages both in the batch file itself and on the video screen. You'll use others only occasionally; for example, once in a while you'll want to use PAUSE in batch files to allow users sufficient time to read information on the screen, or to provide them a convenient time to stop the execution of a batch file.

Still others will be used in specific situations only. In this category, you'll see the FOR subcommand, which allows the repetition of operations, the IF subcommand, which provides decision making, and the GOTO subcommand, which manages the flow of control. This last command, GOTO, allows you to execute commands non-sequentially, according to your own specified order. Changing the order of command execution is known as modifying the flow of control, or simply *branching*.

You'll also have the ability to run one batch file from within another with the CALL subcommand, thereby emulating the powerful feature of high-level programming subroutines. You can also have completely independent values for drive, directory, and environmental variables by using the SETLOCAL and ENDLOCAL subcommands (protected mode only).

Two other subcommands exist in OS/2 that are not often needed, so you'll skip them in this book. They are the SHIFT subcommand, which allows for more than nine variable parameters (%), and the EXTPROC subcommand (protected mode only), which allows you to specify an external batch processor to interpret your batch file instructions.

INCORPORATING MESSAGES INTO BATCH FILES

In simple batch files, the ECHO subcommand is used to suppress the display of succeeding commands while a batch file is processing. However, ECHO has some other uses too. If ECHO is followed by text instead of by ON or OFF, it will print the text. Thus, ECHO can be used to display information on the screen during the execution of a batch file.

To see how this works, create a new batch file called Help1.bat (or Help1.cmd, if you plan to run it in protected mode) containing several ECHO subcommands, each of which contains helpful information for a user (see Figure 8.1). This batch file will explain how the previously created Move.bat file can be used. The figure contains a few sample lines of text to demonstrate the method of using the ECHO subcommand. To run this batch file, type

Help1

at the OS/2 prompt and you will see the results shown in Figure 8.2.

```
@ECHO OFF
REM The Help1 Batch File
CLS
ECHO   The MOVE batch file is designed to
ECHO   transfer a file(s) from one drive or
ECHO   directory to any other drive/directory.
ECHO   =========================================
ECHO   MOVE first copies, then deletes the
ECHO   originals. The general form is:
ECHO        MOVE  Source  Destination
```

Figure 8.1: The Help1 batch file

```
The MOVE batch file is designed to
transfer a file(s) from one drive or
directory to any other drive/directory.
-------------------------------------------------
MOVE first copies, then deletes the
originals.  The general form is:
     MOVE  source  destination
[Prot C:\CHAP8]
```

Figure 8.2: Results of executing the Help1 batch file

Notice that the first two commands set ECHO to OFF and clear the screen, so the remaining "echoed" messages appear without your seeing the actual ECHO subcommand for each line. Regardless of whether ECHO is on or off, the textual information on the ECHO line is always displayed. ECHO OFF only suppresses the display of any succeeding OS/2 commands in the batch file. One additional thing to notice here is the @ symbol in front of the ECHO command. Its sole purpose is to suppress the display of the ECHO OFF command itself, because until ECHO OFF actually executes, that single command would still be displayed.

One of the command lines that is usually suppressed—and purposely so—is a REM statement. You will see many REM statements in batch-file listings. Here is an example:

```
REM This is a simple internal commenting line.
REM So is this... for the Typical.cmd file
```

A REM (remark) statement is used for internal documentation in a batch file. It usually contains notes to the programmer or to the future user of the batch program. Anything from the file name to information about algorithms and techniques will be welcomed by someone trying to understand the inner workings of a batch program. Nearly all of the remaining batch files in this book will have at least one REM statement containing the name of the batch file itself.

If ECHO is set to OFF, the REM statements will not be shown on the video screen during program execution. The more complex or obscure your batch-file logic, the more you need to have several REM lines built into it.

INTERRUPTING BATCH FILES DURING EXECUTION

There are two kinds of interruptions in life: permanent and temporary. OS/2 provides batch-file equivalents to these types of interruptions with the PAUSE subcommand and the Ctrl-Break and Ctrl-C key combinations.

When a PAUSE subcommand is used in a batch file, the execution of the commands in the file stops temporarily, and OS/2 displays the message ''Strike a key when ready....'' When you press the Return key or the Spacebar (or virtually anything else), the next command in the batch file will execute.

The PAUSE subcommand is not necessary to the functioning of the program, but it has a practical function. Filling the screen with a lot of instruction is a sure way to lose a user's attention. Instead, you can display a little information, pause the display, clear the screen,

In a batch file like Help1, which displays text, it's a good idea to add PAUSE as a final command so that the screen information can be read. Information that is displayed to a user is usually only one part of a more complex batch file; pausing the execution allows the user to read the messages before continuing the program.

and display a little more information. This will keep the user alert.

As you saw earlier in the Move batch file, the PAUSE command also gives a user a predefined opportunity to exit from a batch file, depending on earlier results from the batch file operations. If you want to exit from a batch file permanently, use Ctrl-Break or Ctrl-C.

DECISION MAKING IN BATCH FILES

OS/2 can test the value of certain variables and parameters during the execution of a batch file. Performing this test is known as *decision making,* or *logical testing.* A logical test allows branching within a program, which means that different actions will be performed based on the results of the test.

A branching statement (also called a *conditional* statement) might look like this:

If A = B, perform action C. Otherwise, perform action D.

A = B is called a *logical expression.* As in any language, it can stand for such things as Wage = 500 or Lastname = Robbins. If A = B is a true statement, then C will happen. On the other hand, if A = B is false, then action D will take place. This branching ability allows you to create batch files that evaluate circumstances and perform different actions according to the conditions found.

To get an idea of the usefulness of branching, let's create a batch file that uses branching as a development tool. Often, you may be using a valuable application program like Ventura Publisher, but some of its operations perform more slowly than you would like. So you create a RAM disk on your system, copy the appropriate files to it, then run the application program from the RAM disk.

Figure 8.3 shows a batch file that initializes a RAM disk to run Ventura Publisher. This batch file actually creates directories (with the MD command) on the RAM disk (D) for various Ventura files. Lines 7 through 13 perform the necessary directory creation and file copying steps.

Line 2 of this file uses the IF subcommand in an interesting way. Because all the steps of creation and copying can be time-consuming, you don't want to go through all of them each time you run Ventura Publisher. You only want to go through all this the first time. From

Remember that the line numbers in this batch file and in the other files listed in this chapter are there for reference only. If you type in these or similar batch programs for yourself, leave out the line numbers.

```
1    @ECHO OFF
2    IF EXIST D:\Gemsys\Assign.sys GOTO :END
3    SET COMPSEC=D:\Command.com
4    COPY C:\Command.com D:\
5    CD \Gemboot
6    MOUSE
7    MD D:\Gemapps
8    COPY \Gemapps\Vp*.* D:\Gemapps
9    MD D:\Gemapps\Vpsys
10   COPY \Gemapps\Vpsys\*.* D:\Gemapps\Vpsys
11   MD D:\Gemsys
12   COPY \Gemsys\Assign.sys D:\Gemsys
13   COPY \Gemsys\Output.wid D:\Gemsys
14   :END
15   REM The following must be run each time
16   PATH D:\Gemapps
17   CD \Gemsys
18   Gemvdi D:\Gemapps\Vp
19   COPY D:\Gemapps\Vpsys\*.inf C:\Gemapps\Vpsys
20   PATH=D:\;C:\Fw;C:\Dos;C:\;C:\Utility\Misc;C:\Dbase\Db3plus
```

Figure 8.3: RAM disks and batch file subcommands

then on, the necessary files will be in their proper places on drive D, so you can skip these steps and go right on with the actual Ventura program.

If this batch file sequence has already been executed at least once, the file Assign.sys will have already been copied to the Gemsys directory on drive D. The IF statement in Line 2 tests to see if Assign.sys already exists in that RAM disk directory. If it does, the GOTO :END command transfers control to the :END label at line 14, and processing continues there. All the now unnecessary MD and COPY steps are skipped.

USING THE IF SUBCOMMAND   The IF subcommand can be used three ways:

1. IF EXIST or IF NOT EXIST. This form of IF is used to test whether a file exists, as in the previous example.

2. IF A = = B or IF NOT A = = B. This form tests the equality of A and B, where A and B represent character strings. Note that OS/2 uses two equal signs (= =) as the symbol for equality. The character strings can be *literals* or *variables*. A literal (also known as a constant) is any unchanging character string, such as JUDD or END. A variable is one of the changing parameters, %0 through %9, that you learned about earlier in this chapter. For example, the command

   IF %1 = = END

tests to see if the first variable parameter in the batch-file command, %1 (a variable), is equal to the letters END (a literal). This is the most common use of the IF subcommand.

3. **IF ERRORLEVEL #.** This form of the IF subcommand tests to see if the preceding command has executed correctly or has failed. OS/2 or any individual application program can set a return code equal to a number from 0 to 255. Usually, a value of 0 means that the preceding command completed successfully; a number greater than 0 indicates a failure and the value indicates the different reasons for that failure. Several OS/2 commands such as REPLACE, RESTORE, and XCOPY affect this return-code value. Appendix C lists the exit codes for all OS/2 commands that return them. Note that ERRORLEVEL # means a return code of *# or greater.*

When you automate certain operations with batch files, you can use these returned values to test for specific results. If any of these OS/2 commands fail, the error level can be compared to a particular number, #, and different action can be taken depending on the severity of the error. The higher the return code, the more severe the error. The IF statement can control which succeeding section of the batch file receives control, depending on the value of this error level.

In the example of Figure 8.3, the label line (14) does nothing except facilitate jumping from one place in the batch file to another, so the next line actually executed is Line 15. This branching technique is referred to in programming languages as the *flow of control.*

The *GOTO :END* on Line 2 is called an *unconditional transfer of control.* It is necessary in this batch-file language to enable the processing sequence to skip over certain portions of the program. The label :END is again just a placeholder to mark where processing can continue. Line 14 is called a *nonexecutable instruction,* because it does not represent any steps that the processor takes. It is simply a label for that place in the program.

USING SETLOCAL AND ENDLOCAL   Another feature available only in protected mode can improve the processing logic of this batch file. Line 16 changes the system PATH, for the sake of running the

OS/2 usually doesn't care whether information is entered in upper or lowercase letters. However, when you are testing for the equality of groups of characters, as you do with the IF and the FIND subcommands, case does matter. If you enter the lowercase letters *quit* as the first parameter in IF %1 = =QUIT, OS/2 will evaluate the IF as false. If you enter the uppercase letters *QUIT,* the logical expression will be true.

If you use this RAM disk method for improving your system's performance, remember to put the RAM disk on your path *before* any other references to directories that may contain the original copies of the files. Then the fast-access RAM copy of the referenced file is located first, before the slower disk-resident version of the same file.

Gemvdi program seen in Line 18. The former system PATH is restored in Line 20. As the batch file is written, it will run properly as either a .Bat file in real mode or a .Cmd file in protected mode. If you plan to run a batch program like this only in protected mode, you can use two new OS/2 subcommands called SETLOCAL and ENDLOCAL.

Inserting SETLOCAL just before Line 16 will ensure that all adjustments to any environmental parameters (like PATH) will only affect *local* copies of the previous environmental variables. In other words, Line 20 will be unnecessary. When the batch file ends, all environmental variables active before the SETLOCAL command will be automatically restored. In fact, if you wanted to restore the previous environmental parameter values *before* ending the batch file, you would only need to insert the command ENDLOCAL at the desired point.

The task performed by this batch file can be done in other, perhaps simpler, ways. However, you've used an IF subcommand, a GOTO subcommand, and the technique of nonexecutable labels. And you've learned how to use the SETLOCAL and ENDLOCAL commands for managing temporary adjustments in the value of certain environmental variables. You can use these tools to make your own batch files that will do meaningful work on your own system.

USING LOOPING AND REPETITION IN BATCH FILES

The FOR subcommand is similar to commands in other programming languages that facilitate repetition. Often, one or more commands in a program need to be repeated, sometimes a fixed number of times and sometimes a variable number of times. In either situation, the FOR subcommand enables you to meet this need.

The general form of the FOR subcommand is

FOR %%*Letter* IN (*Possibilities*) DO *Command*

Letter can be any single alphabetic letter. It is similar to the variable parameters you saw earlier in this chapter ($\%0$, $\%1$, $\%2$, and so on). In this situation, however, double percent-sign variables are used. The $\%\%$ tells OS/2 that you are referring to a batch-file variable in the looping FOR statement.

The *Command* in the FOR statement that will be executed repeatedly can change slightly during each repetition. This works like the variable parameter method, which required you to write the batch file originally using %1 or %2 to refer to possible first or second input parameters. This method deferred execution so that when the batch file actually executed, it used the actual values typed in after the batch-file name, instead of using the placeholder % expressions.

In a FOR subcommand, execution is similarly deferred until the command executes. At that time, the *Possibilities* are evaluated, and the *Command* is executed for each possibility. When written into a batch file, this command can represent a more concise form of coding. For example, suppose you have a program called Qrtly.exe that generates a quarterly business report. This program requires only that you specify the desired quarter for the current fiscal year. Entering the following at the OS/2 prompt would produce a report for Quarter 3:

    QRTLY 3

At the end of the fiscal year, you might want to generate current copies of the quarterly reports for each quarter. You would enter

    QRTLY 1
    QRTLY 2
    QRTLY 3
    QRTLY 4

and press Return after each line. All four of these successive requests could be replaced in a batch file called Reports.bat with one automatic FOR subcommand, as shown in Figure 8.4.

If you use this looping mechanism, you don't have to wait for each quarterly report to finish before you request the next to begin:

    FOR %%Y IN (1 2 3 4) DO QRTLY %%Y

FOR is a batch-file subcommand. This means it can only be executed from within a batch file.

```
@ECHO OFF
REM The Reports Batch File
REM Produce the Four Quarterly Reports
FOR %%A IN (1 2 3 4) DO QRTLY %%A
```

Figure 8.4: The Reports batch file

Your first reaction might be that this is an awfully complicated-looking expression just to save typing in four simple QRTLY report requests. Again, it just demonstrates the technique. If you had a monthly report program called Monthly.exe, you could just as easily request the printing of twelve monthly reports with

FOR %%Y IN (1 2 3 4 5 6 7 8 9 10 11 12) DO MONTHLY %%Y

As you've seen in the general form of the FOR subcommand, there can be only one *Command* parameter executed after the DO portion of the command. It can be a program name, as you've just seen demonstrated, or it can be another OS/2 command, like DIR or CHKDSK. The following FOR subcommand exemplifies this:

FOR %%A IN (%1 %2 %3 %4) DO DIR %%A

This command would perform a DIR command for each variable parameter (presumably, four different file names). If this FOR subcommand were in a batch file called Hunt.bat, you might invoke Hunt in the following manner to determine if any of the four specified files were located in the current directory:

Hunt Heart.exe, Lungs.exe, Liver.com, Brain.exe

The result would include standard DIR output for each file that was found (see Figure 8.5).

Using a batch subcommand as the object of DO can produce a more concise and attractive result. An IF subcommand can be used to replace the DIR command:

FOR %%A IN (%1 %2 %3 %4) DO
    IF EXIST %%A ECHO %%A FOUND

The results of running Hunt, after rewriting the FOR command to use IF and ECHO instead of DIR, would be

HEART.EXE FOUND
LIVER.COM FOUND

The desired information about whether the files exist is not obscured by any additional OS/2 directory information. In this FOR

```
[Real C:\BIOLOGY]HUNT Heart.exe Lungs.exe Liver.com Brain.exe

  Volume in drive C is ROBBINS
  Directory of  C:\BIOLOGY

HEART     EXE    55424  11-23-85  12:48a
             1 File(s)   5435392 bytes free

  Volume in drive C is ROBBINS
  Directory of  C:\BIOLOGY

File not found

  Volume in drive C is ROBBINS
  Directory of  C:\BIOLOGY

LIVER     COM    62720  12-28-85  10:47a
             1 File(s)   5435392 bytes free

  Volume in drive C is ROBBINS
  Directory of  C:\BIOLOGY

File not found
[Real C:\BIOLOGY]_
```

Figure 8.5: Executing Hunt to repeat an OS/2 command

subcommand, the actual command executed by DO is IF EXIST %%A ECHO %%A FOUND. The important point to note about this example is that subcommands can be nested within subcommands, just as batch files themselves can be nested within batch files.

USING BATCH CHAINS AND BATCH SUBROUTINES

Because a batch file can execute any command that otherwise could be entered directly at the OS/2 prompt, a batch file can invoke another batch file. By simply entering the name of the second batch file, you can pass control from the first to the second file. Execution continues with the instructions in the second batch file and does not return to the first (calling) batch file. This is known as *chaining*. It is different from the calling procedure familiar to programmers.

Look at the listings of the three batch files in Figures 8.6, 8.7, and 8.8. These three files together demonstrate both the capabilities and the limitations of chaining. Carefully read the steps of each of the three batch files, while looking at the output results in Figure 8.9.

```
@ECHO OFF
REM The First Batch File
ECHO Simulated Instruction 1 in First
ECHO Simulated Instruction 2 in First
ECHO Simulated Instruction 3 in First
Second
```

Figure 8.6: The First batch file

```
@ECHO OFF
REM The Second Batch File
ECHO Simulated Instruction 1 in Second
ECHO Simulated Instruction 2 in Second
ECHO Simulated Instruction 3 in Second
Third
ECHO Last Instruction in Second
```

Figure 8.7: The Second batch file

```
@ECHO OFF
REM The Third Batch File
ECHO Simulated Instruction 1 in Third
ECHO Simulated Instruction 2 in Third
ECHO Simulated Instruction 3 in Third
```

Figure 8.8: The Third batch file

```
[Prot C:\CHAP8]FIRST
Simulated Instruction 1 in FIRST
Simulated Instruction 2 in FIRST
Simulated Instruction 3 in FIRST
Simulated Instruction 1 in SECOND
Simulated Instruction 2 in SECOND
Simulated Instruction 3 in SECOND
Simulated Instruction 1 in THIRD
Simulated Instruction 2 in THIRD
Simulated Instruction 3 in THIRD
[Prot C:\CHAP8]
```

Figure 8.9: Batch-file chaining

The first batch file executes three simulated instructions and then invokes the second batch file as its last instruction. These simulated instructions take the place of any other successive batch-file commands that you might write. (You should focus on chaining here, rather than on other command lines; the simulated instructions are displayed merely to give you a representative context for the chaining technique.)

After First is done, it passes control to Second by invoking the name of the file (Second) to which control will be passed as its last instruction. Then batch file Second executes another three simulated instructions before passing control to batch file Third. Third executes its own three simulated instructions before the chain process is complete. However, the line "Last instruction in Second" is never executed, because the third batch file was invoked *in the middle* of the second batch file.

> Proper chaining of batch files requires the new batch-file name to be the last instruction of the preceding batch file in the chain.

True subroutines provide you with the ability to write modular batch files that perform well-defined task sequences, and to temporarily leave one batch file to execute a sequence *without losing your place* in the first batch file. If you need to run a batch file while in the middle of another batch file, you can use the CALL subcommand. The syntax required is

CALL *BatchFileName*

When the batch file has executed all its commands, control will be returned to the very next line in the running batch file—after the one containing the CALL instruction—and execution will continue from there.

Look again at the batch file Third shown in Figure 8.8, and then look at Fourth, shown in Figure 8.10. You can use these two files and the secondary command processor technique to invoke and run the instructions within the Third file, as shown in Figure 8.11. The results are different from the results of chaining.

```
@ECHO OFF
REM The Fourth Batch File
ECHO Simulated Instruction 1 in Fourth
ECHO Simulated Instruction 2 in Fourth
ECHO Simulated Instruction 3 in Fourth
CALL Third
ECHO Last Instruction in Fourth
```

Figure 8.10: The Fourth batch file

```
[Prot C:\CHAP8]FOURTH
Simulated Instruction 1 in FOURTH
Simulated Instruction 2 in FOURTH
Simulated Instruction 3 in FOURTH
Simulated Instruction 1 in THIRD
Simulated Instruction 2 in THIRD
Simulated Instruction 3 in THIRD
Last Instruction in FOURTH
[Prot C:\CHAP8]
```

Figure 8.11: OS/2 supports true subroutines

Running Fourth by this method will result in the same first three simulated instructions as with chaining. When those three have executed, control will be transferred to the Third batch file, at which point its three simulated instructions will execute. However, unlike the previous chaining examples, *control then returns to Fourth*, which can execute its last instruction. If there were another instruction in Fourth, or another hundred instructions, they would then execute. In this way, sophisticated, structured application environments and systems can be built up by using only OS/2 commands and the batch-file mechanism.

CREATING YOUR OWN MENU SYSTEM

Remember that nearly everyone designs and programs differently, and that all of the batch files you see here are demonstrations. Feel free to add embellishments or to design the instruction sequences differently.

It's always helpful to set up a mechanism that makes it easy for you and others to run programs. Hard-disk menu systems are designed to provide that very capability. Of course, you can always buy one. However, an inexpensive way to set up a menu system is to use OS/2's batch-file feature. A series of batch files stored on your hard disk can enable anyone to access the programs you have installed. This section will present one possible design for such a series of batch files.

The first step in creating your own menu system is to create a file that will contain a listing of the programs available on your system. Let's put this display menu into a text file called Menu.scr, as shown in Figure 8.12.

This file of text can be displayed each time you first enter protected or real mode. All you must do is write a Startup.cmd file to automate protected mode operations, or an Autoexec.bat file to automate real mode operations. Either file should contain these two simple commands:

```
CLS
TYPE Menu.scr
```

To make this menu work, you must create other OS/2 batch files for each option listed on the menu. For example, to run your inventory management system, you need to create a batch file called 1. Because the file's base name is the number 1, and you use the correct file extension (.bat in real mode, .cmd in protected mode), typing 1 and pressing Return will execute the commands in that file.

A typical batch file for a menu system would contain a set of actions like the following:

1. Changing the directory to the correct one (for example, C:\Dbms\Invntry).

2. Running the program. For example, to run a dBASE III PLUS customized inventory program called Invent.prg, the batch file would execute the command DBASE Invent.

3. Returning to the root directory after the program has completed.

4. Displaying the menu again, so that the user can make another choice.

Of course, many other things could be done in a file like 1.cmd; for example, it could set a temporary but specialized path (with the SETLOCAL command), or a unique prompt, then reset both at the end of the program.

You could write three batch files called 1.cmd, 2.cmd, and 3.cmd (assuming you're running them in protected mode). Each of these files will perform the actions required for choices 1, 2, and 3 on the menu in Figure 8.12. The 1.cmd file brings up a database management program, the 2.cmd file brings up a spreadsheet program, and the 3.cmd file brings up a word-processing program.

The contents of each of these batch files are almost exactly the same, except that the directory and program must be changed in each. For instance, the 1.cmd file might look like

```
CD \Dbms\Invntry
Dbase Invent
CD \
TYPE Menu.scr
```

Remember to add REM statements for documentation to all batch files that aren't transparently simple. Use them for your successor, for another programmer who uses your batch file, and for yourself—after all, *you* could be the one who, two months later, tries to figure out why a certain statement was included.

The fourth choice on your sample menu, SYSTEM UTILITIES, allows for a flexible multilevel menu system. You could create a batch file called 4.cmd that would contain a new screen display, listing several utility choices. The utility operations could be safely nestled inside other batch files, and another entire set of menu choices could be automated.

If you want your menu system to appear automatically when OS/2 switches to protected mode for the first time, add the command TYPE Menu.scr as the last command in the Startup.cmd file. So

```
                 MENU OF AVAILABLE HARD DISK PROGRAMS

        TO SELECT ONE, TYPE ITS NUMBER AND PRESS <RETURN>



           1  -   INVENTORY MANAGEMENT SYSTEM

           2  -   BUDGET ANALYSIS SYSTEM

           3  -   WORD PROCESSING

           4  -   SYSTEM UTILITIES



           ENTER YOUR CHOICE NOW, PLEASE:
```

Figure 8.12: Menu management file (Menu.scr)

your entire simple but working menu management system consists of the following:

- Menu.scr. This file contains the menu display. It has no OS/2 function. Its only purpose is to tell the user what options are available on the hard disk.

- Startup.cmd. This file executes when the protected mode interpreter Cmd.exe is first executed. It sets initial environmental variables, prepares a specialized prompt, and displays the menu for the user to read.

- 1.bat, 2.bat, 3.bat, 4.bat. These files execute the choices listed on the menu. You should create one batch file for each choice.

- If you want a multilevel batch file system, you would have additional text files containing choices (like Menu.scr) and appropriate other batch files to process user selections.

IMPROVING PERFORMANCE WITH BATCH FILES

There are many ways to improve performance with batch files. In this section, you'll learn a host of simple possibilities for batch files. Since the lines of code are few, you can implement these approaches quickly if you choose.

SIMPLIFYING CONSISTENT SEQUENCES

Most of us are not great typists. Even for those who can speed along, there is great value to be gained in reducing the number of keys to be pressed. In the music world, there is much debate on the value of pressing one button and getting the sound of an entire rhythm section. No such debate rages in the PC world; anything that gets the same result with fewer keypresses receives a broad welcome.

ABBREVIATIONS   Any OS/2 command can be abbreviated to a very simple one-line batch file. For example, the CHKDSK command can be shortened to the letter C simply by creating a batch file called C.bat, and including in it the one instruction

CHKDSK

When you type C at the OS/2 prompt, the batch file C.bat or C.cmd will be given control, and its one instruction will be executed as if you had typed it at the OS/2 prompt.

This technique can also be used for commands that normally take parameters, such as the START or the DETACH command. You could just as easily create a batch file called S.cmd that only contains the one executable instruction

START %1

When you wanted to use this command, you could type S instead of typing START along with the name of the .exe program you wanted to start in protected mode. For instance, if you wanted to start a new protected mode program called Convert under Cmd.exe, you could now type

S CONVERT

OS/2 would quickly discover that S is a batch file, and the job would be handled through the batch-file invocation of the START command, using the parameter (CONVERT) represented as %1.

SHORTHAND FOR COMMAND SEQUENCES Certain commands that perform fixed chores can also be simplified with batch files. For instance, you learned in Chapter 5 how to use the MODE command to manage various aspects of different devices. If your system has both a color and a monochrome monitor, you could use a batch file to invoke the proper version of the MODE command. To switch output to the monochrome monitor, you could enter

MODE Mono

in a batch file called Mono.

To switch output to the color monitor using 80 columns with color enabled, you could enter

    MODE Co80

in a batch file called Color. Then, whenever you needed to switch, you would only have to enter the simple batch name, Mono or Color, to obtain the desired result. With this method a user doesn't have to remember (or even know) the actual OS/2 command or command/ parameter sequence that produces a particular result.

This technique is also useful for turning on compressed printing mode for your Epson or IBM-compatible printer. You could create a batch file called Compress that contains one line:

    MODE Lpt1: 132

You could create another batch file called Normal that would also contain only one line:

    MODE Lpt1: 80

Anyone could now type COMPRESS at the OS/2 prompt to send a wide spreadsheet or database to the printer. When they were done, they could enter the command NORMAL to return the printer to its normal configuration.

Another benefit of this method appears when you acquire new printers at a later date. The inside portion of the batch file has to be changed only once, and only by one knowledgeable person. Everyone else using the system still only has to remember to type COMPRESS or NORMAL.

REPEATED AUTOMATIC INVOCATION

Any time you need to execute the same command repeatedly, the following technique can come in handy. Perhaps you need to find a text string in a series of files located in different directories; or perhaps you just need to obtain a directory listing of several disks successively. This method relies on the fact that %0, as a batch-file variable, represents the actual name of the batch file itself.

Take a look at the following lines from a proposed batch file called Contents:

```
REM The batch file's name is 'Contents' (same as %0)
ECHO Load a disk into drive A
PAUSE
DIR A: /p
%0
```

The ECHO command prompts you to enter a new disk into drive A and the PAUSE command then waits for you to do so. If you press the Return key at this point, you will receive a directory listing of the disk you placed in drive A. However, this is also the point in the batch program at which you can terminate the otherwise unending sequence of directory listings by pressing Ctrl-C. If you do not, the batch file will retype its own name (the word Contents), and then begin to execute again; you will be prompted to enter another disk.

The key to this repetitive behavior is in the final line. The %0 is only a variable parameter that substitutes for the original batch-file name typed at the OS/2 prompt.

PROGRAM SETUP AND RESTORATION

You sometimes perform a recurring series of steps in the computing world. For instance, you may run your word processor (Wp.exe) to create a new document and then, as a matter of course, run your grammar and style checker (Style.com). You may also run a specialized spelling checker (Spell.exe) before you rerun your word processor to implement any suggested changes. The sequence, then, is as follows:

1. Word processor runs

2. Style checker runs

3. Spelling checker runs

4. Word processor runs again

If these programs do not allow parameter passing, you could write a batch file called Write.bat, which would consist of the following lines:

```
WP
STYLE
SPELL
WP
```

On the other hand, many programs allow you to specify a parameter to indicate the name of a file to be selected. If a program allows such a specification, then a batch file can be even more useful. Suppose you are working on a proposal called Proposal.doc. Your Write.bat file could do more work if it contained these lines:

```
WP Proposal.doc
STYLE Proposal.doc
SPELL Proposal.doc
WP Proposal.doc
```

Simply typing WRITE at the OS/2 prompt would bring you successively through all four program invocations, each one bringing in the specified Proposal file.

Here's another example. You may be working on the Great American Novel, and each chapter you write undergoes the same painstaking care and attention as the rest of your word-processed documents. You can take the simplifying process one step further by using the variable parameter technique. Look at the following batch file:

```
WP Chapter%1
STYLE Chapter%1
SPELL Chapter%1
WP Chapter%1
```

If you've named your files Chapter1, Chapter2, and so on, you can then invoke your four-program sequence by typing the chapter number as the parameter at the OS/2 prompt, for example,

```
WRITE 5
```

Keep in mind that if your novel has more than nine chapters, you'll have to name them differently so that you don't exceed OS/2's maximum limit of eight characters in a file name.

INITIALIZING YOUR COLOR MONITOR

You learned in Chapter 5 how to use the PROMPT command with the ANSI escape sequences to set up the foreground and background colors on a color monitor. Having to look up or remember the codes can be tedious. This is a perfect opportunity for a batch file. Rgb.bat (or Rgb.cmd) will expect two parameters, each specifying what colors the monitor should use for the foreground and background. The calling sequence will be

RGB *Foreground Background*

Entering the following sequence at the OS/2 prompt will cause all future output to appear in blue letters on a white background:

RGB BLUE WHITE

The batch file itself can be seen in Figure 8.13.
Several interesting points are demonstrated in this file:

- There are two major sections in the logical flow. The first section (Lines 3–28) controls the setting of the foreground colors, according to the first color parameter specified after the batch-file name RGB. The second section (Lines 30–58) controls the background color settings, based on the value of the second parameter on the batch file line.

- This batch file is not case-sensitive, as other batch programs that relied on the IF subcommand would be. In other words, each of the following commands would produce the same result:

RGB	BLUE	WHITE
rgb	blue	white

- If no color is specified for the foreground or background, you can use the IF ARG = =ARG%1 technique to test for the absence of a variable parameter. This IF test will only be true if the variable (either %1 or %2) is missing.

- ECHO ON and OFF, followed by a screen clearing, is necessary between the setting of the foreground and background colors. The foreground prompt must take effect while

ECHO is off and before the background color is set.

- As written, this RGB file requires that a user enter both parameter values (foreground and background colors). If you enter only one color, the foreground will be set to that color, and the background will not be set at all. However, losing the background color will also lose the pg portion of the

```
 1   REM   Batch File Rgb
 2
 3   ECHO OFF
 4   IF ARG==ARG%1 GOTO BKGROUND
 5   GOTO %1
 6   :BLACK
 7   PROMPT $e[30m
 8   GOTO BKGROUND
 9   :WHITE
10   PROMPT $e[37m
11   GOTO BKGROUND
12   :RED
13   PROMPT $e[31m
14   GOTO BKGROUND
15   :GREEN
16   PROMPT $e[32m
17   GOTO BKGROUND
18   :BLUE
19   PROMPT $e[34m
20   GOTO BKGROUND
21   :MAGENTA
22   PROMPT $e[35m
23   GOTO BKGROUND
24   :CYAN
25   PROMPT $e[36m
26   GOTO BKGROUND
27   :BROWN
28   PROMPT $e[33m
29
30   :BKGROUND
31   ECHO ON
32   ECHO OFF
33   CLS
34   IF ARG==ARG%2 GOTO DONE
35   GOTO BK%2
36   :BKBLACK
37   PROMPT $p$g$e[40m
38   GOTO DONE
39   :BKWHITE
40   PROMPT $p$g$e[47m
41   GOTO DONE
42   :BKRED
43   PROMPT $p$g$e[41m
44   GOTO DONE
45   :BKGREEN
46   PROMPT $p$g$e[42m
47   GOTO DONE
48   :BKBLUE
49   PROMPT $p$g$e[44m
50   GOTO DONE
51   :BKMAGENTA
52   PROMPT $p$g$e[45m
53   GOTO DONE
54   :BKCYAN
55   PROMPT $p$g$e[46m
56   GOTO DONE
57   :BKBROWN
58   PROMPT $p$g$e[43m
59   :DONE
60   ECHO ON
61   CLS
```

Figure 8.13: Batch file Rgb sets foreground and background colors

Remember that if you use programs like Rgb in real mode, you must include the line DEVICE = Ansi.sys in your Config.sys file. If you run Rgb in protected mode, you must be sure that ANSI is set to ON (see the ANSI command in Chapter 5).

prompt. This program, like all programs, could be improved by separating the setting of the background color from the pg. You could include PROMPT pg at the end of the batch file so it would always be executed (after line 59). Try it now as an exercise. Remember to include an ECHO ON, ECHO OFF sequence.

The overall flow of this program can be seen in Figure 8.14.

CREATING SOPHISTICATED BATCH FILES

This section deals with some specific batch files used by experienced operating system users. People's perceptions of advanced

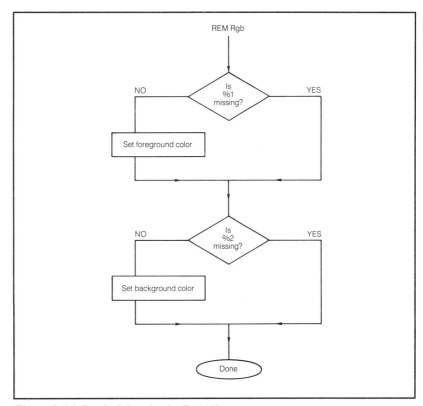

Figure 8.14: Logical flow in the Rgb file

CH.8

subjects differ dramatically; what one person views as sophisticated, another views as old hat. The batch-file techniques presented here are beneficial. If they're new to you, that's all the better. If they're old hat, perhaps you'll learn some new approaches by the manner in which these batch programs are implemented.

CUSTOMIZED SYSTEM HELP SCREENS

Some systems are used by many people at different times. A desirable feature for such a system is customizable help screens. You can use the batch-file mechanism in OS/2 to easily set up this capability. All it takes is the Info batch file, shown in Figure 8.15.

Once you've installed this batch file in your path, you can use it from any directory. All you need to do is write a text file with an .hlp extension. This file should contain the text information you'd like displayed when anyone requests help. Your users, in turn, will only need to run the Info batch file and specify the first parameter as the topic for which they need help.

For example, if there is a subject named Newhires for which you wish to provide users with helpful on-line information, you should place the information in a text file called Newhires.hlp. Then the user need only enter

INFO Newhires

to display the predefined textual information. If help is not available on your system (that is, an .hlp file does not exist for the subject), a

In this example of a help file, no CLS instruction is executed. If you were to write a similar Info system for yourself, you might want to consider inserting CLS instructions before Lines 5 and 9, the output lines in the Info batch file.

```
 1  @REM Batch File Info
 2
 3  @ECHO OFF
 4  IF EXIST %1.HLP   GOTO OK
 5  ECHO Sorry.  No help available for %1
 6  GOTO END
 7
 8  :OK
 9  TYPE %1.HLP
10  PAUSE
11
12  :END
```

Figure 8.15: Customizable help screens with the Info batch file

simple message to that effect is given

```
INFO LISP
Sorry. No help available for LISP
```

The program in Figure 8.15 can be understood quickly by looking at the logic-flow diagram in Figure 8.16. The heart of the batch program begins at Line 4, after the initial REM and ECHO OFF statements. If an .hlp file exists for the subject (entered as %1), the batch file continues executing at Line 8. This is really only the label :OK, which is needed by the GOTO statement in Line 4. The TYPE statement in Line 9 tells OS/2 to present the help information to the user. The PAUSE statement ensures that the user will have time to read the information before anything else appears on the screen or before the screen is cleared.

If no help file exists, the IF statement in Line 4 causes Line 5 to be executed next. The ECHO statement displays a "Sorry ..." message to the user, and the batch program ends immediately. This is handled by the GOTO statement in Line 6, which ensures that none of the instructions between Lines 7 and 11 execute.

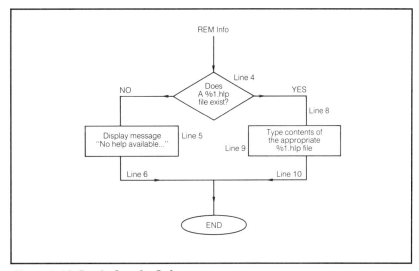

Figure 8.16: Logic flow for Info

APPOINTMENT REMINDER SYSTEM

Some computer systems offer the luxury of automatic appointment reminders. In addition, some utility packages like SideKick permit the entry and retrieval of date-oriented information (however, this is not automatic). The following example can take away the problem of forgetting to check your message or appointment log.

Unless you're very self-disciplined, the easiest way to implement this method begins by including a couple of reminders in your Autoexec.bat or Startup.cmd file. For instance, these three lines should jog your memory:

```
ECHO  Remember to enter the following command to
ECHO  get your messages for today (or any day).
ECHO  TODAY mm-dd-yy
```

When you want to see the message or appointment file for, say, September 26, 1988, you only need to enter

```
TODAY 09-26-88
```

The results of this sequence can be seen in Figure 8.17.

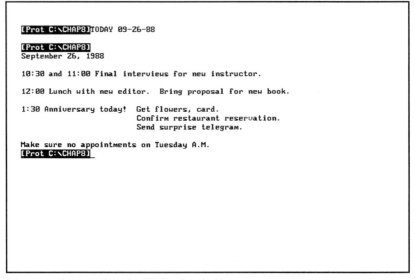

```
[Prot C:\CHAP8]TODAY 09-26-88

[Prot C:\CHAP8]
September 26, 1988

10:30 and 11:00 Final interviews for new instructor.

12:00 Lunch with new editor.  Bring proposal for new book.

1:30 Anniversary today!  Get flowers, card.
                        Confirm restaurant reservation.
                        Send surprise telegram.

Make sure no appointments on Tuesday A.M.
[Prot C:\CHAP8]
```

Figure 8.17: Running the Today batch file

The naming convention for date files must be adhered to precisely. If you use dashes or leading zeros to create the text files, then you must also use them when you run the TODAY batch file.

Remember to erase your older date files when you no longer need them. These type of information files tend to proliferate quickly if they are not erased after use.

The actual batch file that manages this simple operation is shown in Figure 8.18. As you can see, it is only a variation on the help method of the preceding section. The date files are text files, differing only in name and content from the .hlp files.

The way that these text files are used (via the TYPE command) also reflects a similar batch-file approach. With the Info method, all the files were similarly named with an .hlp extension, and their base names reflected the actual topic for which help was desired. In this appointment reminder system, the actual file name is understood to be the date itself (via %1), a simple enough naming convention. The batch file types out the text file by that precise name. You cannot assume that the batch-file code has the intelligence of the OS/2 DATE command; in other words, 09-26-88 could not be replaced by 9/26/88 or any other variation.

BROADCASTING SYSTEM MESSAGES

Yet another variation on the theme of this section can be seen in the Announce.bat file of Figure 8.19. This batch program uses an area in memory called the *OS/2 environment,* which contains a set of variables and the values assigned to them. The OS/2 environment always includes the COMSPEC variable and the values you assign to PATH and PROMPT variables, as well as other arbitrarily named

```
1   @REM Batch File Today
2
3   @ECHO OFF
4   IF NOT EXIST %1 GOTO ERROR
5
6   TYPE %1
7   GOTO END
8
9   :ERROR
10  ECHO No messages for %1
11
12  :END
```

Figure 8.18: The Today batch file

```
1   @REM Batch File Announce
2
3   @ECHO OFF
4   ECHO Current System Messages:
5   TYPE %message%
```

Figure 8.19: The Announce batch file

variables used by some programs or by the batch files described here.

A little-known technique of referencing OS/2 environment variables from within batch files allows you to broadcast messages to your system's users. This technique is useful for systems that have a number of different users, with perhaps one primary user. The goal is to have a simple command like

ANNOUNCE

display all current system messages for a user (see Figure 8.20).

In this figure, the key to the technique lies in a required startup step. You must initialize an OS/2 environment variable, such as MESSAGE, equal to the name of this week's message file. In this case, the primary system operator only has to make the assignment of Week34.txt to MESSAGE once, usually at the beginning of the day:

SET MESSAGE = Week34.txt

For the rest of the time that the system is up, simply typing Announce at the OS/2 prompt will display the current message file.

```
[Prot C:\CHAP8]ANNOUNCE week34

[Prot C:\CHAP8]
Current System Messages:
Messages for Week 34 of FY88:
        Ted Bishop is on vacation.  Susanne Powers will be filling in.
        Next Saturday is the company picnic.  Mary has the tickets.
        Don't forget.  Backup, backup, backup.
        Time cards due on Thursday this week!
[Prot C:\CHAP8]
```

Figure 8.20: Announce displays all current system messages

Only the system operator needs to know the name of the actual message file, and from week to week, everyone's procedure for displaying system messages remains the same. Even the naming conventions can change, and the system operator is the only one who needs to know it.

This batch program can be modified slightly to allow for recurring messages that don't change from week to week. For instance, you could insert another line before Line 5, like

```
TYPE Always.txt
```

Then the Always.txt file could contain any relatively constant information that you wished to display at any time, regardless of the week. This could contain such things as the operator's name and phone number, the service bureau's phone number, the security guard's extension, and so forth.

This technique of setting the values of named environmental variables prior to running a batch file, then referencing those variables by enclosing their name in % signs, is a sophisticated method of passing information. Numbered parameters (%1, %2, and so on) are limited to nine unique values to be used as input to a batch file. Named parameters (%name1%, %name2%, and so on) are more understandable, and are not limited to the number of them that you can define and use. However, in real mode, the total number of bytes consumed by them is limited by the total environmental space allocated in Command.com.

TIPS, TRICKS, AND TECHNIQUES

So far, you have learned several batch files that will be useful in your system either directly or with slight modification. They represent stand-alone batch files that can provide you and others with useful additional tools, like the customized help screens or the color monitor initialization. This section will present a number of techniques that you can apply to your batch files. You can use these methods as you see them, or you can incorporate them into the more sophisticated batch programs you write.

USING RAM DISKS EFFECTIVELY

If you want to run a word processor on your RAM disk, you could use the lines

```
CD C:\Wp
D:
WP
C:
CD\
```

to create a file called Ramwp.bat.

Storing the Ramwp.bat file in your root directory, and assuming your root is on your PATH, you could switch to rapid RAM-based word processing easily and quickly by simply typing

```
RAMWP
```

This naturally assumes that you've already copied all necessary word processing system and support files to your RAM disk. You can use the same technique for your database management program, or for any other program that is slow because of normal disk-access speed. A variation of the Ramwp.bat file for a database management system might contain these lines:

```
CD C:\Dbms
D:
Dbase
C:
CD\
```

This batch file also makes the C hard-disk directory the obvious one for containing your document or data files. D, the RAM disk, is made the current drive so that the Wp or Dbase program that executes is the one found on the RAM disk. Any references to C alone, with no directory path, will access the files in the current default directory on the C drive (in this case, either \Wp or \Dbms).

If you use this RAM drive technique for running more than one major program (for example, both a word processor and a Dbms), you must have enough space reserved for both. If you do not, you may need to write a separate batch program to copy the required programs onto the RAM drive. Of course, you can use the IF and EXIST subcommands to check the RAM drive itself. They will do the work for you, determining what files are needed and whether any existing files need to be erased to make room for the new ones.

CONTROLLING USER ACCESS

Entire books have been written on the subject of password protection. Even more advanced tomes discuss the subject of *resource allocation*, which involves usage as well as access. Resource allocation means controlling access to both the contents of data files and the running of program files. Let's look at a simple but subtle form of password protection that you can implement with OS/2 alone.

The OS/2 environment affords you a special password feature. You can initialize a PASSWORD variable at the OS/2 prompt or in another batch file. This is another example of the use of named variables in OS/2 batch files, as opposed to the %n numbered variable technique. For instance, you can enter

```
SET PASSWORD = EELS
```

The following code segment can be contained in a batch file that will restrict access to only those people who know the password:

```
IF %PASSWORD% = = EELS GOTO RUN
IF %PASSWORD% = = eels GOTO RUN
ECHO Sorry. That's an invalid password.
GOTO END
:RUN
PROGRAM
:END
```

If PASSWORD was set correctly to EELS before a batch file containing this code was run, PROGRAM will run. Otherwise, the invalid password message will be echoed, and the batch file will terminate. In short, only those users who know that the password is EELS and set it correctly will be able to run the particular program. The program to be run could be any .exe or .com file, or even another batch file, and of course, the batch file could properly reset the directory if necessary in the :RUN section.

The password feature can easily be extended by using several OS/2 environment variables, each containing different passwords. Your batch programs can check for the proper values. For instance, you can have three passwords controlling access to the inventory, personnel, and accounting programs. Doing this might require several blocks of code like the code just seen, and three passwords, PASS1, PASS2, and PASS3, controlling access to Inventry.exe, Prsonnel.exe, and Accounts.exe.

You might have a menu system that passes control to three batch files (shown below) instead of directly to the three main programs.

This password code uses IF statements to check for entry of the password in uppercase and in lowercase. You never know what case a user's keyboard might be in when he or she tries to run your batch file or menu system.

Only users who knew and set the appropriate OS/2 environment variable would be allowed access to the program they chose from the menu. Notice that the third password contains digits only, so IF tests for upper and lowercase do not have to be performed.

The following code controls access to the main inventory program:

```
IF %PASS1% = = STORE GOTO RUN1
IF %PASS1% = = store GOTO RUN1
ECHO Sorry. That's an invalid password.
GOTO END1
:RUN1
INVENTRY
:END1
```

This code controls access to the main personnel program:

```
IF %PASS1% = = JOSHUA GOTO RUN2
IF %PASS1% = = joshua GOTO RUN2
ECHO Sorry. That's an invalid password.
GOTO END2
:RUN2
PRSONNEL
:END2
```

Finally, the code below controls access to the main accounting program.

```
IF %PASS1% = = 1812 GOTO RUN3
ECHO Sorry. That's an invalid password.
GOTO END3
:RUN3
ACCOUNTS
:END3
```

In all of these password examples, clearing the password after use is a good idea. This ensures that subsequent users can't gain access without themselves knowing the actual password. This could be done by inserting a line at the end of the batch file:

```
SET PASSWORD =
```

SUMMARY

In this chapter, you took a close look at the OS/2 batch-file mechanism. It extends the power of your operating system by allowing you to build your own new set of commands. The new set of commands can be used just like any existing OS/2 command, except that it is your customized batch file that executes when requested, and not a prewritten command provided by OS/2.

You learned the following key points about batch files:

- A batch file that will run in real mode must have a .bat extension; a batch file that will run in protected mode must have a .cmd extension.

- You can terminate the execution of your batch program by pressing the Break key combination. In real mode, you are asked if you mean to terminate the batch file. In protected mode, the batch file is immediately cancelled.

- Your Autoexec.bat and Startup.cmd files offer you a host of useful applications. Besides automating the system startup, you can change the default system prompt and automate anything you wish at power-up time. This ranges from automatically running any OS/2 command, to starting a program in a new screen group, to even detaching a separate background process that requires no keyboard input.

- Batch files can contain a series of sequentially executed commands or programs, or even other batch files.

- Batch files can be invoked as easily as any OS/2 command, by simply typing the name of the batch file. This allows you to create your own set of specialized add-on OS/2 commands.

- Variable parameters make your batch files very flexible in terms of when and how you can use them. These variables are referred to as %0, %1, %2, %3, and so on through %9.

- Variable parameters that have names, rather than numbers, can be created as environmental variables and then referenced from within batch files as *%name%*.

- OS/2 has a variety of specialized commands that only work from within batch files. These subcommands provide OS/2 with the kind of features normally reserved for a high-level computer language.

- Messages can be included for internal documentation with the REM subcommand. You can also choose to display or suppress messages and command lines during the execution of the batch program with the ECHO ON or OFF subcommand and the @ character.

- Batch files can contain the standard logic seen in most programming languages. Branching is managed by the GOTO subcommand in conjunction with simple labels, decision making is provided with the IF subcommand, and you can implement true programming subroutines by using the CALL subcommand.

- The FOR subcommand controls the sophisticated features of looping and command repetition.

- You can interrupt your own batch program temporarily with the PAUSE subcommand or permanently with the Break key combination.

- The SETLOCAL command enables you to create temporary copies of environmental variables for use during a protected mode batch file. The previous variable values are restored by OS/2 when the batch file ends, or when you issue the ENDLOCAL command.

- The EXTPROC command gives sophisticated users the ability to substitute their own batch file processor for the standard one included in Cmd.exe.

- Batch files can be used to create simple but functional menu systems to drive the most sophisticated application setup.

- Batch files can simplify consistent instruction sequences and variable parameters allow you to repeat critical application tasks automatically.

- A batch file quickly and automatically invokes any application program that is nested in its own subdirectory structure. The current directory and OS/2 path can be set up before program execution and restored afterwards.

- You can make batch files that will prepare and initialize your RAM disk automatically. This increases system efficiency and improves response time.

- Color monitors can be controlled easily through judicious batch-file development. You saw how a single batch file can make short work of setting the foreground and background colors on color screens.

- With batch files, you can create customized system help features, as well as an appointment reminder system. You can also broadcast messages to system users. These features can be very useful on systems that involve many people sharing the computer at different times.

- You also learned a couple of new tricks for dealing with RAM disks. Batch programs can load main word processing, spreadsheet, or database programs onto a RAM disk, and then execute the RAM-resident version of the main program using data files from your hard disk.

- The OS/2 environment can also be used with batch files to manage a password control system.

Congratulations! There is nothing more you need to know about batch files in OS/2. You can now develop your own new batch files whenever you like, adding to the customized flexibility of your OS/2 system. Batch files give you the ability to collect and coalesce OS/2 features, and to essentially create your own new commands. The subject of the next chapter is the system configuration file. With Config.sys and an incredibly broad range of special commands, you can go inside your OS/2 system to customize it even further.

CUSTOMIZING YOUR OS/2 SYSTEM

NEARLY ALL THE FEATURES YOU'VE LEARNED ABOUT in OS/2 have their own well-specified syntax, function, and results. Behind the scenes, however, you'll find additional important features over which you have considerable control. If you understand and use them, you can create a personalized operating system that is both flexible and efficient. In this chapter, you'll take a detailed look at how you can customize your system and contour it to your exact uses. You'll find out how to reconfigure OS/2 by resetting any of the parameters available to you in the Config.sys file.

CONFIGURING OS/2'S INTERNAL SETTINGS

Customization takes many faces in OS/2. It can involve specifying the country in which you are using your machine, setting up memory management options like task swapping, or even scheduling algorithms for determining time allocation to tasks. Each setup variable is controlled by a single specification line of the Config.sys file. If the Config.sys file is not created by you or the installation task, or if it is later removed or deleted, OS/2 initializes itself with a set of default values for all of these variables. Table 9.1 lists these default values.

The Config.sys file must reside in the root directory of the boot disk. You can use OS/2's TYPE command to display the current contents of the Config.sys file by typing

    TYPE Config.sys

CONFIGURATION COMMAND	**DEFAULT VALUE**
BREAK	OFF
BUFFERS	10
CODEPAGE	437(United States)
COUNTRY	001
DEVICE	none
DEVINFO	none
DISKCACHE	0
FCBS	16,8
IOPL	YES
LIBPATH	C:\
MAXWAIT	3
MEMMAN	swap,move(hard disk) noswap,move(floppy disk)
PRIORITY	DYNAMIC
PROMPT	YES
PROTECTONLY	NO
PROTSHELL	Cmd.exe
REM	none
RMSIZE	variable
RUN	none
SHELL	Command.com
SWAPPATH	C:\
THREADS	50
TIMESLICE	variable

Table 9.1: Config.sys Default Values

If no Config.sys file is currently on your disk, you can create it by using a line editor or a word processor. If a Config.sys file already exists, make any necessary replacements, corrections, or additions to that file. But be sure you fully understand the purpose of every line before you remove or replace any of them with additional configuration commands.

Both real and protected modes are initialized with Config.sys, the only configuration file OS/2 uses or needs. Some commands are relevant to both modes, while others apply only to real mode. However, none of your adjusted Config.sys lines will take effect until after you reboot the system. OS/2 reads and sets internal parameters at startup, and this is the only time the Config.sys file is read and acted on.

There are three primary classes of configuration commands. Table 9.2 summarizes all the commands within each class, and presents a brief definition of their functions. This chapter discusses each command in detail. They are presented alphabetically within each of the three major sections.

The most useful commands for the average user are the standard configuration commands. You will often find it necessary to set the values they control to ensure that your application environment will work at all. Commands in this category include BREAK, BUFFERS, DEVICE, FCBS, LIBPATH, PROMPT, REM, RMSIZE, RUN, and SWAPPATH.

The second major classification of configuration commands offer advanced control of operating system parameters. These commands are not needed by the average user; in fact, you should not adjust them unless you understand them clearly and an application specifically requires them. Inappropriate setting of these commands can severely impede the proper processing of applications and tasks run under OS/2. The commands include IOPL, MAXWAIT, MEM-MAN, PRIORITY, PROTSHELL, PROTECTONLY, SHELL, THREADS, and TIMESLICE.

The commands in the last group relate to country-specific operations of OS/2 and are also infrequently used. Use the CODEPAGE, COUNTRY, and DEVINFO commands if you are running OS/2 outside the United States, or are working with files created by DOS or OS/2 users in another country. These commands, as well as the others mentioned earlier, are compatible in format, purpose, and functionality with the latest national language support commands in DOS 3.3.

BREAK is the only configuration command that can be run at the OS/2 prompt. The rest must be included in the Config.sys file if they are to have any impact at all on system configuration.

	COMMAND NAME	FUNCTION
Standard Config.sys commands:	BREAK	Controls checking for Ctrl-C keypresses
	BUFFERS	Indicates number of memory buffers
	DEVICE	Specifies device driver
	FCBS	Indicates number of file control blocks
	LIBPATH	Indicates directory with dynamic link modules
	PROMPT	Displays message on error
	REM	Documents remarks
	RMSIZE	Allocates physical memory to real mode
	RUN	Loads and runs application tasks
	SWAPPATH	Specifies swapping file directory
Advanced Config.sys commands:	DISKCACHE	Creates memory buffer to speed up disk I/O
	IOPL	Grants input/output privileges
	MAXWAIT	Indicates maximum wait time before priority adjustment
	MEMMAN	Manages swapping and segment relocation

Table 9.2: Classes of Configuration Commands

	COMMAND NAME	FUNCTION
Advanced Config.sys commands (continued):	PRIORITY	Specifies dynamic versus absolute
	PROTECTONLY	Controls whether real mode is configured
	PROTSHELL	Specifies the protected mode shell program
	SHELL	Sets up alternate real mode command processor
	THREADS	Indicates number of threads to be managed
	TIMESLICE	Defines time allocation for task processing
Country-specific commands:	CODEPAGE	Sets character set tables used by devices
	COUNTRY	Initializes display/printing values
	DEVINFO	Prepares physical device for code page switching

Table 9.2: Classes of Configuration Commands (continued)

USING THE STANDARD CONFIGURATION COMMANDS

The commands in this section are the most commonly-used in any OS/2 environment. Nearly all applications require you to expand the value of the OS/2 BUFFERS command or to set the amount of memory reserved for real mode. Because the standard configuration commands control these and other commonly-used variables, they will probably be the most important commands you will learn.

STOPPING TASK EXECUTION

The BREAK command tells OS/2 how frequently to check the keyboard for the Ctrl-C keypress. The only time OS/2 normally looks for a Ctrl-C is when it is communicating with your screen or printer, but you can configure OS/2 to test more frequently by setting the BREAK parameter on. The syntax of this command is

BREAK = [ON | OFF]

The default value is BREAK = OFF. If you set BREAK on, OS/2 checks for Ctrl-C each time a program issues a system call. This happens often, and gives you closer control over when to interrupt an executing program. BREAK works only in real mode, and only if the PROTECTONLY command (see later in this chapter) is set to NO, or does not exist at all in your Config.sys file.

CONTROLLING THE NUMBER OF DISK BUFFERS

A *disk buffer* is a 512-byte portion of memory used by OS/2 for temporary placement of data when reading or writing to a disk. The default number of disk buffers (10) used by OS/2 is only marginally acceptable to any serious business environment. The BUFFERS command allows you to increase the number of buffers OS/2 uses. The syntax for this command is

BUFFERS = *n*

No one buffer setting is perfect for every use. A buffer setting of 10 might be perfect for a simple word processing environment, a setting of 20 might do for a database environment, but a setting of 40 might be best for an environment in which one task recalculates spreadsheet values, while another performs database management operation. Experimenting with the BUFFERS value to find the proper number for a particular application environment has always guided DOS users, and the same is true for OS/2. Setting a BUFFERS value of 40 or 50 is probably reasonable for an unknown but average OS/2 operating environment.

Don't forget that each buffer takes up 512 bytes, so a setting of BUFFERS = 50 costs you 25K of available physical memory. You can see why you should have *at least* 1.5 megabytes of real physical memory before running any serious applications under OS/2. Two megabytes is probably a more appropriate minimum for installed RAM, especially if you will be using real mode in addition to protected mode.

INSTALLING ADDITIONAL DEVICE DRIVERS

The DEVICE configuration command allows you to specify a file name that contains the device information for controlling extra OS/2 devices. Chapter 2 looked at the standard devices included with OS/2: Ansi.sys, Com.sys, Ega.sys, Extdskdd.sys, Mouse*xx*.sys, and Vdisk.sys. The syntax required to include one of these installable device drivers is

DEVICE = *drivername* [*parameters*]

Remember that installing a mouse device driver (Mouse*xx*.sys) also requires you to install the special driver for pointing devices. This is done with a DEVICE = Pointdd.sys entry in your Config.sys file.

Anything other than the standard device drivers usually requires a new .sys file from the manufacturer. All of your .sys files must be kept in the root directory of the boot drive, because at bootstrap time, the OS/2 file system does not have enough information about the directory structure to look anywhere but in the root.

DEFINING THE NUMBER OF OPEN FILE CONTROL BLOCKS

The FCBS real mode command is necessary only with older applications, because file handles have replaced file control blocks (FCBs) as the method for accessing files. If you are running an older DOS application that requires an FCB setting, this command allows compatibility with the old requirement. The syntax is

FCBS = *x,y*

x represents the total number of files that OS/2 real mode keeps open, ranging from 1 to 255. *y* specifies the number of files that *must* remain open no matter what else goes on. This value of *y* ranges from from 0 to 255, and must be less than or equal to the *x* value.

The default values of *x* and *y* are 16 and 8, respectively. Remember that because this old style setting works only in real mode, the PRO-TECTONLY command in Config.sys either must be set to NO, or shouldn't exist at all as a command entry in Config.sys.

LOCATING THE DYNAMIC LINK MODULES

OS/2 makes it easier for programmers to prepare smaller and more flexible applications. It allows special linking libraries to be stored in a particular subdirectory. The LIBPATH configuration command allows you to specify the location of the dynamic link libraries in your directory structure. Its format is

LIBPATH = *drive:path*[;*drive:path*][...]

This configuration command looks somewhat like the well-known DOS PATH environmental variable, which is also available in OS/2. When DOS or OS/2 use the PATH setting, the default directory is always searched before the path is followed. When OS/2 uses the LIBPATH setting, however, it searches one or more directories in the listed order. The default directory is not even searched unless it is on the LIBPATH.

A common technique might be to define a subdirectory called Library, and store all dynamic link library modules there. In this case, include a line in your Config.sys file of the following sort:

LIBPATH = C:\Library

If you do not specify a LIBPATH entry in your Config.sys file, it is assumed that the root of your boot disk contains any required dynamic link libraries.

HANDLING ERRORS DURING CONFIGURATION

The PROMPT command instructs OS/2 how to acknowledge errors during configuration. It is completely different from the OS/2

PROMPT command that controls the appearance of your command line prompt (see Chapter 5). The syntax is straightforward:

PROMPT = ON | OFF

If this is omitted, the default setting is ON, and the system will pause when any configuration command error occurs. The message ''Press ENTER to continue'' will appear, enabling you to decide whether to continue.

If you set PROMPT to OFF, OS/2 will ignore any errors it encounters and it will not display an error message. Configuration will continue with the next line in the Config.sys file.

DOCUMENTING YOUR CONFIGURATION FILE

The REM command in the Config.sys file permits the inclusion of simple text remarks. Similar to the REM subcommand in batch files, it is designed to allow you to document your configuration file. Simply enter

REM *textstring*

where *textstring* is any explanatory message you want to incorporate into your Config.sys file at any point.

RESERVING MEMORY FOR REAL MODE APPLICATIONS

The RMSIZE command is critical to running DOS applications in an OS/2 environment. It allows you to specify the portion of total physical memory to be reserved for real mode operations. DOS 3.x uses physical memory entirely for itself and its applications. OS/2 goes well beyond that. In order to run DOS programs, you must carve out a portion of physical memory in OS/2. The syntax for this request is

RMSIZE = *x*

x specifies the number of kilobytes to allocate to real mode operations, and can range from 0 to 640.

Use this command along with the Config.sys PROTECTONLY command, which must either be set to NO, or not be included in the Config.sys file at all. In that case, task operations are not then restricted to only protected mode.

RUNNING TASKS AT SYSTEM INITIALIZATION TIME

The RUN command loads up and initiates an application task during system initialization. Required syntax is

RUN = [*drive:*][*path*]filename [*parameters*]

> Programs that are RUN directly from the Config.sys file must be specified completely; that is, you must include the .com or .exe extension as part of the file name.

You can initiate more than one protected mode program from the Config.sys file by including several RUN commands. All device commands are treated first, even if they follow RUN commands in the Config.sys file. You might use RUN to initiate programs that always need to be up and running in your system, such as a program managing seat assignments in a theater box-office system.

LOCATING THE DISK SWAPPING FILE

Swapping is a sophisticated action taken by OS/2 when multiple tasks are running and there is insufficient physical memory for all of them to be in memory simultaneously. *Segments*, or logical portions of the running task, can be temporarily written out to disk, freeing up memory areas to be used for another task. OS/2 uses an advanced scheduling algorithm to decide which task will take priority. Tasks placed on temporary hold by OS/2 may have portions of their operating memory written out to a special file on the disk, the *swap file*. The configuration command, SWAPPATH, defines the drive and an optional path on that drive to which OS/2 writes any temporarily created swap files. Required format for this command is

SWAPPATH = [*drive:*][*path*]

You can define the swapping path to be any drive or directory (the root directory of the boot drive is the default), but it is best to define it as the root directory of your fastest available hard disk drive. The speed of system operations often depends on how quickly portions of a task can be swapped out and later swapped back in. From the point of view of your hardware, the fastest disk assures that this occurs as quickly as possible. From the point of view of your software, placing the swapping path in the root directory of that drive assures that there will be the least possible overhead in finding the physical site on the disk for the swapping file.

ADVANCED OPERATIONAL CONTROL COMMANDS

This second class of configuration commands includes advanced features rarely adjusted by most users. Nearly all of these commands control advanced operating system aspects, or manage the subtle interplay among tasks. All require you to have a sophisticated understanding of OS/2 design and performance in order to make an informed decision about adjusting their values. The fact that they are provided at all suggests an important advance in the operating system that will most benefit advanced programmers and systems designers wishing to adjust the performance of a sophisticated application processing environment.

SETTING UP DISK CACHING

The DISKCACHE configuration command allows you to specify a portion of memory to be reserved for disk caching operations. The principle behind this sophisticated disk buffering scheme is seen in Figure 9.1. An application task requiring code or data information from a disk file requests OS/2 to obtain that information from the disk drive. Under normal conditions, OS/2 fulfills the request and transfers the information directly to the application task. When a disk cache is set up, however, OS/2 first transfers that information to a memory buffer (cache) and then transfers it to the application. The extra step slightly increases overhead on system operation, but occurs at such fast memory speeds that this increase is insignificant.

The advantage of a disk cache is that later requests for the same data can be very quickly satisfied. OS/2 realizes that the requested data has already been placed in memory and can immediately make

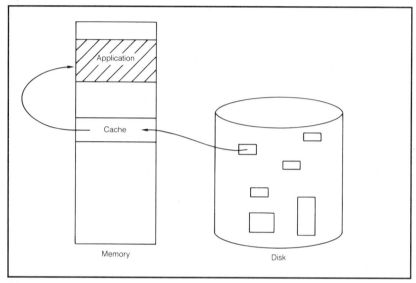

Figure 9.1: Disk caching in OS/2

a direct transfer from the memory resident portion of the cache buffer to the application, instead of undergoing the much slower task of locating and reading in the information from its disk location. The format for this command is

DISKCACHE = *nnn*

nnn represents the number of kilobytes that you wish OS/2 to allocate from available physical memory for caching operations. When you use memory as a cache buffer, you achieve speedup based on a reduced frequency of disk access. However, you take memory away from other multitasking operations. This may potentially force more frequent disk references.

There is no single formula to guide you in deciding whether to use a disk cache and selecting the amount of memory you want to allocate. Sophisticated performance measurements often underlie your final decision. Consider assigning no more than 25 percent of your physical memory to the disk cache, and reduce it to below 25 percent if you plan to increase the number of simultaneously running tasks. For example, if your system has two megabytes of physical memory, you might consider setting DISKCACHE to 512. However, if your system will be running spreadsheet recalculations as one task, communications transfer as another task, database updating as a third task, and a C compilation as yet a fourth task, you should consider reducing the cache buffer size to 256.

GRANTING INPUT/OUTPUT PRIVILEGES

Sophisticated programs sometimes use direct I/O instructions. In OS/2, this represents advanced and potentially complex ground. The IOPL configuration command allows you to specify whether I/O activity is to be permitted by any task requesting it. The syntax of this command is

    IOPL = YES | NO

The default is IOPL = YES. This means that the privilege of performing data input and output is granted to any task that asks for it. Because the default is YES, you need to include this line only if you or your application program specifically wants to inhibit this I/O privilege.

AFFECTING THE SCHEDULING ALGORITHM

Scheduling is at the heart and soul of any sophisticated multitasking operating system. No task may run until the OS/2 scheduler gives control to it. To ensure that tasks will not necessarily have to wait forever, OS/2's MAXWAIT configuration command gives you some control over the automatic adjustment factor in the scheduling algorithm.

The required format is

    MAXWAIT = n

where n is the maximum number of seconds a task may wait before OS/2 increases its standing in the priority queue. Normally, any task that has not had a chance to execute in three seconds (the default value of n) has its priority adjusted upward by OS/2. This makes it more likely that the task will have a chance to run during the current execution cycle.

CONTROLLING
THE MEMORY MANAGEMENT ALGORITHM

Specifying combinations of memory management algorithms used by OS/2 is useful only in certain dedicated or time dependent system environments. The MEMMAN configuration command requires the following syntax:

MEMMAN = *swapvalue,movevalue*

The *swapvalue* either enables (= swap) or disables (= noswap) memory swapping. The *movevalue* allows OS/2 to relocate data segments (= move) or not (= nomove). The three valid combinations of these parameters are discussed below.

MEMORY MANAGEMENT FOR HARD DISKS The setting for hard disks (shown below) includes memory swapping and automatic relocation of data segments as needed:

MEMMAN = swap,move

This is the most efficient setting for a typical hard disk based system. OS/2 uses a timesharing algorithm to provide limited physical memory resources to all requesting tasks. Requesting tasks can address up to one gigabyte of virtual memory, but no more than 16MB of physical memory. In fact, if swapping is permitted, all tasks will have a chance to execute, regardless of the size of physical memory.

OS/2 swaps segment information assigned to one task into a swapping file (specified by the SWAPPATH configuration parameter), whenever necessary. This usually occurs when physical memory is required by a higher priority task, and an insufficient amount of free memory currently exists. When the first task needs to execute again, swapping occurs in reverse order; the first task will be assigned physical memory as necessary to allow it to run. In the typical multitasking environment, many tasks are trying to run at the same time. If there is not enough physical memory for all of these tasks to be resident concurrently, system performance in a busy environment measurably improves when swapping is enabled.

MEMORY MANAGEMENT FOR FLOPPY DISKS The setting for OS/2 systems booted from a floppy disk should not include automatic swapping:

MEMMAN = noswap,move

Swapping is disabled because of the relatively slow access time of a floppy disk system, but segment relocation (which can occur at memory speed) is permitted to enhance internal performance.

MEMORY MANAGEMENT FOR DEDICATED SYSTEMS If you are running a system devoted to a special purpose application only, you should disable the overhead of disk-based swapping, as well as the overhead of internal segment relocation. This then reduces the OS/2 performance overhead, and increases your application program's performance.

MEMMAN = noswap,nomove

This setting should only be used for dedicated time-critical system operations, such as robotic-controlled factories or radar tracking systems.

CONTROLLING TASK PRIORITIES

You have some control over OS/2 prioritization, the mechanism that decides the order in which tasks will run. You can specify the priority configuration command, PRIORITY, with a value of either absolute or dynamic:

PRIORITY = ABSOLUTE | DYNAMIC

OS/2 typically defaults this value to dynamic. A sophisticated, priority-based algorithm is used here to determine which one of perhaps several tasks should run within each timeslice (see the section on the TIMESLICE command later in this chapter). Normal OS/2 tasks have 32 internal priority levels, which OS/2 sets. As OS/2 runs it allocates resources to tasks, and these priority values are adjusted dynamically up or down both to fit the algorithm and to assure a reasonable and fair distribution of system usage and resources.

If you have an unusual system that is quite limited in the kind of tasks it runs, you can set PRIORITY to ABSOLUTE. This switches off the variable algorithmic logic, and switches on a simplistic first-come first-served logic. A standard office environment should never set the priority to ABSOLUTE, but instead should accept the default value. Most tasks are interactive, and require only small resources for small amounts of time. An absolute priority scheme can subjugate every task to the whims of one demanding program.

SELECTING BETWEEN PROTECTED AND REAL OPERATIONS

The PROTECTONLY configuration command allows protected mode only operations in OS/2 if it is set to YES. You can also set it to NO, although this is already the default if you do not include the command in your Config.sys file. The syntax is

PROTECTONLY = YES | NO

This command is one of OS/2's many double-edged swords. If you set PROTECTONLY to YES, you allow OS/2 to use all available physical memory for protected mode application tasks. If you set PROTECTONLY to NO, a portion of physical memory will be reserved for real mode application, but won't be available for protected tasks. The amount of physical memory reserved for real mode operations is based on the RMSIZE command seen earlier in this chapter.

If you intend to run any former DOS programs (3.x and earlier), you must make sure that PROTECTONLY is set to NO, either explicitly or by default.

LOADING A DIFFERENT PROTECTED MODE COMMAND PROCESSOR

The PROTSHELL configuration command allows you to specify a completely different executable module to be used as the protected mode command shell. A *command shell* is a program that interprets the commands you enter at the system prompt. With care and skill, you can create a modified version of the Cmd.exe shell program provided to you with OS/2. The version of this command usually included in your Config.sys file (even in the default Config.sys supplied with your system) is

PROTSHELL = [drive:][path]Shell.exe Cmd.exe [parameters]

This version of the command requires that both the Shell.exe and your Cmd.exe files be accessible.

The default assumption is that Cmd.exe will be read in from disk and used as the protected mode command processor. System programmers designing their own protected mode command shell program should use the PROTSHELL command to tell OS/2 the location of their customized command processor.

Since Cmd.exe does take two possible switches (see the CMD command in Chapter 5), you can add either the /c or /k switches at the end of the PROTSHELL command line. This way, you can ensure that the environment is initialized for *each new protected mode session*:

PROTSHELL = Shell.exe Cmd.exe /k C:\Initenv

In this example PROTSHELL entry, OS/2's standard protected mode command processor (Cmd.exe) is loaded. Using the /k switch directs Cmd.exe to be kept in memory, after running the specified batch file C:Initenv.cmd. This standard Initenv.cmd batch file included with your system initializes several environment variables; any other program or batch file could be substituted on this line, however, and it would be run at the start of each new protected mode session.

LOADING THE REAL MODE COMMAND PROCESSOR

In real mode, OS/2 reads in Command.com as its standard real mode shell program. As with DOS 3.x, you can write or modify your own command processor, and use the SHELL command to tell OS/2 where to find this new or modified real mode shell program. The syntax is

SHELL = [*drive:*][*path*]program [*parameters*]

The SHELL command only affects real mode operation, and is meaningful only if OS/2 has been configured to run real mode (PROTECTONLY = NO).

SPECIFYING THE NUMBER OF TASK THREADS

As a user, you know what application tasks your computer is running. Internal to each of those tasks are a number of executing *threads*. A thread in a task is a logical sequence of instructions that can be independently scheduled by OS/2. Threads are fundamental to multitasking and simultaneous operations. A task can contain one or more threads, depending on how many simultaneous operations can be programmed into that task. Multiple tasks can therefore contain multiple threads. OS/2 itself requires additional system resources to manage multiple threads. During configuration, you can specify the maximum number of threads that your operating environment will demand. The syntax is

    THREADS = n

OS/2 defaults the number of threads to 50, but you can increase it to 255. The more programs and complex tasks that you run, the larger the value of threads must be. The default of 50 is sufficient for simple operations. Consult your applications documentation for advice on increasing this number. But don't blindly increase it. The larger it becomes, the fewer system resources remain for OS/2 operations, and the greater the performance impact on your operating environment.

SETTING THE TIMESLICE VALUES

OS/2 schedules tasks to run for a certain amount of time (a slice). The TIMESLICE configuration command specifies the minimum amount of time allocated to a task, and can also allocate the maximum allowable time. The conventional view of timeslices is shown in Figure 9.2, where time is divided into small slices, the smallest one being the minimum amount of time that the operating system can manage. In OS/2 this minimum amount of time, represented by x, is

31 milliseconds. The syntax for this command is

TIMESLICE = $x[,y]$

OS/2 sets timeslice values according to its internal algorithm, unless you specify this command line in your Config.sys file. x is the minimum, and when specified, y is the maximum time in milliseconds that OS/2 allows a given task before it interrupts to check on the demands and needs of other running tasks. The y value is optional; if it is not set, OS/2 sets both minimum and maximum timeslice values according to the value you give to x.

SUPPORTING NATIONAL LANGUAGE OPERATIONS

This final class of configuration commands is necessary only if your OS/2 system operates outside the United States, or if you work

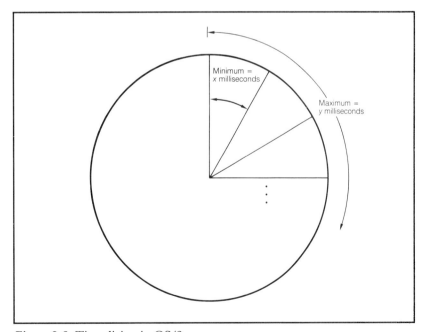

Figure 9.2: Timeslicing in OS/2

with files created in other countries or for users in other countries. The CODEPAGE command specifies the set of characters used for displays, printers, and keyboards. The COUNTRY command specifies time, date, and currency symbols for different countries. The DEVINFO command prepares a specialized output device for switching between code pages.

SELECTING A SYSTEM CODE PAGE

An OS/2 code page is a table of characters defining the symbols (letters, numbers, punctuation, and graphics) that you can display or print on your system at any given moment. Because there are five possible sets of these characters (see Table 9.3), the CODEPAGE command permits you to configure your system to include all of the different characters on these different code pages. The required syntax is

CODEPAGE = *xxx*[,*yyy*]

xxx and *yyy* allow you to specify up to two of the five different code page values listed in Table 9.3. These are the same code page values available in DOS 3.3.

If you don't include the CODEPAGE command in your Config.sys file, OS/2 uses standard default values for a monitor, keyboard, and printer. If you use code pages with certain devices that can support the related character sets, you must also use the DEVINFO command. (DEVINFO is fully discussed in a later section.)

VALUE	CODEPAGE NAME
437	United States
850	Multilingual
860	Portuguese
863	Canadian French
865	Nordic

Table 9.3: Code Page Values

SELECTING A COUNTRY OF OPERATION

The COUNTRY command allows you to customize some aspects of the keyboard, display, and printer operations. At a minimum, it specifies which country's character set is to be used. The required syntax is

COUNTRY = *xxx*

Code *xxx* indicates the country for which your system is being initialized. Table 9.4 shows the correspondence between your selected country code and the default code pages, as well as the assumed keyboard layout for that country. Country codes and code page definitions are constantly being added to OS/2, so Table 9.4 is a partial list only. Your OS/2 users manual carries the current complete list.

PREPARING DEVICES FOR CODE PAGE SWITCHING

The DEVINFO command works with the CODEPAGE command to allow specific input/output peripheral devices to switch between code pages. The syntax is

DEVINFO = *devtype,subtype,[path]filename,[ROM = [(]xxx[,yyy)]]*

You need one DEVINFO command in your Config.sys file for each device that you want to switch between code pages. Table 9.5 clarifies each of the parameters in the DEVINFO command line.

SUMMARY

Each time OS/2 boots up, it searches in the root directory of the boot drive for Config.sys, the file that configures your OS/2 system to operate in both real and protected modes. Config.sys gives you the ability to customize OS/2 according to your own needs. The wide range of operating parameters are controlled by simple command lines you may add to, change, or delete. Some of these commands work only for real mode. There are three classes of these configuration commands: standard, advanced, and country-specific.

COUNTRY CODE	COUNTRY NAME	CODE PAGES
001	United States	437,850
002	Canada (French)	863,850
003	Latin America	437,850
031	Netherlands	437,850
032	Belgium	437,850
033	France	437,850
034	Spain	437,850
039	Italy	437,850
041	Switzerland	437,850
044	United Kingdom	437,850
045	Denmark	865,850
046	Sweden	437,850
047	Norway	865,850
049	Germany	437,850
061	Australia (English)	437,850
351	Portugal	860,850
358	Finland	437,850

Table 9.4: Partial List of Country Codes

The standard configuration commands most frequently employed for OS/2 system configuration are listed below:

- BREAK: Controls how frequently OS/2 checks in real mode for Ctrl-C key presses.

- BUFFERS: Sets the number of memory buffers to be used by OS/2.

- DEVICE: Adds a new device driver to the system.

- FCBS: Sets the number of file control blocks.

- LIBPATH: Indicates which directory contains the dynamic link modules.

Parameter	Function
devtype	Specifies the type of device as either Lpt1, Lpt2, Lpt3, Prn, Kbd, Scr.
subtype	Specifies the precise physical device type, such as an EGA display.
filename	Specifies the file name containing the necessary keyboard translation tables (for a keyboard device) or the code page tables (for a display or printer). If the path is not specified, OS/2 looks in the root directory of the boot drive.
ROM	Indicates one or two code pages available in an output device's ROM or available in a cartridge for insertion into that output device. *xxx* identifies the primary code page, while *yyy* identifies the secondary code page.

Table 9.5: Parameter Specifications for the DEVINFO Command

- PROMPT: Controls whether or not an error will pause the configuration process.

- REM: Inserts text documentation into the Config.sys file.

- RMSIZE: Specifies the portion of physical memory to be allocated for real mode operations.

- RUN: Loads and begins an application task at the end of the system initialization procedure.

- SWAPPATH: Defines the location of the OS/2 swapping file.

The second class of configuration commands, the advanced operational control commands, includes the following:

- DISKCACHE: Assigns a variable length memory buffer to be used as a holding site for disk sector information, thereby speeding up disk I/0.

- IOPL: Enables or disables input/output privileges for requesting tasks.

- MAXWAIT: Influences the amount of time any task will wait before it moves up the priority ladder.

- MEMMAN: Controls whether swapping and segment relocation occur.

- PRIORITY: Controls whether the standard dynamic prioritization occurs, or whether tasks will be serviced on a first-come, first-served, absolute basis.

- PROTECTONLY: Indicates whether all memory is to be allocated for protected mode operations (PROTECT-ONLY = YES), or whether a certain amount (specified by RMSIZE) will be reserved for real mode operations (PRO-TECTONLY = NO).

- PROTSHELL: Specifies the protected mode shell program to use (usually Cmd.exe).

- SHELL: Specifies use of an alternate real mode command processor (instead of Command.com).

- THREADS: Indicates how many unique, simultaneously executing threads can be managed by your configured OS/2. The more threads you allow, the fewer system resources remain available to each of your tasks.

- TIMESLICE: Sets minimum and maximum processing times for execution of each task.

Country-specific configuration commands are necessary only for computer systems outside the United States, or for files created in other countries or for users in other countries. They include the following commands:

- CODEPAGE: Defines which character set tables will be used by any device.

- COUNTRY: Enables OS/2 to use the appropriate foreign punctuation and values for time, date, and currency indicators.

- DEVINFO: Prepares each physical device for code page switching.

Now that you've learned the extensive set of configuration capabilities in OS/2, there remains only one last major arena to cover in this presentation of OS/2: programming. Chapter 10 will deliver a necessary and useful introduction to this complex subject.

INTRODUCTION TO
PROGRAMMING IN OS/2 ___

CHAPTER *10*

IN THIS CHAPTER, YOU STEP INTO THE WORLD OF programming with OS/2. In a general and introductory way, you will learn more of what goes on behind the scenes: how OS/2 supports virtual memory and how it maps one gigabyte of virtual memory into 16MB of physical memory. This chapter discusses multitasking from the programmer's point of view, and explains how OS/2 assures memory protection between tasks. It compares the three methods for communicating between tasks—pipes, semaphores, and queues—and explains which method you should use for different applications. You'll find out more about scheduling and interrupt handling, and about the existence of multiple threads within individual OS/2 tasks.

You will be introduced to the range of system calls in OS/2 protected mode, as well as the subset of real mode system calls that facilitate compatibility between DOS and OS/2 environments. The new CALL mechanism is contrasted with the old Int 21H, and OS/2 error handling and programmer utilities are briefly presented.

MULTITASKING IN OS/2

As you've seen in this book, multitasking allows you to run a number of application programs at the same time. Individual applications can still be designed like old style application programs in DOS, which means that you can choose to have the application do one thing at a time. But this logical mechanism is not necessarily efficient. OS/2 allows you to design applications that can handle these formerly sequential steps in a simultaneous manner.

OS/2 interrupts real mode and protected mode applications in a similar way (based on CPU clock ticks). However, real mode applications receive this kind of service only after you consciously switch OS/2 to real mode.

Simultaneous operations in OS/2 are not limited only to multiple executing tasks visible from the Session Manager. You've learned that a number of background tasks, like print spooling, can be run at the same time as tasks visible on the Session Manager screen. A background task does not usually appear on the Session Manager, and must responsibly terminate itself when it is completed. Just as this large scale multitasking occurs, so can smaller scale *multithreading* occur within the tasks themselves. Most real mode tasks have only one executing thread, but it is possible to run multiple executing threads in one protected mode task. This is called multithreading. A thread is a logical sequence of instructions that receives systems services from OS/2. If these threads can be grouped and are relatively independent, they can be handled simultaneously by OS/2, which assigns CPU execution cycles to each thread according to a timeslicing algorithm. The important priority-based OS/2 scheduler program makes sophisticated assignments to threads within the tasks, based on TIMESLICE and PRIORITY values set up in the Config.sys file.

From a user's point of view, a task is simply an application program. The more formal definition of a task is an application program executing with OS/2-defined system resources like memory, disk space, or pipes. From the programmer's point of view, the one or more threads within each task are the real elements being allocated time by the processor. The programmer can opt to design an application that has several separate tasks, or multiple threads within a single task, or a combination of these two options.

For example, in Figure 10.1 you see a database management task (called DBMS) with four threads. Thread 1 represents a portion of internal code whose sole purpose is to look for keyboard interrupts and then accept the user input. Once user input is completed, information entered by the user is passed along to Thread 2 that can update a database file. Thread 1 becomes active again, waiting for more input, while Thread 2 manages its updating simultaneously. Thread 3, meanwhile, contains code that manages the preparation and spooling of a printed report based on the data updating the database. Threads 1, 2, and 3 operate simultaneously, while Thread 4 displays information on the screen at specific times. For instance, Thread 4 could keep the user informed by displaying the status of the updating process (Record 500 updated, Record 1000 updated, Record 1500 updated. . .), or it could display the status of the report preparation (a graphic thermometer symbol could indicate the percentage of a report already prepared, or actually spooled out for printing), or it could do both.

These four threads would have to be sequentially programmed to run in DOS, but with OS/2's multitasking and multithreading capabilities, the system designer can overlap them. But even with OS/2, multithreading works only to the extent that the threads are independent of one another, but still logically reference the same information. The speed of overall application throughput can be significantly increased by using the multithreading technique.

The example DBMS process we just looked at in Figure 10.1 might be visible on the Session Manager screen as a program called Dbms.exe, along with other programs like Wksheet.exe and Wp.exe. Figure 10.2 shows these three example tasks running simultaneously. All three rely on OS/2 to access system resources such as memory, disk files, and various hardware devices. The tasks themselves each have unique identification numbers, each may be assigned a unique swapfile when necessary, and each may be given access to various files, system pipes, program and data files, and virtual and physical memory. The threads existing in each task are the

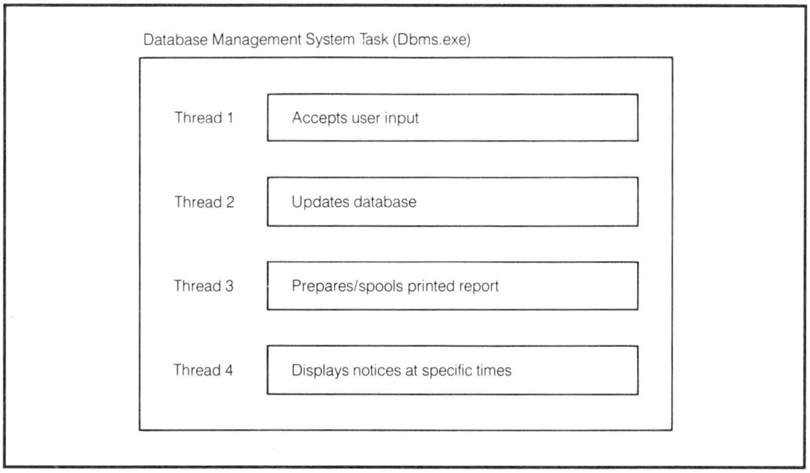

Figure 10.1: Inside an OS/2 task

actual units of execution, and receive specific amounts of time from the processor. Each thread is responsible for the nitty-gritty interaction with elements like stack pointers, and the state of any processor chips (i.e., 80286, 80287). When OS/2 switches between tasks as in Figure 10.2, it decides which thread in the task gains service based on issues like priority and length of time since last being serviced.

System calls create and terminate tasks and threads within the tasks. When you decide to write code using these system service calls (see Appendix D), be aware that built-in separation and protection between

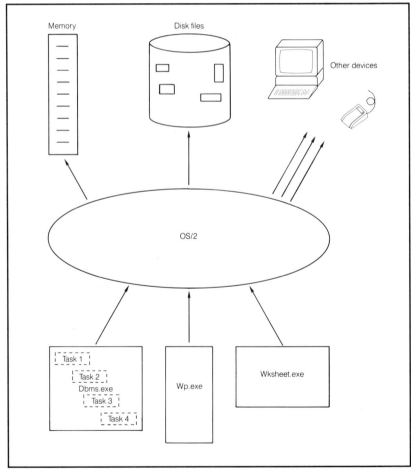

Figure 10.2: Multitasking and multithreading in OS/2

tasks means that creation and termination mechanisms are much faster for threads than for tasks. It is assumed that threads within a task are working in concert and support one another, and that they have been written by the same hand or by a team of programmers. Each thread within a task naturally has access to the same address space as every other thread. It is therefore far easier to share data between threads, and faster as well. You have many more options for manipulating data used by several threads than you have for manipulating data used by several tasks. For further information, refer to the section on interprocess communication later in this chapter.

MEMORY MANAGEMENT IN OS/2

OS/2 memory management allows an application to request and receive an apparent amount of memory (virtual memory) exceeding the actual physical memory available in the system. The previous DOS physical memory application limit of 640K is extended to 16MB with OS/2. OS/2 uses an ingenious memory management program to facilitate each task addressing up to an apparent one gigabyte (2^{30}) of virtual memory. Sophisticated techniques like storage overcommitment, segment movement, segment discard, and address and segment protection all support OS/2 memory management. In this section, you will explore the process of mapping virtual to physical memory, and the logical use of segment registers to enable this procedure. You will also see what local and global descriptor tables look like, and find out how they are used in this memory management procedure.

Figure 10.3 illustrates the OS/2 logical mapping procedure. Each process can believe it is addressing up to one gigabyte. The Memory Manager actually decides how to assign, or *map*, these virtual addresses to the more limited physical memory and real addresses available in your own OS/2 system. The swapping mechanism enables the Memory Manager to swap out the contents of various physical memory segments in order to free up memory for a task's referenced virtual addresses.

Running DOS applications under OS/2 requires that real mode be enabled through the RMSIZE command in Config.sys. As you learned in Chapter 1, all data segments and actual code for protected applications are loaded above the real mode area.

Figure 10.4 depicts how DOS programs manage memory. In the real mode environment, the programmer uses a segment plus offset address to locate the actual instruction or piece of data. This means that segment registers contain actual physical addresses, limiting real mode application to execution below one megabyte. Because the area between 640K and one megabyte is reserved for special ROM and video buffers, a DOS application executes below the real memory maximum of 640K.

In contrast, a protected mode application can execute at any address. Only the lowest 640K of physical memory is significantly

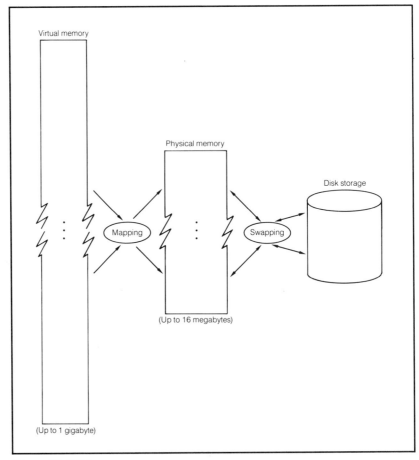

Figure 10.3: Memory management

affected when real mode is configured. If real mode is not configured, this lowest portion of physical memory is freed up for protected mode code and data segments. The new approach for addressibility in these applications is seen in Figure 10.5. Protected mode segment registers contain logical, not physical, segments. Each of the 16K segments contains 64K of virtual memory, totalling 16K times 64K, or one gigabyte.

Each application program has a unique address space providing potential access to the entire one gigabyte of virtual memory. Descriptor tables are used for mapping from the virtual address space of one gigabyte to the physical address space of up to 16MB.

A descriptor table like that in Figure 10.6 accounts for both the privacy or separateness of tasks and the mapping of virtual to physical memory. OS/2 provides each application (or task) with a *local descriptor table* (LDT). Each local descriptor table contains a series of the assigned logical segments discussed earlier. These logical segments are mapped by the Memory Manager into available memory at physical memory segments. Whenever necessary, the Memory Manager manages the swapping of physical memory segment contents out to a swap file to free up memory. The segment numbers in the affected local descriptor tables are adjusted. OS/2 maintains its

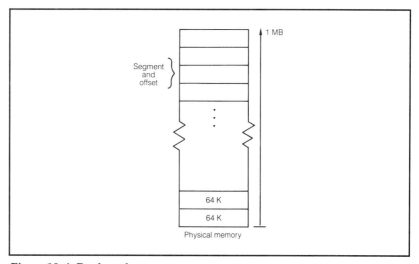

Figure 10.4: Real mode memory management

separateness from all executing tasks by mapping itself into actual physical memory addresses.

OS/2 also maintains one *global descriptor table* (GDT) for system-wide data and programs shared across all applications. Memory protection between programs is enforced by using the descriptor table concept seen again in Figure 10.7. Notice how virtual memory segment numbers for three separate tasks are listed in their own local descriptor tables. The globally shared logical selectors are listed in the special global descriptor table. The Memory Manager keeps track of the physical segments assigned to each task. Because the Memory Manager assures that no two virtual segments are simultaneously assigned to the same real physical segment, there can be no possible overlap of addressibility between separate tasks. As you can see, the

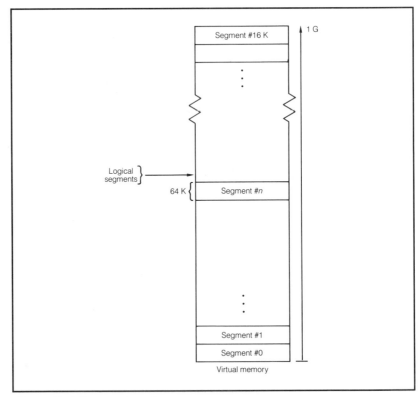

Figure 10.5: Protected mode memory management

protected mode system provides a close to ideal situation. It is not completely ideal because real mode programs are not truly isolated from protected mode programs; errors in real mode addressibility can still impact protected mode code and data.

None of this applies when any real mode program runs. A real mode program has the ability to address memory beyond itself, and can in effect crash the system. Because of its ability to run Int 21H service calls, it has the power to bring down the entire system if it does not work properly.

Two additional OS/2 operating system techniques are *segment discard* and *segment movement*. With segment discard, OS/2 uses a physical memory segment containing shared code or data (a *pure segment*) not currently used by a task, yet still existing in the descriptor table for

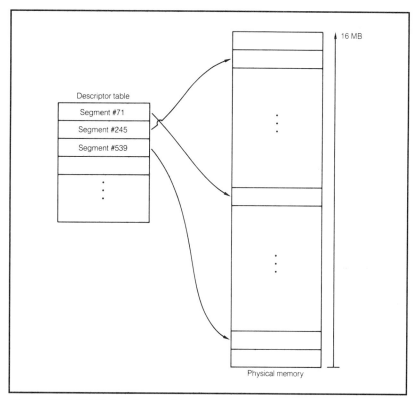

Figure 10.6: OS/2 descriptor tables

that application. Because there is no new information that has been written into this pure segment, OS/2 can immediately use the segment by simply discarding its contents and reassigning the physical memory segment to another task. If the discarded virtual segment is needed later, a new copy can be read in from the disk.

Because segments can be assigned and reassigned, and because they can be of variable lengths, gaps can occur in physical memory. In an active system, these individual gaps may be insufficient to meet a system request for additional memory. OS/2 segment movement moves segments as necessary (see the MEMMAN configuration command in Chapter 9), and merges them to generate a sufficient contiguous block of memory to satisfy the memory request.

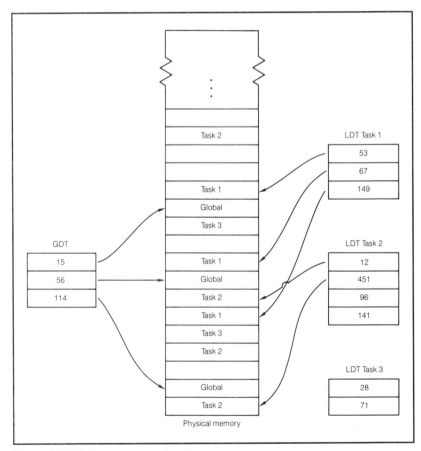

Figure 10.7: Memory protection between programs

USING INTERPROCESS COMMUNICATIONS IN OS/2

There are three basic methods of interprocess communications (IPC): semaphores, pipes, and queues. These mechanisms provide a wide range of possible communication services to use between tasks, as well as between threads within individual tasks. They greatly extend the nominal ability to pass information between a parent and child process.

A parent process can sometimes communicate information by using command strings or environment variables. In other cases, a child process can send an exit code back to the parent process, allowing the parent process to make decisions based on this exit code. (See Appendix C for more information on exit codes.) A more powerful way to communicate information, however, is to use one of the three mechanisms described in this section.

USING SEMAPHORES FOR HIGH-PERFORMANCE COMMUNICATIONS

Semaphores (sometimes called flags) are traditionally used for two purposes: to control access to shared code segments and to serially reusable resources (SRR). These resources are usually accessed by the code within a thread. A shared code segment is in essence a form of SRR, and can be treated by OS/2 in the same way.

Serially reusable resources are peripheral devices, files, or memory addresses, that cannot be successfully accessed by more than one thread at a time. They can be accessed and reused sequentially or serially, but not simultaneously. Semaphores give programmers a cooperative method to assure that these shared code segments, devices, or system resources are not simultaneously used. A semaphore representing the designated resource is a simple indicator that is either set or cleared. If it is set, it means that the resource is in use and no other thread needing that resource should use it. Threads can suspend or block themselves from continuing to execute while waiting to obtain ownership of the semaphore. By convention, no thread or task is allowed to access a resource unless it owns the representing semaphore.

There are two types of OS/2 semaphores. A RAM semaphore is a double word of data storage used either for simple signaling or to control resource contention between multiple threads in a single task. The semaphore itself is located in the task's address space and can be manipulated very quickly by any thread in the task.

The second type of semaphore, a system semaphore, is used for synchronization or signaling between tasks. Although it is also RAM resident, the double word of memory used is in OS/2's address space. Tasks can access it by using a pseudodirectory, called Sem, nominally in the root. For example, a semaphore called *animal* is accessible from different tasks by using the standard file naming convention: \Sem\Animal.

Use RAM semaphores to signal between threads. Use system semaphores to synchronize between tasks. RAM semaphores are far more common than system semaphores.

STRIKING A BALANCE WITH PIPES

Pipes are the interprocess communicators at the next level of power (see Chapter 6 for a discussion of automatically generated pipes). Unlike semaphores, they are not limited to a double word signal or indicator, but can contain up to 65,504 bytes of information. Because information is kept memory resident, the performance level of a pipe is similar to that of a semaphore. Pipes are usually used to pass information between tasks and to allow OS/2 to use a portion of memory to manage the number, location, and size of information being communicated.

Pipes are limited to a maximum size of approximately 64K. They are usually used to communicate between tasks rather than between threads. They are most commonly used for the automatic OS/2 communication of input and output between a parent and a child task, in contrast to using keyboard and screen as standard input and output devices. Reading and writing to a pipe is similar to reading and writing to a file, except that pipes in OS/2 are memory resident (unlike in DOS), and the transfer of information is thus much faster.

USING QUEUES FOR TOP-OF-THE-LINE COMMUNICATIONS

Queues are by far the slowest, yet by far the most flexible and powerful IPC supported in OS/2. A message queue is an arranged list of memory segments that can be shared. Each segment consists of separate information to be communicated, and can be as large as 64K. Queues are slow because the overhead to manage them is greatest. Since larger queue segment information is stored to a large extent on disk, the Memory Manager is intimately involved in the overhead.

Information communicated through queues is not copied, but rather passed along as shared memory segments. Since the shared memory segments are virtual, the Memory Manager determines how much of the communicated information can be placed in free memory, and how much should be put in swapping file storage on the disk. The possibility of storing shared memory segments in the swap file accounts for the overall slowness of an OS/2 queue.

OS/2 provides a series of system calls (see Appendix D) to create, open, close, read, and write information in queues. The queue name is similar to the semaphore structure. For programming, it takes a form like the following: \Queues\Filename. OS/2 returns a system handle whenever a queue is created, providing subsequent queue access. This means that any task can open and write queue information. Although each record in a queue represents a separately allocated portion of memory (up to 64K), total queue size has no limit (except the obvious limit on free memory and swap file space).

All records placed in a queue can be examined and removed selectively, so that standard First-In-First-Out (FIFO), Last-In-First-Out (LIFO), or other prioritization mechanisms can be implemented.

TRADEOFFS IN INTERPROCESS COMMUNICATION METHODS

Figure 10.8 summarizes some of the key characteristics of the three IPC methods supported by OS/2.

Semaphores, the simplest and fastest method, indicate that a task or thread owns a system resource; they can also symbolize a system event. Because you can implement the semaphore mechanism as a double word of memory storage (therefore resident), semaphores are fast and short, but cannot convey a lot of information. Tasks and threads employ semaphores by simply setting them, testing them, and clearing them to mark the availability of a serially reusable resource, or to mark the occurrence of an event.

Because the content of communicated information is memory resident, pipes are also reasonably fast, but they are still limited to a maximum created size of 64K. Unlike semaphores, pipes allow you to pass more than a double word of information, and the length and content of that information can vary. Pipes are usually used to communicate information between relatively independent tasks that intend to share input or output information.

Queues are the most powerful and flexible IPC method, though still the slowest. Multiple records of information can be passed from task to task with a queue, and each record can be as large as a single 64K pipe. The total amount of data is limited only by the amount of free memory and swapping space. This means that all of your system's virtual memory can be used in support of the queueing mechanism.

Although there are many variations on use and a reasonable degree of overlap, the most common programming usage of these

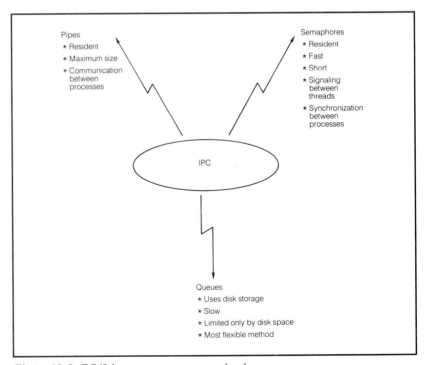

Figure 10.8: OS/2 interprocess communications

three IPC techniques is the following:

- Semaphores signal resource usage and event occurrence between threads within a task.

- Pipes communicate modest amounts of information between two loosely related tasks.

- Queues communicate a large amount of data from multiple tasks to a single task. The data records can be prioritized and treated in some logical order by the single task, manipulating data sent into the queue by the multiple submitting tasks. A printing or spooling task is a good example of just such an application arena, and perfectly fits the mechanism for which queues are designed.

APPLICATIONS PROGRAMMING FOR SOFTWARE DEVELOPERS

OS/2 offers two application programming interfaces for software developers. There are approximately two hundred system calls available in the complete OS/2 environment. All of these system functions are available via the call-return method, unlike old-style Int 21H system calls. (OS/2 still supports old-style system calls for programs running only in real mode.)

The protected mode supports all of OS/2's call-based services for managing files, memory, tasks, and devices. They constitute the kernel of OS/2, called the Application Programming Interface (API). There are a number of benefits to this new API call-return mechanism. Because the 80286 and 80386 chips can copy parameters from the requesting program's stack, the call mechanism represents a flexible means to achieve addressibility and system services, assuming variable parameters are pushed onto the stack prior to a protected mode call.

Additionally, high-level language programs can now make OS/2 calls directly by using the same structure used to invoke standard library routines in the high-level language, creating a more intuitive and easier to read body of program code. You can now access these calls directly from the high-level language, instead of having to go through high-level language library routines as in DOS applications.

The OS/2 *dynamic link* facility provides a major improvement in program development. With this new facility, linkage to called subroutines is not resolved until run time, a sharp contrast to static DOS mechanisms. Because common code modules do not have to be linked into each load module, each of the executable versions of files will be smaller. Special routines for handling exceptions do not have to be loaded initially, but can be automatically loaded at the necessary time. Because library modules are not bound (copied) into the final executable modules, the overall application programs can also be updated more easily. Only the library needs to be updated, rather than each separate executable program that references a library module. Each version of each program that has already been linked and loaded does not have to be rebound. Even if OS/2 changes some of its dynamic link modules, or one of your application packages changes, you don't have to modify final application code. Only the affected (dynamically linked) library module must be updated.

Using OS/2's dynamic link feature is no more difficult than DOS static linking is. When you declare external code to be EXTERNAL FAR, your high-level language compiler generates a standard external reference. During linking, dynamic link definition records are actually entered into the bound module. At execution time, these entries provide the connection between the referenced entry point and the file containing the actual code routine being called.

All of the complex IPC techniques are implemented through a variety of these API functions. Sophisticated programs should be much easier to write when you use these OS/2 functions for all operations. Appendix D lists each function available in OS/2 for applications programming development, along with a brief description of its use and the class of function it represents (*i.e.*, tasking, IPC, memory management, etc.).

A portion of the Applications Programming Interface is the subset of functions known as the Family Applications Programming Interface, or FAPI. You can use this subset in both protected and real mode. Any application using only FAPI can be linked to run in OS/2's protected mode, as well as in real mode. Some of these FAPI functions have specific restrictions in real mode. See the OS/2 programmer's guide for details about these restrictions. But see Appendix D for a list of system service calls unique to FAPI, as well as the ones that are restricted in real mode.

TIPS AND TECHNIQUES FOR OS/2 PROGRAMMING

If you program in assembly language under DOS or under OS/2 and are familiar with the 80286 or 80386 processor, you know that some instructions on these processors were not even defined and cannot be emulated on an 8088 or 8086 machine. If you intend to write programs to run under OS/2's protected mode, as well as on a DOS 3.x machine, avoid any of these instructions (see Appendix D). Using only FAPI functions is the best way to assure compatibility. Certain real-mode-only programming practices must be avoided if the application you write is to work in both protected mode on an 80286 machine, and on an 8088/8086 DOS 3.x machine. Some of the practices you should avoid are listed below; however, please refer to the *Microsoft Operating System/2 Programmer's Reference* for explanatory details.

- Do not rely on segment register contents to represent physical addresses. On DOS machines, segment registers contain physical address displacements, while on OS/2 machines, segment registers contain indexes into descriptor tables, which then contain the displacement values.

- Do not use segment registers for temporary value storage, or for segment arithmetic. Do not use tricks such as wraparound segment offsets.

- Do not address beyond the allocated size of a segment. In OS/2, doing so generates a hardware interrupt that aborts the task.

- Do not mix code and data in the same segment.

- Do not modify the contents of a code segment, because the 80286 does not allow writeable code segments.

- Use the appropriate OS/2 system calls for manipulating specific I/O ports.

- Do not use the CLI instruction; it generates a hardware interrupt (protection trap) on an 80286 machine. In protected mode, interrupts are not disabled by an INT instruction.

- Do not use shift counts in excess of 31. The number of bits used for masking differs on 80286 and 8086 processors. If you handle divide trap errors, you will have to process the code stream differently in each of the two different processors.

- Do not write any code that is dependent on the CPU speed.

- Do not single step an INT instruction, because the 8086 and 80286 chips work differently.

- Do not use the POPS instruction; it does not work the same way on the two different processors.

- Do not directly address video memory; always use OS/2 calls for this interface.

- Do not use old .com formats; they are direct memory images loaded at a particular memory address. Use the newer OS/2 .exe format, because these files are relocatable and provide additional header information to OS/2.

- Do not use any ROM support provided by your OEM.

- Use file handles instead of FCBs.

SUMMARY

Programming under OS/2 is a broad topic. Effective, correct, and successful programming requires an understanding of the nearly two hundred system calls enabling an application to manage multitasking, memory, interprocess communication, and a range of other system services. (See Appendix D for a summary of the system calls.)

- *Multitasking* in OS/2 is supported in protected mode. Many application programs can be run simultaneously.

- In addition to simultaneous tasks, each task can have its own set of logical code sequences called threads. Multithreading allows each task to run many of these code threads simultaneously. A thread is the actual entity scheduled by OS/2's priority-based, interrupt-driven scheduling algorithm.

- System resources are doled out and assigned to executing threads based on dynamic priorities. The Config.sys file allows a measure of control over the number of threads, the type of priority, and the timeslice assigned to executing threads.

- OS/2 maps virtual memory addresses and tasks to your system's physical memory by using special descriptor tables.

- The descriptor table technique enforces memory protection between programs. Entries in the descriptor table are never duplicated from task to task. This way, no two tasks can address the same physical location.

- Each task has its own local descriptor table (LDT). Segment registers in OS/2 contain logical entries into these descriptor tables, which then contain the actual offset into physical memory addresses. By contrast, DOS segment registers contain actual displacement values.

- A global descriptor table (GDT) shares system-wide information among many tasks.

- Each OS/2 logical segment can contain 64K of virtual memory. Because there are 16K segments, there is a total of one gigabyte (16K × 64K) of virtual memory available per application.

- OS/2 uses segment discard for discarding and reusing memory segments containing shared code or data.

- Segment movement is used to reduce memory gaps by coalescing available memory sections into contiguous blocks of memory.

- A serially reusable resource (SRR) is any resource, such as a printer, that cannot be used by more than one task simultaneously.

- There are three methods of interprocess communications (IPC) in OS/2: semaphores, pipes, and queues.

- Semaphores (or flags) are simple double words of memory used for signaling event occurrences or for managing the allocation of serially reusable resources; they are the fastest

IPC mechanism. Semaphores are most effectively used for quick synchronization and information passing between threads within a single task.

- Pipes are the middle-of-the-road IPC technique, and usually communicate information between parent and child tasks. Pipes are most effective when the information to be communicated is of a modest size (less than 64K).

- The third IPC area is a queue. It is the slowest technique because it uses disk storage, but it is the most powerful and flexible. Messages are essentially unlimited and can be accessed from the queue in any order, not necessarily the order in which they were stored. The queue mechanism is used most often when one task (server) receives variable length information from multiple other tasks (clients), and then deals with this information in a variety of ways (FIFO, LIFO, or priority).

- OS/2 has approximately two hundred system service calls available through a call-return mechanism, in contrast to the DOS method of using Int 21H. Together, these system service calls are known as the Applications Programming Interface (API).

- The subset of service calls that allow program applications to run in both OS/2 protected mode and in DOS 3.x machines is called the Family Applications Programming Interface (FAPI). There is a big overlap between these calls and those available in DOS 3.x. A number of the overlap calls do bear some restrictions when used in the OS/2 real mode environment.

Congratulations! You have successfully completed this introductory volume on Microsoft's Operating Sytem/2. You've been introduced to the fundamentals of the multitasking world of OS/2, and learned how real and protected modes enable you to run your newer OS/2 applications, without losing the ability to run DOS applications. You have seen how to install and start up OS/2 and how to make powerful use of OS/2's large virtual memory address space. You explored the many new OS/2 commands available at the real and protected mode command prompts, from within the configuration module (Config.sys), and from inside batch files. Your introduction to OS/2 programming gave you a glimpse of the more formalized mechanisms OS/2 uses in the programming arena.

PART 4

APPENDICES

Four appendices are included to make your use of OS/2 a little easier. Appendix A is a glossary of the important computer terms used in this book. Appendix B is a detailed presentation of the FDISK command for partitioning your hard disk. Although you won't need to run FDISK often, the material presented here is a useful reference for those occasional times when you do need it.

Appendix C presents a list of the commands in OS/2 that provide exit codes and the values they return. This appendix will be useful whenever you are developing sophisticated programs or batch files that make decisions based on the outcome of certain OS/2 commands.

Lastly, Appendix D presents concise definitions of the system service calls available in OS/2's Application Programming Interface (API). These service calls are grouped by function (i.e., multitasking, interprocess communications, etc.) for easy reference. The subset of these calls that can be used in simultaneous DOS-OS/2 development is called the Family API, or FAPI. The Appendix specifies which calls fall into this category, as well as which are restricted in some way when used in this FAPI programming environment.

APPENDIX *A* *GLOSSARY*

This appendix defines all of the important OS/2-related terms used in this book. Although these terms are defined in the text when they are first introduced, the glossary presented here offers concise definitions that will refresh your memory when you read a chapter later in the book, or when you simply can't remember the meaning of a particular term.

active partition　The section of a hard disk containing the operating system to be used when the hardware powers up.

ANSI driver　A device driver, contained in the Ansi.sys file, that loads additional support for advanced console features.

application program　A program that performs or replaces a manual function, such as balancing a checkbook or managing inventory.

Application Programming Interface (API)　The set of all OS/2 system service calls accessible through the call-return technique.

archive bit　A bit in a file specification used to indicate whether the file in question needs to be backed up.

ASCII　American Standard Code for Information Interchange; the coding scheme whereby every character the computer can access is assigned an integer code between 0 and 255.

assembly language　A symbolic form of computer language used to program computers at a fundamental level.

asynchronous communications　*See* serial communications.

Autoexec.bat　A batch file executed automatically the first time that real mode is entered in OS/2.

background task　An additional program running simultaneously on your computer; often a printing or communications operation that shares the CPU with your main foreground task. Background tasks typically do not require any interaction with the user at the console.

base name The portion of a file name to the left of the period separator; it can be up to eight characters long.

BASIC Beginners All-purpose Symbolic Instruction Code. A computer language similar to the English language.

batch file An ASCII file containing a sequence of OS/2 commands that, when invoked, will assume control of the computer, executing the commands as if they were entered successively by a computer user.

baud rate The speed of data transmission, usually in bits per second.

binary A numbering system that uses powers of the number 2 to generate all other numbers.

bit One-eighth of a byte. A bit is a binary digit, either 0 or 1.

bit mapping The way a graphics screen is represented in the computer. Usually signifies point-to-point graphics.

booting up *See* bootstrapping.

boot record The section on a disk that contains the minimum information OS/2 needs to start the system.

bootstrapping When the computer initially is turned on or is restarted from the keyboard with Ctrl-Alt-Del, it "pulls itself up by its bootstraps." *See also* warm booting, cold booting.

branching The transfer of control or execution to another statement in a batch file. *See also* decision making.

break key The control-key combination that interrupts an executing program or command; activated by pressing the Scroll Lock key while holding down the Ctrl key.

buffer An area in memory set aside to speed up the transfer of data, allowing blocks of data to be transferred at once.

byte The main unit of memory in a computer. A byte is an eight-bit binary-digit number. One character usually takes up one byte.

cache A portion of memory reserved for the contents of recently referenced disk sectors. Facilitates faster reaccess of the same sectors.

case sensitivity Distinguishing between capital letters and lower-case letters.

chaining Passing the control of execution from one batch file to another. This represents an unconditional transfer of control.

character set A complete group of 256 characters that can be used by programs or system devices. Consists of letters, numbers, control codes, and special graphics or international symbols. *See also* code page.

cluster   A group of contiguous sectors on a disk. This is the smallest unit of disk storage that OS/2 can manipulate.

code page   A character set that redefines the country and keyboard information for non-U.S. keyboards and systems.

cold booting   When the computer's power is first turned on and OS/2 first starts up. *See* bootstrapping.

Command.com   The command interpreter for OS/2's real mode.

command line   The line on which a command is entered. This line contains the command and all of its associated parameters and switches. It may run to more than one screen line, but it is still one command line.

command processor   The program that translates and acts on commands.

command shell   A program that interprets and acts on all keyboard entries.

compatibility box   Another name for real mode.

compressed print   Printing that allows more than 80 characters on a line of output (usually 132 characters, but on some printers, can be up to 255 characters per line).

computer-aided design program (CAD)   A sophisticated software package containing advanced graphics and drawing features. Used by engineers, architects, and designers for drawing and design applications.

concatenation   The placing of two text files together in a series.

conditional statement   A statement in a batch file that controls the next step to be executed in the batch file, based on the value of a logical test.

Config.sys   An ASCII text file containing system configuration commands.

configuration   An initial set of system values, such as the number of buffers OS/2 will use, the number of simultaneously executing threads it will allow, and the specific devices that will be supported.

console   The combination of a system's monitor and keyboard. Only one real console typically exists in a system, while each screen group writes to its own virtual console.

contiguity   The physical adjacency on a disk of the disk sectors used by a file.

control codes   ASCII codes that do not display a character but perform a function, such as ringing a bell or deleting a character.

copy protection   Special mechanisms contained in disks to inhibit copying by conventional commands.

CPU   Central Processing Unit. The main chip that executes all individual computer instructions.

Ctrl-Z   The end-of-file marker.

cursor   The blinking line or highlighted box that indicates where the next keystroke will be displayed or what the next control code entered will affect.

cutting and pasting   Selecting text from one part of a document or visual display and moving it to another location.

cylinder   All tracks that are in the same position on both sides of all platters of a disk drive. For example, Side 0 Track 30, Side 1 Track 30, Side 2 Track 30, and Side 3 Track 30 form a cylinder.

daisy-wheel printer   A printer that uses circular templates for producing letter-quality characters.

data area   The tracks on a disk that contain user data.

database   A collection of data organized into various categories. A phone book is one form of a database.

database management system   A software program designed to allow the creation of specially organized files, as well as data entry, manipulation, removal, and reporting for those files.

data bits   The bits that represent data when the computer is communicating.

data disk   A disk that has been formatted without the /s switch. The disk can contain only data; no room has been reserved for system files.

data stream   The transmission of data between two components or computers.

dead key   A reserved key combination on international keyboards that outputs nothing itself, but allows the next keystroke to produce an accent mark above or below the keystroke's usual character.

debugging   The process of discovering what is wrong with a program, where the problem is located, and what the solution is.

decimal   A numbering system based on ten digits.

decision making   A point in a batch file at which execution can continue in at least two different paths, depending on the results of a program test. Also known as logical testing or branching.

default   The standard value of a variable or system parameter.

deferred execution   In a program or batch file, when execution is delayed until a value for some parameter is finally entered or computed.

delimiter   A special character, such as a comma or space, used to separate values or data entries.

descriptor table   A list of virtual memory segments assigned to a process.

destination   The targeted location for data, files, or other information generated or moved by an OS/2 command.

device   Any internal or external piece of peripheral hardware.

device driver   Also known as an interrupt handler. A special program that must be loaded to use a device. Adds extra capability to OS/2.

device name   Logical name that OS/2 uses to refer to a device.

digital   A representation based on a collection of individual digits, such as 0's and 1's in the binary number system.

digitizer   A device with a movable arm that can take an image and break it up into small parts, which the computer translates into bits.

directory   A grouping of files on a disk. These files are displayed together and may include access to other directories (subdirectories).

directory tree   The treelike structure created when a root directory has several subdirectories, each of the subdirectories has subdirectories, and so on.

disk drive   A hardware device that accesses the data stored on a disk.

disk optimizer   A program that rearranges the location of files stored on a disk in order to make the data in those files quickly retrievable.

DOS   Disk Operating System. A set of programs that manages computer-user interaction, program execution, and all hardware in a computer system.

dot-matrix printer   A printer that represents characters by means of tiny dots.

double-density disk   A floppy disk on which magnetic storage material is arranged twice as densely as usual, allowing the storage of twice the usual amount of data. Generally refers to a 360K, 5$^1/_4$-inch disk.

drive identifier   A single letter assigned to represent a drive, such as drive A or drive B. Usually requires a colon after it, such as A:.

dual tasking   Two tasks or programming events occurring simultaneously.

dynamic linking   Linkage to subroutines and library routines at run time, rather than at load time.

echoing   Displaying the keystrokes you type in on your video monitor.

EDLIN   The OS/2 real mode line editor.

end-of-file marker   A Ctrl-Z code that marks the logical end of a file.

environment   The context within which OS/2 interfaces with you and with your commands.

error code   *See* exit code.

error level   A code set by programs as they conclude processing that tells OS/2 whether an error occurred, and if so, indicates the severity of that error.

exit code   A value returned after an OS/2 command executes, indicating whether any error occurred during the execution of that program or command.

expansion cards   Add-on circuit boards through which hardware can increase the power of the system, such as adding extra memory or a modem.

expansion slots   Connectors inside the computer in which expansion cards are placed so that they tie in directly to the system.

extended ASCII codes   ASCII codes between 128 and 255, which usually differ from computer to computer and from code page to code page.

extended OS/2 partition   A hard-disk partition used to exceed the 32MB, single-disk barrier; it can be divided into logical disk drives.

extended memory   Additional physical memory beyond 1MB.

extension   The one to three characters after the period following the base name in a file specification.

external buffer   A device connected to the computer and another device that acts as a buffer.

external commands   Commands that are accessible as separately defined and named disk files, usually with extensions of .exe or .com. Batch files in protected mode (.cmd) and batch files in real mode (bat.) can also be considered external commands.

Family Application Program Interface (FAPI)   The suggested subset of OS/2 function calls that allow a developed program to run in either real or protected mode.

file   A collection of bytes, representing a program or data, organized into records and stored as a named group on a disk.

file allocation table (FAT)   A table of sectors stored on a disk, which tells OS/2 whether a given sector is good, bad, continued, or the end of a chain of records.

file name   The name of a file on the disk. Usually refers to the base name, but can include the extension as well.

file version   Indicates which developmental copy of a software program is being used or referenced.

filter   A program that accepts data as input, processes it in some manner, and then outputs the data in a different form.

fixed disk   IBM's name for a hard disk.

floppy disk   A flexible, oxide-coated disk used to store data. (Also called a diskette.)

flow of control   The order of execution of batch-file commands; how the control flows from one command to another, even when the next command to be executed is not located sequentially in the file.

foreground task   The main program running on your computer, as opposed to a less visible background task.

formatting   The placement of timing marks on a disk to arrange the tracks and sectors for subsequent reading and writing.

fragmentation   A condition in which many different files have been stored in noncontiguous sectors on a disk.

function keys   Special-purpose keys on a keyboard that can be assigned unique tasks by OS/2 or by application programs.

gigabyte   1024 megabytes (2^{30} bytes).

global characters   *See* wild cards.

global descriptor table (GDT)   A system-wide table of shared virtual memory segments containing code and data available to all applications.

graphics mode   The mode in which all screen pixels on a monitor are addressable and can be used to generate detailed images. Contrasts with text mode, which usually allows only 24 lines of 80 characters.

hard disk   A rigid platter that stores data faster and at a higher density than a floppy disk. Sealed in an airtight compartment to avoid contaminants that could damage or destroy the disk.

hardware   The physical components of a computer system.

hardware interrupt   A signal from a device to the computer, indicating a request for service or support from the system.

head   A disk-drive mechanism that reads data from and writes data to the disk.

head crash   Occurs when the head hits the disk platter on a hard disk, physically damaging the disk and the data on it.

help file   A file of textual information containing helpful explanations of commands, modes, and other on-screen tutorial information.

hexadecimal   A numbering system in base 16. A single eight-bit byte can be fully represented as two hexadecimal digits.

hidden files   Files whose names do not appear in a directory listing. Usually refers to OS/2's internal system files, but can also refer to certain files used in copy-protection schemes.

high-capacity disk   A 1.2MB, 5¼-inch floppy disk.

high-resolution mode   The mode on a video monitor in which all available pixels are used to provide the most detailed screen image possible. On a color monitor, this mode reduces the possible range of colors that can be output.

horizontal landscape   When output to a printer is not done in the usual format, but rather with the wider part of the printed image laid out horizontally, as in a landscape picture.

hot key   A key combination used to signal that a background program, or a waiting process thread should begin operation. In OS/2, the Ctrl-Esc key combination will interrupt any running screen group and call up the Session Manager screen. The Alt-Esc combination can switch successively from any one running screen group to all other screen groups.

housekeeping   Making sure the directory stays intact and well organized, and that unnecessary files are deleted.

hub   The center hole of a floppy disk.

IF   A conditional statement in a batch file.

ink-jet printer   A printer that forms characters by spraying ink in a dot pattern. *See* dot-matrix printer.

interface   The boundary between two things, such as the computer and a peripheral.

interprocess communications   Refers to three OS/2 mechanisms used to transfer information between processes, or between threads within processes. *See* semaphore, pipe, queue.

internal commands   OS/2 commands that are built into the memory-resident portion of the command interpreter (Command-.com in real mode, Cmd.exe in protected mode).

interrupt   A signal sent to the computer from a hardware device or a software program, indicating that some event has taken place, and that system service is requested.

keyboard translation table   An internal table, contained in the keyboard driver, that converts hardware signals from the keyboard into the correct ASCII codes.

key combination   When two or more keys are pressed simultaneously, as in Ctrl-ScrollLock or Ctrl-Alt-Del.

key redefinition   Assigning a nonstandard value to a key.

kilobyte (K)   1024 bytes.

laser printer   A printer that produces images (pictures or text) by shining a laser on a photostatic drum, which picks up toner and then transfers the image to paper.

line editor   A program that can make textual changes to an ASCII file, but can only make changes to one line of the file at a time.

line feed   When the cursor on a screen moves to the next line, or when the printer advances the paper by one line.

literal   Something that is accepted exactly as it was submitted.

local descriptor table (LDT)   A per-process descriptor table of assigned virtual memory segments.

lockup   Occurs when the computer will not accept any input. Requires that the computer be warm or cold booted to resume operating.

log file   A separate file, created with the BACKUP command, that keeps track of the names of all files written to the backup disk(s).

logging on   Signing onto a remote system, such as a mainframe or telecommunications service.

logical   Something that is defined based on a decision, not by physical properties.

logical drives   Disk drives, created in an extended OS/2 partition, that do not physically exist, but OS/2 thinks they do. A means for OS/2 to access a physical disk that has more than 32MB available.

logical segment   Virtual memory addressed by tasks (up to 64K/segment).

logical testing   *See* decision making.

machine language   The most fundamental way to program a computer, using instructions made up entirely of strings of 0s and 1s.

macro   A set of commands, often memory-resident. When executed, they appear to the program executing them as if they were being entered by you.

mapping   Mapping assigns a real system resource to a program's logical or virtual value. The Session Manager maps, or assigns, only one of many virtual consoles to the actual system console. The Memory Manager maps, or assigns, physical memory addresses to the programs that reference logical or virtual memory addresses.

medium-resolution mode   The mode on a Color Graphics Adapter in which only 320 × 200 pixels of resolution are allowed.

megabyte (MB)   1024 kilobytes.

memory   The circuitry in a computer that stores information. *See also* RAM and ROM.

Memory Manager   The software code, internal to OS/2, that keeps track of the mapping between virtual memory (as used by programs) and physical memory (as managed by the operating system).

memory-resident   Located in physical memory, as opposed to being stored in a disk file.

menu   A set of choices displayed in tabular format.

meta symbols   Special single-character codes used by the PROMPT command to represent complex actions or sequences to be included in the OS/2 prompt.

microfloppy disk   The 3½-inch floppy disk format used in the Personal System/2 and many other computers.

modem   A device that transmits digital data in tones over a phone line.

monitor   The device used to display images; a display screen.

monochrome   Using two colors only—the background and foreground.

mouse   A device that moves the screen cursor by means of a hand-held apparatus moved along a surface such as a desk. The computer can tell how far and in which direction the mouse is being moved.

multithreading   Running more than one code sequence within a process simultaneously. *See* thread.

multitasking   Running multiple programs simultaneously.

national language support operations   The OS/2 feature that supports displays and printers, using a new range of code and character groupings.

network   Several computers, connected together, that can share common data files and peripheral devices.

nibble   Four bits, or half of a byte.

nonexecutable instruction   A label in a batch program that is merely a place holder to facilitate transfer of control. It represents no additional processing steps.

octal   A numbering system in base 8.

on-line help Provides explanations for every OS/2 system message, along with a course of suggested action based on the nature of the message. The HELPMSG command supports this feature.

operating system *See* OS/2.

OS/2 Operating System/2. The set of programs that allows computer/user interaction, manages memory, enables swapping, and facilitates multitasking.

OS/2 environment A part of memory set aside to hold the defaults needed in the current processing environment, such as COMSPEC, PATH, and PROMPT.

OS/2 prompt Usually C> or [C:\]. The visual indication that OS/2 is waiting for a command or prompting you for input.

overlay files Files containing additional command and control information for sophisticated and complex programs. An overlay file is usually too large to fit into memory along with the main .exe or .com file.

overwriting Typing new data over what is already there.

parallel communications Data transmission in which several bits can be transferred or processed at one time.

parameter An extra bit of information, specified with a command, that determines how the command executes.

parity The bit, added to the end of a stream of data bits, that is assigned a 0 or 1 depending on the sum value of the data bits.

partition The section of a hard disk that contains an operating system. There can be at most four partitions on one hard disk.

password A sequence of characters that allows entry into a restricted system or program.

path The list of disks and directories that OS/2 will search through to find a command file ending in .com, .bat (real mode), .cmd (protected mode), or .exe.

peripheral Any physical device connected to the computer.

PID *See* process identification number.

pipe The temporary memory storage that contains the output of one process, to be used as the input to another process. The information being communicated between processes constitutes the metaphorical pipe, while the two processes involved represent the ends of the pipe.

piping   Redirecting the input or output of one program or command to another program or command.

pixel   The smallest unit of display on a video monitor—in short, a dot—that can be illuminated to created text or graphics images.

platter   The rigid disk used in a hard-disk drive.

plotter   A device that draws data on paper with a mechanical arm.

port   A doorway through which the computer can access external devices.

precedence   A prioritization method used by OS/2 to decide which file to use (.exe, .com, or .bat/.cmd) when more than one file with the same base name is found. Also applies to the order in which the protected mode interpreter, Cmd.exe, treats commands connected with special grouping symbols (e.g. ^, (), >, <, >>, ¦, &&, ¦¦, and &).

primary OS/2 partition   Up to the first 32MB of a hard disk. Contains the boot record and other OS/2 information files.

printer   A device that outputs data onto paper using pins (dot matrix), a daisy wheel, ink jets, laser imaging, and so on.

process   *See* task.

process identification number (PID)   An internal number used by OS/2 to keep track of multiple tasks or processes. Each task receives a unique number, but only background tasks initiated by you will cause OS/2 to display that task's PID to you.

protected mode   The principal operating environment of OS/2 that supports multitasking, process protection, and advanced memory management.

public domain   Something not copyrighted or patented. Public domain software can be used and copied without infringing on anyone's rights.

queue   A series of information messages transmitted by several separate processes and waiting to be retrieved and dealt with by one other process. OS/2 implements this as a list of shared memory segments.

RAM   Random Access Memory. The part of the computer's memory to which you have access; stores programs and data while the computer is on.

RAM disk   An area of RAM that acts as if it were a disk drive. All data in this area of memory is lost when the computer is turned off or warm booted. Also known as a virtual disk.

range   A contiguous series of values (minimum to maximum, first to last, and so on).

read-after-write verification   An extra level of validity checking, invoked with the VERIFY command or the /v switch. Rereads data after writing it to disk, comparing the written data to the original information.

read-only status   Indicates that a file cannot be updated but can be read.

read/write bit   The bit in a file specification that indicates whether a file can accept changes or deletions, or can only be accessed for reading.

real mode   The single tasking unprotected operating environment that runs old DOS programs under OS/2.

redirection   Causing output from one program or device to be routed to another program or device.

REM statement   A line in an OS/2 batch file containing remarks or comments for program explanation or clarification.

reserved names   Specific words in a programming language or operating system that should not be used in any other application context.

resident commands   Commands located in random-access memory.

resource allocation   Making system facilities available to individual users or programs.

reverse video   Black letters on a white background.

ROM   Read-Only Memory. The section of memory from which you can only read. This contains the basic computer operating system and system routines.

root directory   The first directory on any disk.

scan code   The hardware code representing a key pressed on a keyboard. Converted by a keyboard driver into an ASCII code for use by OS/2 and application programs.

screen group   The collection of all programs that are executing in the same OS/2 session. All of these programs can output to the same virtual console; the Session Manager can switch among the different screen groups.

scrolling   What the screen does when you're at the bottom of it and press Return: all of the lines roll up.

secondary command processor   A second copy of Command.com or Cmd.exe, invoked either to run a batch file or to provide a new context for subsequent OS/2 commands.

sector   A division of a disk track; usually, 512 bytes.

segment discard   The reassignment of a real memory segment containing shared code or data that is not currently in use by a process, but still exists in some process's descriptor table.

segment movement   Relocation of assigned memory segments to create sufficient contiguous blocks of memory to satisfy application requests for memory.

segmentation   The partitioning of memory by logical addresses instead of by physical addresses, enabling you to run programs that can reference more memory than actually exists.

semaphore   A simple two word indicator that can be set, queried, or cleared to indicate possession of a system resource by a thread or task, or to indicate the occurrence of a system event.

serial communications   Data transmission in which data are transferred and processed one bit at a time. Also known as asynchronous communications.

serially reusable resource (SRR)   A system resource (i.e. file, peripheral device) that cannot be accessed simultaneously by multiple processes, but must be accessed sequentially or serially.

Session Manager   The program that maps one virtual console's output (out of all possible active processes) to the one actual system console.

software   The programs and instruction sets that operate the computer.

software interrupt   A signal from a software program that calls up a resident OS/2 routine. Also, a software signal to the computer that the software program has finished, has a problem, and so on.

source   The location containing the original data, files, or other information to be used in an OS/2 command.

spooling   Simultaneous Peripheral Operations On-Line. Using a high-speed disk to store input to or output from low-speed peripheral devices while the CPU does other tasks.

spreadsheet program   An electronic version of an accountant's spreadsheet; when one value changes, all other values based on that value are updated instantly.

SSE   A full-screen protected mode file editor.

start bit   The bit sent at the beginning of a data stream to indicate that data bits follow.

Startup.cmd   A batch file that is executed automatically the first time protected mode is entered in OS/2.

stop bit   The bit sent after the data bits, indicating that no more data bits follow.

storage overcommitment   The ability of OS/2 to allow programs to address an apparent memory space that exceeds actual memory. A process in OS/2 can address up to one gigabyte of virtual memory, while OS/2 will actually support physical memory addresses up to only 16MB.

string   A series of characters.

subcommands   Several specialized commands used only within batch files.

subdirectory   A directory contained within another directory or subdirectory. Technically, all directories other than the root directory are subdirectories.

subtask   Any task that is initiated by or from within another task.

swap file   *See* swapping.

swapping   Copying the contents of a portion of physical memory out to a disk file (the swap file), then reassigning the memory to another process that needs it.

switch   A parameter included in OS/2 commands, usually preceded by the slash symbol (/), that clarifies or modifies the action of the command.

synchronization   The coordination of a sending and receiving device, so that both simultaneously send and receive data at the same rate.

system disk   A disk containing the necessary OS/2 system files for system booting.

task   A program and the set of system resources that it uses.

text mode   The mode in which standard characters can be displayed on a monitor.

thread   A logical sequence of code within a program or process. This is the entity that is assigned system resources by OS/2.

timeslice   A minimum amount of time used by OS/2 to provide attention and service to requesting tasks (actually to threads within tasks).

toggle   A switch or command that reverses a value from off to on, or from on to off.

track   A circular stream of data on the disk. Similar to a track on a record, only not spiraling.

transient command   A command whose procedures are read from the disk into memory, executed from memory, and then erased from memory when finished.

utility   A supplemental routine or program, stored in a disk file, designed to carry out a specific operation, usually to modify the system environment or perform housekeeping tasks.

utility command   *See* external command.

variable parameter   A named element, following a command, that acts as a placeholder; when you issue the command, you replace the variable parameter with the actual value you want to use.

verbose listing   A listing of all files and subdirectories contained on the disk and path specified in the command. Activated by the CHKDSK command with the /v switch.

vertical portrait   The conventional 8½ by 11-inch output for printed information, with the long side of the paper positioned vertically.

virtual console   A memory buffer that mimics an actual output device. Multiple processes in OS/2 perform their input/output to virtual consoles. The Session Manager decides at any particular moment which one of these processes is connected to the actual system console.

virtual disk *See* RAM disk.

volume label A name, consisting of up to 11 characters, that can be assigned to any disk during a FORMAT operation or after formatting with the LABEL command.

warm booting Resetting the computer using the Ctrl-Alt-Del key combination. *See* bootstrapping.

wide directory listing An alternate output format that lists five columns of file names.

wild cards Characters used to represent any other characters. In OS/2, * and ? are the only wild-card symbols.

word processor A computerized typewriter. Allows the correction and reformatting of documents before they are printed.

write-protection Giving a disk read-only status by covering the write-protect notch.

Hard disks are usually so large that they can contain more than one type of operating system. For example, you can have OS/2 manage one part of a disk and UNIX manage another. Each of these sections is called a *partition*. You can have from one to four partitions on a disk.

Partitions are used to make the hard disk, especially a very large one, a more economical investment. They allow you to effectively have up to four completely different computer systems resident in one set of hardware. However, since they do not share a common software environment, they cannot share data directly.

Two types of partitions can be set up for OS/2: a *primary OS/2 partition* and an *extended OS/2 partition*. The primary OS/2 partition is the partition that contains OS/2, and is the first partition on the disk. This is usually the only partition on a typical user's hard disk, if that disk is no larger than 32MB. The extended OS/2 partition is a separate partition that cannot be used for booting, but can be divided into separate logical drives.

If you have more than 32MB available on your hard disk, you will need to create an extended OS/2 partition, which is assigned the next logical drive letter. For example, if you had a 60MB hard-disk drive and wanted access to all of it, you would create a 32MB primary partition and a 28MB extended partition. The primary partition could be accessed as drive C, while the extended partition would be called drive D. You could also subdivide the extended partition into more logical drives (up to the letter Z).

You must create partitions before using a hard-disk drive. You will probably take the easiest route by simply making the entire disk into one primary partition. The FDISK program presented here, however, is also necessary in several more advanced situations. For example, you may plan on using multiple operating systems from the same disk.

If your disk is already being used and you wish to make a new partition, you will have to first back up all of your data and then run FDISK from a system disk. Then, you'll need to reformat your disk before restoring your files to it.

FDISK will let you set up unique partitions for each system. (Each of these would be a primary partition, but only one could be designated the active partition, the one that will gain control at boot up.) Then again, you may be using one of the large hard disks (40–70MB) that are increasingly common. Since OS/2 can only access individual logical drives of 32MB or less, you'll need to partition a larger physical drive into multiple logical drives. This is the only way you can store and retrieve information on the larger hard disk.

CONFIGURING AN OS/2 PARTITION

In this section, you will learn exactly how to use the FDISK command. This procedure is very important, and it can have serious consequences if done incorrectly. However, when done properly, it can make your system more efficient. You can use FDISK on hard-disk systems only.

Invoking the FDISK command is as simple as typing

FDISK

and pressing Return. (Remember to have your path set properly to include the directory containing the FDISK command file.) After this command creates the appropriate partition(s), you must then logically format the disk. All data on your disk will be destroyed when you create partitions with FDISK.

All data on your disk will be destroyed when you create partitions with FDISK.

When you first execute FDISK, the screen will clear and the FDISK Options screen shown in Figure B.1 will appear. This contains the menu used to get around in FDISK. As you can see, there are four choices. If you have a system with more than one hard-disk drive, the number in the "Current Fixed Disk Drive: 1" line would be changed to reflect which drive is being partitioned. Also, a fifth option, "Select Next Fixed Disk Drive," would be displayed on the screen. You can only work on one hard-disk drive at a time, but you can switch from the drive you are working on to another drive. For now, let's assume you have one hard-disk drive and that you'll receive the four choices shown.

```
FDISK Options

Current Fixed Disk Drive: 1

Choose one of the following:

        1. Create Microsoft Operating System/2 Partition
           or Logical Drive
        2. Change primary partition
        3. Delete Microsoft Operating System/2 Partition
            or Logical Drive
        4. Display Partition Data

Enter choice: [1]


Press Enter when ready
Press ESC to return to Microsoft Operating System/2.
```

Figure B.1: The main FDISK Options menu

CREATING A PARTITION

> If you plan to use your hard disk to support another operating system, do not partition the whole disk. Leave some room so that another system can be loaded onto the disk.

The first option on the FDISK Options menu is to create an OS/2 partition. Since you are using OS/2, and not another operating system like UNIX, you can only create OS/2 partitions. Should you wish to put another operating system onto the disk, that system would have its own version of FDISK that would create its own partitions next to OS/2's. Choosing the first option to create an OS/2 partition results in Figure B.2.

Assuming you are starting from scratch, you would select choice 1 to create the primary OS/2 partition. You will then see the screen shown in Figure B.3.

If you want to use the whole disk for OS/2, answer Y on this screen. Doing so makes OS/2 use the whole disk. The computer will allocate the entire disk, and then come back with the message

The system will now restart.

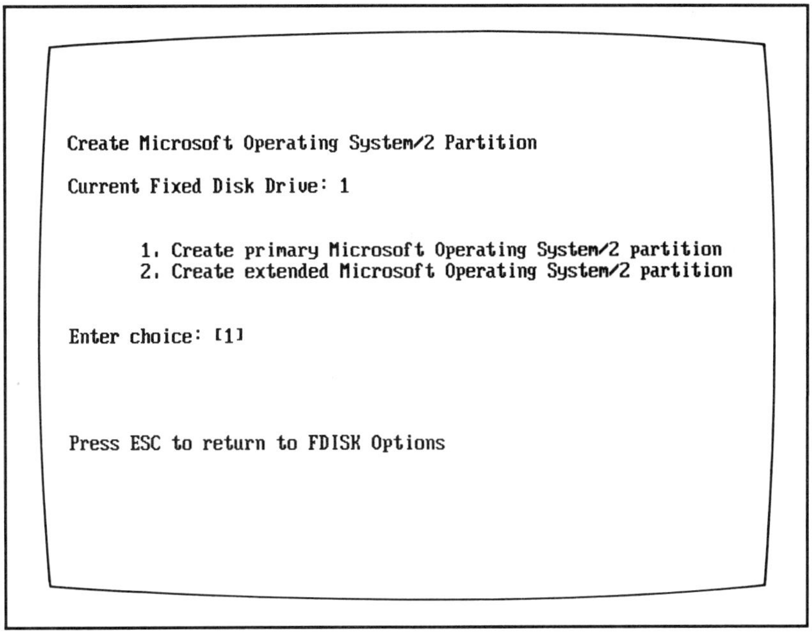

```
Create Microsoft Operating System/2 Partition

Current Fixed Disk Drive: 1


        1. Create primary Microsoft Operating System/2 partition
        2. Create extended Microsoft Operating System/2 partition


Enter choice: [1]



Press ESC to return to FDISK Options
```

Figure B.2: The Create OS/2 Partition menu

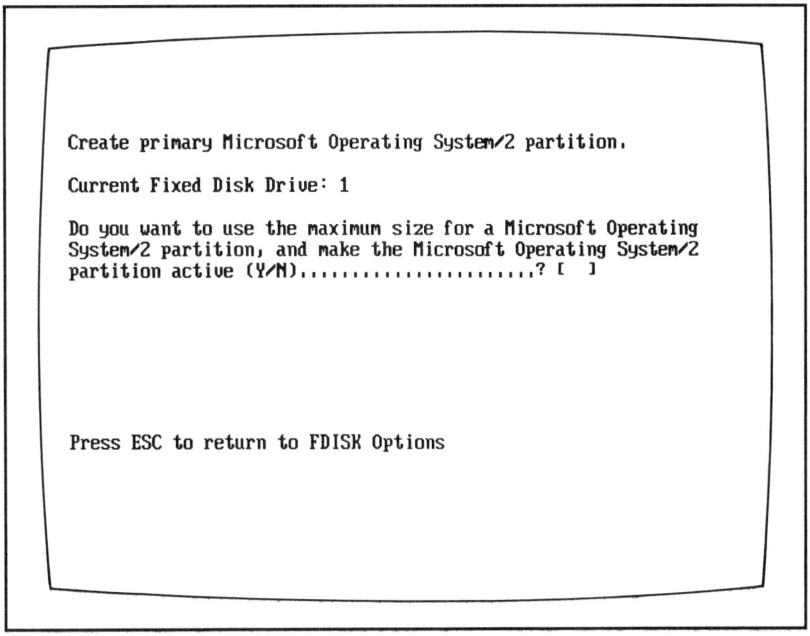

```
Create primary Microsoft Operating System/2 partition.

Current Fixed Disk Drive: 1

Do you want to use the maximum size for a Microsoft Operating
System/2 partition, and make the Microsoft Operating System/2
partition active (Y/N).......................? [  ]




Press ESC to return to FDISK Options
```

Figure B.3: Creating the primary MS OS/2 partition

Insert the Microsoft Operating System/2 diskette in drive A:
and press Ctrl + Alt + Del

Since you just created the partition, there is now nothing on the
hard disk. The system must be rebooted from the disk drive. You can
now format the entire hard disk just as you would a floppy disk.

On the other hand, if you answer N, you'll have the opportunity to
create a smaller partition. Let's just review terminology for a
moment (see Figure B.4). A hard disk consists of several platters,
similar to a disk; each platter consists of a series of concentric tracks
made up of sectors. Each platter lies above another and is read by a
different disk head. Viewed vertically, a series of tracks (with the
same track number, but on different platters) located one above the
other constitute a cylinder. OS/2 will display the number of cylinders
available on your hard disk.

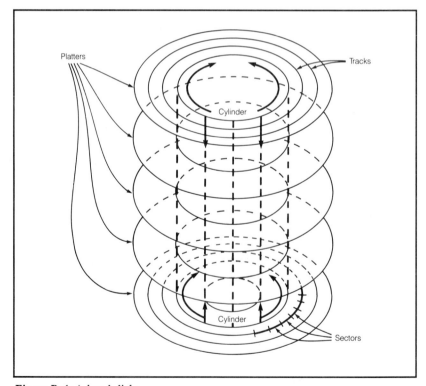

Figure B.4: A hard disk

If you are using your disk for OS/2 alone, you should accept the default maximum cylinder value. All disk space will then be available for OS/2 and your OS/2 files. If you plan on splitting up your disk between OS/2 and another operating system, however, you'll have to decide for yourself what percentage of total disk space is needed for the other operating system.

For example, let's say you intend to create an extended OS/2 partition on a hard disk that contains 854 cylinders. You intend to create three logical drives: C, D, and E. By entering N to the question in Figure B.3, you will then be shown the current number of cylinders on the disk, and asked to enter how many of them you wish to use for the first partition. As seen in Figure B.5, you might enter 500 to be used for this primary partition, disk C.

The message near to the bottom of the screen, "No partitions defined", only reflects the fact that you have not yet created any disk partitions. That's what you're about to do. Entering 500 results in the screen shown in Figure B.6. This screen tells you that the partition you just created on drive C is a primary OS/2 partition

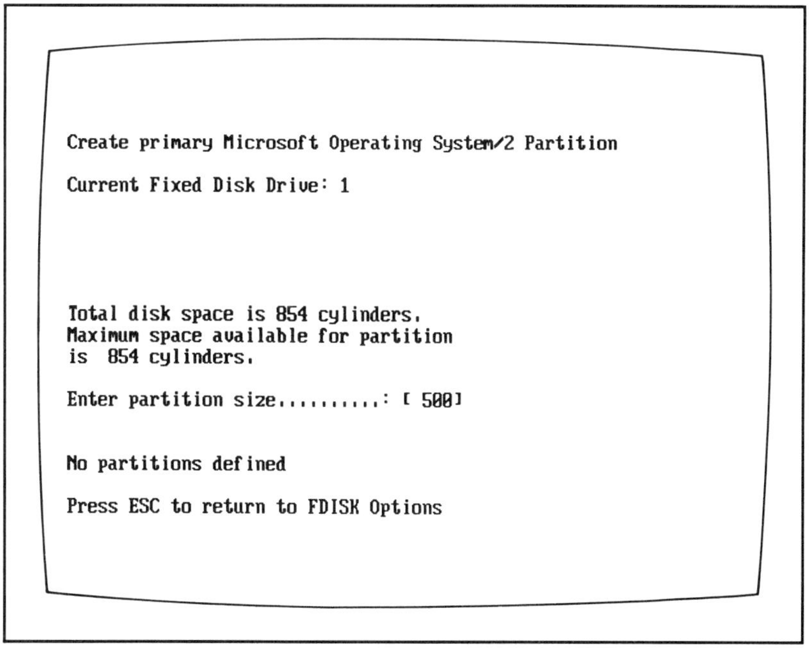

```
Create primary Microsoft Operating System/2 Partition

Current Fixed Disk Drive: 1




Total disk space is 854 cylinders.
Maximum space available for partition
is  854 cylinders.

Enter partition size..........: [ 500]


No partitions defined

Press ESC to return to FDISK Options
```

Figure B.5: Specifying the size of the primary OS/2 partition

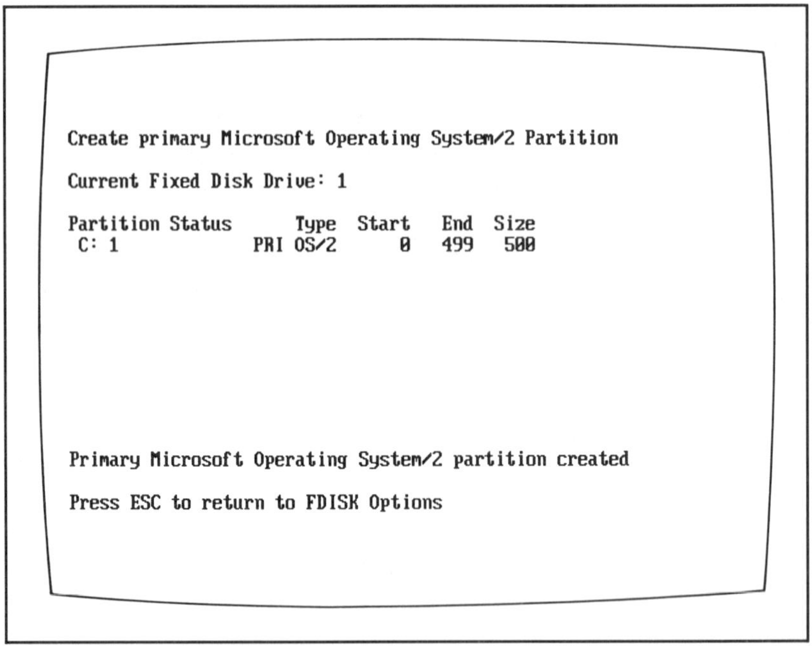

```
Create primary Microsoft Operating System/2 Partition

Current Fixed Disk Drive: 1

Partition Status        Type  Start  End  Size
   C: 1                PRI OS/2    0   499  500




Primary Microsoft Operating System/2 partition created

Press ESC to return to FDISK Options
```

Figure B.6: Primary OS/2 partition screen

(PRI OS/2) that starts at cylinder 0 and ends at cylinder 499, constituting a total of 500 cylinders. Pressing Esc at this point returns you to the FDISK Options menu.

In this example, you have only used 500 cylinders out of a possible 854, so you can now make an extended OS/2 partition. To do so, you select choice 1 on the FDISK Options menu (see Figure B.1) and then select choice 2 on the Create menu (see Figure B.2).

The resulting screen (see Figure B.7) allows you to create an extended OS/2 partition. This screen tells you the current partition information—there are 854 total cylinders available for use—and also tells you that 354 cylinders remain unused. The 354 value is used as the default entry at this stage, and is displayed initially within the square brackets. You only need to type in a number over the 354 to override the default. In Figure B.6, 200 was entered for the desired extended OS/2 partition, leaving 154 cylinders unused on the disk for another operating system.

There can only be one primary OS/2 partition. When OS/2 boots up, the system files from this partition are loaded into memory for your operations.

```
Create Extended Microsoft Operating System/2 Partition

Current Fixed Disk Drive: 1

Partition Status      Type Start  End  Size
  C: 1                PRI OS/2    0    499  500



Total disk space is  854 cylinders.
Maximum space available for partition
is  354 cylinders.

Enter partition size...........: [ 200]



Press ESC to return to FDISK Options
```

Figure B.7: Creating an extended OS/2 partition

The screen will now clear, redisplay the partition information (including that on the new extended OS/2 partition), and print the following message near the bottom of the screen:

Extended OS/2 Partition created
Press ESC to return to FDISK Options

Pressing Esc will result in the next step of the process. The main Creation menu will now show a third choice, namely the ability to create logical drives within the now existing extended partition (see Figure B.8).

If you select choice 3, OS/2 tells you the total available cylinders in the extended partition (200) and asks you to enter a size for the logical drive (see Figure B.9).

Let's say you enter 100. This creates logical drive D, and leaves only 100 cylinders unassigned in the extended partition. You could run through the same menu sequence again to assign this last 100 cylinders to another logical drive (E). The resulting screen will contain

```
Create Microsoft Operating System/2 Partition

Current Fixed Disk Drive: 1


        1. Create primary Microsoft Operating System/2 partition
        2. Create extended Microsoft Operating System/2 partition
        3. Create logical drive(s) in
             the extended Microsoft Operating System/2 partition



Enter choice: [1]




Press ESC to return to FDISK Options
```

Figure B.8: Modified main creation menu

```
Create Logical Microsoft Operating System/2 Drive(s)



No logical drives defined


Total partition size is   200 cylinders.

Maximum space available for logical
drive is   200 cylinders.

Enter logical drive size.......: [  100]


Press ESC to return to FDISK Options
```

Figure B.9: Creating logical drives in an extended partition

the logical drive information (drive name, starting cylinder, ending cylinder, and total cylinders used):

Drv	Start	End	Size
D:	500	599	100
E:	600	699	100

CHANGING THE ACTIVE PARTITION

The *active* partition is the partition that is used to boot the system. It is the default partition. Choosing option 2 on the main FDISK Options menu leads you to a menu like that shown in Figure B.10, in which the partition information is displayed along with the total number of cylinders available on the disk. FDISK now wants to know the number of the partition that you wish to make active.

Typically, you type the number 1 so that the primary OS/2 partition will have control when the system comes up. Pressing Return will result in a message that Partition 1 has been made active.

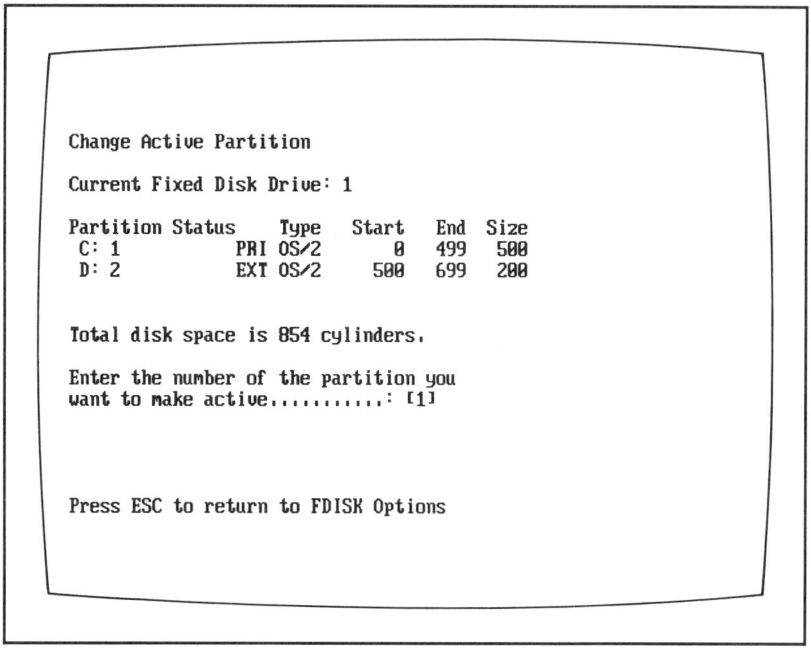

```
Change Active Partition

Current Fixed Disk Drive: 1

Partition Status    Type    Start   End  Size
  C: 1              PRI OS/2     0   499   500
  D: 2              EXT OS/2   500   699   200


Total disk space is 854 cylinders.

Enter the number of the partition you
want to make active............: [1]



Press ESC to return to FDISK Options
```

Figure B.10: The Change Active Partition menu

DISPLAYING PARTITION INFORMATION

Option 4 on the FDISK Options menu is used to display information about the partitions. This is useful because no extra functions will be executed at the same time; you can simply look at the information. Choosing option 4 yields the screen shown in Figure B.11.

The information at the top of the screen is familiar by now. But what if you want to see information about the logical drives that have been defined? Look at the bottom half of the screen, where you are asked you if you want to see this information. Replying with Y results in a display of information about these logical drives, including their drive identifiers (D and E), their sizes (each 100 cylinders), and their Start-End cylinder numbers (500–599, and 600–699). Pressing Esc at that point will return you to the FDISK Options menu.

```
Display Partition Information

Current Fixed Disk Drive: 1

Partition Status    Type    Start   End   Size
   C: 1       A    PRI OS/2     0    499   500
   D: 2       N    EXT OS/2   500    699   200


Total disk space is 854 cylinders.


The Extended Microsoft Operating System/2
partition contains logical drives. Do you
want to display logical drive information? [Y]


Press ESC to return to FDISK Options
```

Figure B.11: Displaying partition information

DELETING OS/2 PARTITIONS

As with most things, what OS/2 giveth, OS/2 can taketh away— with a little prodding from you. Selecting choice 3 on the FDISK Options menu produces the Delete OS/2 Partition menu, shown in Figure B.12.

Using this menu, you can delete any of the information you've already set up. You may want to expand or contract other partitions, or you may no longer want to use a partition in the manner you originally designed. In any case, you can only make changes in a certain order. You cannot delete the primary OS/2 partition without first deleting the extended OS/2 partition.

In addition, you cannot delete an extended OS/2 partition without first "undefining" (deleting) the logical drives in that partition. Trying to delete the extended OS/2 partition before deleting the drives in

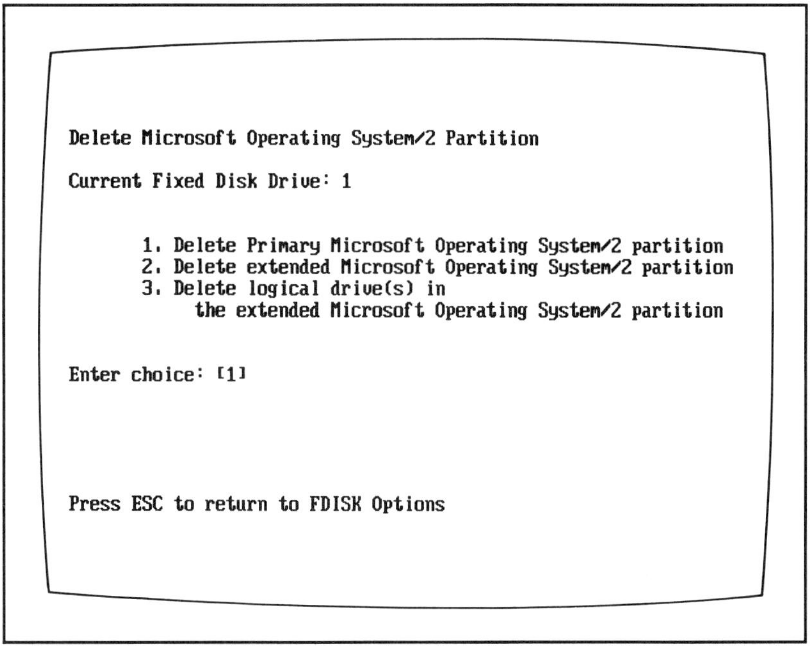

```
Delete Microsoft Operating System/2 Partition

Current Fixed Disk Drive: 1


        1. Delete Primary Microsoft Operating System/2 partition
        2. Delete extended Microsoft Operating System/2 partition
        3. Delete logical drive(s) in
             the extended Microsoft Operating System/2 partition



Enter choice: [1]




Press ESC to return to FDISK Options
```

Figure B.12: The Delete OS/2 Partition menu

it will simply display the current partition information with a message similar to

Cannot delete Extended OS/2 partition
while logical drives exist.
Press ESC to return to FDISK options

Choice 3 in the Delete OS/2 Partition menu is probably the first selection you will need to make; you work your way backward in the order in which you created things. (Actually, you will find that this is a fairly natural process.) Selecting choice 3 produces a screen that contains the logical drive information and the size of the extended OS/2 partition that contains the drives. You are also warned that any data contained in the logical disk drive to be deleted will also be deleted.

If you still want to delete the drive, simply enter the drive identifier. You will then be asked to confirm this step. You will enter Y to do this. If you enter N, you are returned to the FDISKOptions menu.

Once FDISK deletes the logical drive, it updates the display at the top of the screen and asks for another drive to delete. If you wanted to regain all the space used by this partition, you would enter drive D, then Y to confirm your entry. Pressing Esc twice at this point will bring you back up through the menu screens to the main FDISK Options menu.

Now that the logical drives are gone, you can delete the extended OS/2 partition itself if you choose to do so. Choosing option 2 on the Delete OS/2 Partition menu results in the familiar form of an FDISK screen. Again, you are shown the partition information display, warned that data will be lost, and asked if you really want to delete the extended OS/2 partition. If you reply Y, the screen will be updated to show only the primary OS/2 partition and a message that the extended OS/2 partition has been deleted. Press Esc to return once again to the FDISK Options menu.

APPENDIX *C* *OS/2 COMMAND EXIT CODES*

In this appendix, you will learn which OS/2 commands return exit values. When any program or command ends, it can return a value to the invoking program. This return value, or exit code, is a number indicating whether the command completed successfully or not. If any error occurred during the running of the program or the command, a nonzero value is returned. This appendix lists the values returned by commands in OS/2.

Not all commands in OS/2 are designed to return an exit code. The eight commands that do return exit codes are listed in this appendix along with the values of those return codes. Since most of these return codes represent error conditions, the code itself is sometimes called an error code.

The ERRORLEVEL command along with the GOTO command used in batch files can be used to test for any of these values. In this way you can use the exit code values to control the flow of execution during any of your customized batch files. In each of the following eight commands the exit code value represents the listed operational meaning.

BACKUP

EXIT CODE	MEANING
0	Successful backup of specified files
1	No files meet specification
2	Backup not complete due to sharing conflict
3	User termination
4	Termination due to other error

DISKCOMP

EXIT CODE	*MEANING*
0	Two disks matched completely
1	There were differences on the compared disks
2	User termination (Ctrl-C)
3	An unrecoverable hard disk error (read or write) occurred
4	The command could not begin because of insufficient memory, invalid command syntax, or invalid drive specification

DISKCOPY

EXIT CODE	*MEANING*
0	The disk copied completely
1	A non-fatal read/write error occurred and the command was aborted
2	User termination (Ctrl-C)
3	An unrecoverable hard disk error occurred (read or write)
4	The command could not begin because of insufficient memory, invalid command syntax, or invalid drive specification

FORMAT

EXIT CODE	*MEANING*
0	The disk formatted successfully
3	User termination (Ctrl-C)
4	An unrecoverable fatal error for any reason

5	User termination with the answer N to the format prompt, "Proceed with format (Y/N)?"

GRAFTABL

EXIT CODE	MEANING
0	Successful loading of the new character set
1	Table already loaded into memory
2	Termination due to file error

REPLACE

EXIT CODE	MEANING
0	Successful replacement of specified files
2	Specified file not found
3	Specified path not found
5	Unsuccessful replace due to read only status
8	Insufficient memory for the command operations
11	Illegal command line syntax
15	Invalid drive
22	Inexplicable command specification

RESTORE

EXIT CODE	MEANING
0	Normal completion of restoration operations
1	Specified files could not be found
2	Some files could not be restored due to sharing conflicts
3	User termination (Ctrl-C)
4	Other error termination

XCOPY

EXIT CODE	MEANING
0	All files copied successfully
1	No specified files were found to copy
2	User termination (Ctrl-C)
4	The command could not begin because of insufficient memory, invalid command syntax, or invalid drive/path specification
5	User termination while Interrupt 24 routine was processing I/O to or from the disk

This appendix lists the set of system service calls available in OS/2 for software development. All function names and brief descriptions of the services they perform are included. Unless otherwise noted in the column labeled CLASS, these functions are standard Application Programming Interface functions.

If the function is part of the special subset called Family API, or FAPI, it is noted in that additional middle column. Software that uses only functions noted as FAPI can be linked to run in either DOS 3.x machines or in the protected mode of OS/2. Some API functions are available to run in DOS mode, but their overall functionality may be limited in some way. This limitation is denoted by an asterisk next to the FAPI indicator.

ASYNCHRONOUS SIGNALING SERVICES

FUNCTION NAME	*CLASS*	*DESCRIPTION*
DosHoldSignal	FAPI*	Disables/enables signal
DosSetSigHandler	FAPI*	Handles signal

I/O (DEVICE) SERVICES

FUNCTION NAME	*CLASS*	*DESCRIPTION*
DosBeep	FAPI	Generates sound from speaker
DosCLIAccess		Requests CLI/STI privilege
DosDevConfig	FAPI	Gets device configuration

DosDevIOCtl	FAPI*	Controls I/O for devices
DosPortAccess		Requests port access

I/O (KEYBOARD) SERVICES

FUNCTION NAME	CLASS	DESCRIPTION
KbdCharIn	FAPI	Reads character scan code
KbdClose		Closes logical keyboard
KbdDeRegister		Deregisters keyboard subsytem
KbdFlushBuffer	FAPI	Flushes keyboard buffer
KbdFreeFocus		Frees keyboard focus
KbdGetFocus		Gets keyboard focus
KbdGetStatus	FAPI	Gets keyboard status
KbdOpen		Opens logical keyboard
KbdPeek	FAPI*	Peeks at character scan code
KbdRegister	FAPI	Registers keyboard subsystem
KbdSetFgnd		Sets foreground keyboard priority
KbdSetStatus	FAPI	Sets keyboard status
KbdShellInit		Initializes keyboard shell
KbdStringIn	FAPI	Reads character string

KbdSynch		Synchronizes keyboard access
KbdXlate		Translates keyboard scan code

I/O (MOUSE) SERVICES

FUNCTION NAME	*CLASS*	*DESCRIPTION*
MouClose		Closes current screen group mouse device
MouDeRegister		Deregisters mouse subsystem
MouDrawPtr		Releases screen area for device driver
MouFlushQue		Flushes mouse event queue
MouGetDevStatus		Gets pointing device status flags
MouGetEventMask		Gets pointing device one-word event mask
MouGetHotKey		Gets system hot key button
MouGetNumButtons		Gets number of buttons
MouGetNumMickeys		Gets number of mickeys-per-centimeter
MouGetNumQueEl		Gets queue status for pointing device
MouGetPtrPos		Gets mouse pointer coordinates
MouGetPtrShape		Gets mouse pointer shape

MouGetScaleFact	Gets pointing device scale factors
MouInitReal	Initializes real-mode mouse device driver
MouOpen	Opens mouse for current screen group
MouReadEventQue	Reads pointing device event queue
MouRegister	Registers mouse subsystem
MouRemovePtr	Reserves screen area for application use
MouSetDevStatus	Sets mouse driver status flags
MouSetEventMask	Sets current pointing device event mask
MouSetHotKey	Sets system hot key
MouSetPtrPos	Sets mouse pointer coordinates
MouSetPtrShape	Sets pointer shape and size
MouSetScaleFact	Sets scale factors for mouse
MouShellInit	Initializes mouse shell
MouSynch	Synchronizes mouse driver access

I/O (VIDEO) SERVICES

FUNCTION NAME	CLASS	DESCRIPTION
VioDeRegister		Deregisters video subsystem
VioEndPopUp		Deallocates a pop-up display screen

VioGetAnsi		Gets ANSI state
VioGetBuf	FAPI	Gets logical video buffer
VioGetConfig		Gets video configuration
VioGetCurPos	FAPI	Gets cursor position
VioGetCurType	FAPI	Gets cursor type
VioGetFont		Gets font selector
VioGetMode		Gets display mode
VioGetPhysBuf	FAPI	Gets physical video buffer
VioGetState		Gets video state
VioModeUndo		Restores mode undo
VioModeWait		Restores mode wait
VioPopUp		Allocates pop-up display screen
VioPrtSc		Prints screen
VioPrtScToggle		Toggles print screen
VioReadCellStr	FAPI	Reads character-attribute string
VioReadCharStr	FAPI	Reads character string
VioRegister		Registers video subsystem
VioSavReDrawUndo		Undoes screen, save, redraw
VioSavReDrawWait		Activates screen, save, redraw, wait
VioScrLock	FAPI*	Locks screen
VioScrollDn	FAPI	Scrolls screen down
VioScrollLf	FAPI	Scrolls screen left

VioScrollRt	FAPI	Scrolls screen right	
VioScrollUp	FAPI	Scrolls screen up	
VioScrUnLock	FAPI	Unlocks screen	
VioSetAnsi		Sets ANSI on or off	
VioSetCurPos	FAPI	Sets cursor position	
VioSetCurType	FAPI	Sets cursor type	
VioSetFont		Sets video font	
VioSetMode	FAPI	Sets display mode	
VioShowBuf	FAPI	Displays logical buffer	
VioWrtCellStr	FAPI	Writes character-attribute string	
VioWrtCharStr	FAPI	Writes character string	
VioWrtCharStrAttr	FAPI	Writes character string with attribute	
VioWrtNAttr	FAPI	Writes N attributes	
VioWrtNCell	FAPI	Writes N character-attributes	
VioWrtNChar	FAPI	Writes N characters	
VioWrtTty	FAPI	Writes TTY string	

DEVICE MONITOR SERVICES

FUNCTION NAME	CLASS	DESCRIPTION
DosMonClose		Closes connection to OS/2 device
DosMonOpen		Opens connection to OS/2 device
DosMonRead		Reads monitor structure input

| DosMonReg | | Registers buffers as monitor |
| DosMonWrite | | Writes monitor output structure |

DYNAMIC LINKING SERVICES

FUNCTION NAME	CLASS	DESCRIPTION
DosFreeModule		Frees dynamic-link module
DosGetModHandle		Gets dynamic-link module handle
DosGetModName		Gets dynamic-link module name
DosGetProcAddr		Gets dynamic-link procedure address
DosGetResource		Gets resource segment selector
DosLoadModule		Loads dynamic-link module

ERRORS AND EXCEPTIONS

FUNCTION NAME	CLASS	DESCRIPTION
DosErrClass		Classifies error code
DosError	FAPI*	Enables hard error processing
DosSetVec		Establishes handler for exception vector
DosSystemService		Activates system process services

FAMILY API SERVICES

FUNCTION NAME	*CLASS*	*DESCRIPTION*
BadDynLink	FAPI	Indicates bad dynamic link
DosGetMachineMode	FAPI	Returns current processor mode

FILE I/O SERVICES

FUNCTION NAME	*CLASS*	*DESCRIPTION*
DosBufReset		Commits file cache buffers
DosChdir	FAPI	Changes current directory
DosChgFilePtr	FAPI	Changes file read/write pointer
DosClose	FAPI	Closes file handle
DosDelete	FAPI	Deletes file
DosDupHandle	FAPI	Duplicates file handle
DosFileLock	FAPI*	Manages file lock
DosFindClose	FAPI*	Closes find handle
DosFindFirst	FAPI*	Finds first matching file
DosFindNext	FAPI*	Finds next matching file
DosMkdir	FAPI	Makes subdirectory
DosMove	FAPI	Moves file or subdirectory
DosNewSize	FAPI	Changes file size
DosOpen	FAPI*	Opens file

DosPhysicalDisk		Supports partitionable disk
DosQCurDir	FAPI	Queries current directory
DosQCurDisk	FAPI	Queries current disk
DosQFHandState		Queries file handle state
DosQFileInfo	FAPI*	Queries file information
DosQFileMode	FAPI	Queries file mode
DosQFSInfo	FAPI	Queries file system information
DosQHandType		Queries handle type
DosQVerify	FAPI	Queries verify setting
DosRead	FAPI	Reads from file
DosReadAsync		Reads from file asynchronously
DosRmdir	FAPI	Removes subdirectory
DosScanEnv		Scans environment segment
DosSearchPath		Searches path for file name
DosSelectDisk	FAPI	Selects default drive
DosSetFHandState	FAPI*	Sets file handle state
DosSetFileInfo	FAPI	Sets file information
DosSetFileMode	FAPI	Sets file mode
DosSetFSInfo		Sets file system information
DosSetMaxFH		Sets maximum file handles

DosSetVerify	FAPI	Sets/resets verify switch
DosWrite	FAPI	Writes to file synchronously
DosWriteAsync		Writes to file asynchronously

INTERPROCESS COMMUNICATION SERVICES

FUNCTION NAME	CLASS	DESCRIPTION
DosCloseQueue		Closes queue
DosCloseSem		Closes system semaphore
DosCreateQueue		Creates queue
DosCreateSem		Creates system semaphore
DosFlagProcess		Sets process external event
DosMakePipe		Creates pipe
DosMuxSemWait		Waits for a semaphore to be cleared
DosOpenQueue		Opens queue
DosOpenSem		Opens existing system semaphore
DosPeekQueue		Peeks at queue
DosPurgeQueue		Purges queue
DosQueryQueue		Queries queue
DosReadQueue		Reads from queue
DosSemClear		Clears semaphore
DosSemRequest		Requests semaphore
DosSemSet		Sets semaphore to owned

DosSemSetWait	Sets semaphore; waits for next clear
DosSemWait	Waits for semaphore to be cleared
DosWriteQueue	Writes to queue

MEMORY MANAGEMENT SERVICES

FUNCTION NAME	CLASS	DESCRIPTION
DosAllocHuge	FAPI*	Allocates huge memory
DosAllocSeg	FAPI*	Allocates segment
DosAllocShrSeg		Allocates shared segment
DosCreateCSAlias	FAPI	Creates CS alias
DosFreeSeg	FAPI	Frees segment
DosGetHugeShift	FAPI	Gets shift count
DosGetSeg		Gets access to segment
DosGetShrSeg		Accesses a shared segment
DosGiveSeg		Gives access to segment
DosLockSeg		Locks segment in memory
DosMemAvail		Gets size of largest free memory block
DosReAllocHuge	FAPI*	Changes huge memory size
DosReAllocSeg	FAPI*	Changes segment size
DosSubAlloc	FAPI	Suballocates memory within segment

DosSubFree	FAPI	Frees suballocated memory
DosSubSet	FAPI	Initializes or sets allocated memory
DosUnLockSeg		Unlocks segment

MESSAGES

FUNCTION NAME	CLASS	DESCRIPTION
DosGetMessage	FAPI	Gets system message
DosInsMessage	FAPI	Inserts variable text message strings
DosPutMessage	FAPI	Outputs message text to handle

NATIONAL LANGUAGE SUPPORT

FUNCTION NAME	CLASS	DESCRIPTION
DosCaseMap	FAPI*	Performs binary case mapping
DosGetCollate		Gets collating sequence
DosGetCP		Gets process code page
DosGetCtryInfo	FAPI*	Gets country-dependent information
DosGetDBCSEv		Gets DBCS environmental vector
DosPFSActivate		Activates font
DosPFSCloseUser		Closes font user instance

DosPFSInit	Initializes code page and font
DosPFSQueryAct	Queries active font
DosPFSVerifyFont	Verifies font
DosSetCP	Sets process code page
KbdCustCP	Installs custom translate table
KbdGetXT	Gets loaded translate table ID
KbdSetXT	Sets translate table
VioGetCP	Gets code page
VioSetCP	Sets code page

PROGRAM STARTUP

FUNCTION NAME	CLASS	DESCRIPTION
DosGetEnv	FAPI	Gets address of process
DosGetVersion	FAPI	Gets DOS version number

TASKING SERVICES

FUNCTION NAME	CLASS	DESCRIPTION
DosCreateThread		Creates another executing thread
DosCWait	FAPI*	Waits for child termination
DosEnterCritSec		Enters critical execution section
DosExecPgm	FAPI*	Executes program

DosExit	FAPI*	Exits program
DosExitCritSec		Exits critical execution section
DosExitList		Obtains routine process termination list
DosGetInfoSeg		Gets address of system variables segment
DosGetPrty		Gets process priority
DosKillProcess		Terminates process
DosPTrace		Interfaces for program debugging
DosResumeThread		Resumes thread execution
DosSelectSession		Selects foreground session
DosSetPrty		Sets process priority
DosSetSession		Sets session status
DosStartSession		Starts session
DosStopSession		Stops session
DosSuspendThread		Suspends thread execution

TIMER SERVICES

FUNCTION NAME	CLASS	DESCRIPTION
DosGetDateTime	FAPI	Gets current date and time
DosSetDateTime	FAPI	Sets current date and time
DosSleep	FAPI	Delays process execution

DosTimerAsync	Starts asynchronous timer
DosTimerStart	Starts periodic interval timer
DosTimerStop	Stops asynchronous or interval timer

INDEX

SYBEX Computer Books are different.

Here is why . . .

At SYBEX, each book is designed with you in mind. Every manuscript is carefully selected and supervised by our editors, who are themselves computer experts. We publish the best authors, whose technical expertise is matched by an ability to write clearly and to communicate effectively. Programs are thoroughly tested for accuracy by our technical staff. Our computerized production department goes to great lengths to make sure that each book is well-designed.

In the pursuit of timeliness, SYBEX has achieved many publishing firsts. SYBEX was among the first to integrate personal computers used by authors and staff into the publishing process. SYBEX was the first to publish books on the CP/M operating system, microprocessor interfacing techniques, word processing, and many more topics.

Expertise in computers and dedication to the highest quality product have made SYBEX a world leader in computer book publishing. Translated into fourteen languages, SYBEX books have helped millions of people around the world to get the most from their computers. We hope we have helped you, too.

For a complete catalog of our publications:

SYBEX, Inc. 2021 Challenger Drive, #100, Alameda, CA 94501
Tel: (415) 523-8233/(800) 227-2346   Telex: 336311

Essential OS/2:
The Companion Disk and The OS/2 Newsletter

THE COMPANION DISK

If you have found *Essential OS/2* to be useful to you, you'll be glad to learn that every one of the batch files in this book is contained in a companion disk. Save time, energy, and money—and avoid the drudgery of typing these excellent programs—by ordering the *Essential OS/2* Companion Disk now ($19.95).

OS/2 NEWSLETTER

The OS/2 Newsletter summarizes key developments in the OS/2 marketplace, and contains a wealth of up-to-the-minute tips, techniques, problem resolutions, and Q&A for OS/2 users. This essential monthly newsletter is available for $19.00 ($24.00 foreign) annually.

Use the order form below to order this or any of the other fine products (listed below) produced by Judd Robbins. Mail today with complete payment to Computer Options, 198 Amherst Avenue, Berkeley, CA 94708.

_____ copies of *Essential OS/2* Companion Disk at $19.95 each   _____
_____ annual subscription to *OS/2 Newsletter*
      at $19.00 ($24.00 foreign)   _____

DOS Only materials:

_____ copies of the Companion Disk to *Mastering DOS*
      at $19.95 each   _____
_____ copies of *ReComm*, the DOS Command Reissuing Utility
      at $19.95 each   _____
_____ copies of *Introduction to DOS* Audio Cassette Training
      at $49.00 each   _____
_____ Shipping and Handling (add $2.50 per item)   _____
_____ California sales tax
      (please add appropriate amount for your city/county)   _____

TOTAL ORDER: _____

Name: _____

Company: _____

Address: _____

City, State, Zip: _____

Telephone: _____

CODE PAGE FOR UNITED STATES

Hex Digits 1st / 2nd	0-	1-	2-	3-	4-	5-	6-	7-	8-	9-	A-	B-	C-	D-	E-	F-
0-		▶		0	@	P	`	p	Ç	É	á	░	└	╨	α	≡
1-	☺	◀	!	1	A	Q	a	q	ü	æ	í	▒	┴	╤	β	±
2-	☻	↕	"	2	B	R	b	r	é	Æ	ó	▓	┬	╥	Γ	≥
3-	♥	‼	#	3	C	S	c	s	â	ô	ú	│	├	╙	π	≤
4-	♦	¶	$	4	D	T	d	t	ä	ö	ñ	┤	─	╘	Σ	⌠
5-	♣	§	%	5	E	U	e	u	à	ò	Ñ	╡	┼	╒	σ	⌡
6-	♠	▬	&	6	F	V	f	v	å	û	ª	╢	╞	╓	µ	÷
7-	•	↨	'	7	G	W	g	w	ç	ù	º	╖	╟	╫	τ	≈
8-	◘	↑	(	8	H	X	h	x	ê	ÿ	¿	╕	╚	╪	Φ	°
9-	○	↓	)	9	I	Y	i	y	ë	Ö	⌐	╣	╔	┘	Θ	∙
A-	◙	→	*	:	J	Z	j	z	è	Ü	¬	║	╩	┌	Ω	·
B-	♂	←	+	;	K	[	k	{	ï	¢	½	╗	╦	█	δ	√
C-	♀	∟	,	<	L	\	l	|	î	£	¼	╝	╠	▄	∞	ⁿ
D-	♪	↔	-	=	M	]	m	}	ì	¥	¡	╜	═	▌	φ	²
E-	♫	▲	.	>	N	^	n	~	Ä	Pt	«	╛	╬	▐	ε	■
F-	☼	▼	/	?	O	_	o	△	Å	ƒ	»	┐	╧	▀	∩	

CODE PAGE FOR MULTILINGUAL OPERATIONS

Hex Digits 1st / 2nd	0-	1-	2-	3-	4-	5-	6-	7-	8-	9-	A-	B-	C-	D-	E-	F-
0-		▶		0	@	P	`	p	Ç	É	á	░	└	ð	Ó	-
1-	☺	◀	!	1	A	Q	a	q	ü	æ	í	▒	┴	Ð	β	±
2-	☻	↕	"	2	B	R	b	r	é	Æ	ó	▓	┬	Ê	Ô	=
3-	♥	‼	#	3	C	S	c	s	â	ô	ú	│	├	Ë	Ò	¾
4-	♦	¶	$	4	D	T	d	t	ä	ö	ñ	┤	─	È	õ	¶
5-	♣	§	%	5	E	U	e	u	à	ò	Ñ	Á	┼	ı	Õ	§
6-	♠	▬	&	6	F	V	f	v	å	û	ª	Â	ã	Í	µ	÷
7-	•	↨	'	7	G	W	g	w	ç	ù	º	À	Ã	Î	þ	¸
8-	◘	↑	(	8	H	X	h	x	ê	ÿ	¿	©	╚	Ï	Þ	°
9-	○	↓	)	9	I	Y	i	y	ë	Ö	®	╣	╔	┘	Ú	¨
A-	◙	→	*	:	J	Z	j	z	è	Ü	¬	║	╩	┌	Û	·
B-	♂	←	+	;	K	[	k	{	ï	ø	½	╗	╦	█	Ù	¹
C-	♀	∟	,	<	L	\	l	|	î	£	¼	╝	╠	▄	ý	³
D-	♪	↔	-	=	M	]	m	}	ì	Ø	¡	¢	═	¦	Ý	²
E-	♫	▲	.	>	N	^	n	~	Ä	×	«	¥	╬	Ì	¯	■
F-	☼	▼	/	?	O	_	o	△	Å	ƒ	»	┐	¤	▀	´	

SUMMARY OF OS/2 COMMANDS*

COMMAND	DESCRIPTION	SYNTAX
KEYB	Loads in new keyboard translation table	[*D:path*]KEYB *xx*
LABEL	Defines or changes existing disk volume label	[*D:path*]LABEL [*D1:*][*string*]
MKDIR (MD)	Creates a new subdirectory	MD [*D:path*][...]
MODE	Defines attributes for all of the ports and code pages	[*D:path*]MODE LPT*x*: [*CPL*][,*LPI*][,P] [*D:path*]MODE LPT*x*: = COM*y* [*D:path*]MODE COM*y*[:]*baud*[,[*parity*] [,[*bits*][,P] [*D:path*]MODE *type*
MORE	Pauses the display of long files	[*D:path*]MORE
PATCH	Makes byte-by-byte corrections to disk files	PATCH [*D:path*] [/a]
PATH	Defines search list for .exe, .com, and .bat files	PATH [*D1:path1*][;*D2:Path2*...]
PRINT	Queues files for printing	[*D:path*]PRINT [/c][/t][/d:*device*][*filespec*...]
PROMPT	Changes the system prompt	PROMPT [*string*]
RECOVER	Rescues damaged files	[*D:path*]RECOVER[*D*][*filespec*]
RENAME (REN)	Changes the names of files	REN *oldfile newfile*
REPLACE	Selectively copies, adds, and updates programs	[*D:path*]REPLACE *sourcefile* [*dest*:][/a][/p][/r][/s][/w]
RESTORE	Reads backup file back onto disk	[*D:path*]RESTORE *sourceD filespec* [/s][/p][/b:*mm-dd-yy*] [/a:*mm-dd-yy*][/m][/n][/l:*hh-mm-ss*][/e:*hh-mm-ss*]
RMDIR (RD)	Deletes empty directories	RD [*D:path*]
SET	Changes defaults and definitions in the OS/2 environment	SET [*name* = [*param*]]

*See Chapter 5, "OS/2 Command Reference," for a complete description of commands and their parameters.